Sep. 9, 2020
ccu

To President Donald Swt
From Gregmoor
I hope you find this +
of interest.
Thank you for your
faithfulness + leadership
in these trying times.

Greg Moor

Niebuhrian International Relations

Niebuhrian International Relations

The Ethics of Foreign Policymaking

GREGORY J. MOORE

OXFORD

UNIVERSITY PRESS

OXFORD
UNIVERSITY PRESS

Oxford University Press is a department of the University of Oxford. It furthers
the University's objective of excellence in research, scholarship, and education
by publishing worldwide. Oxford is a registered trade mark of Oxford University
Press in the UK and certain other countries.

Published in the United States of America by Oxford University Press
198 Madison Avenue, New York, NY 10016, United States of America.

Library of Congress Cataloging-in-Publication Data
Names: Moore, Gregory J., author.
Title: Niebuhrian international relations : the ethics of
foreign policymaking / Gregory J. Moore.
Description: New York, NY : Oxford University Press, [2020] |
Includes bibliographical references and index. |
Identifiers: LCCN 2019044897 (print) | LCCN 2019044898 (ebook) |
ISBN 9780197500446 (hardback) | ISBN 9780197500460 (epub) | ISBN 9780197500477 (online)
Subjects: LCSH: Niebuhr, Reinhold, 1892–1971—Political and social views. |
International relations—Philosophy. | International relations—Moral and ethical aspects. |
Christianity and international relations. | Political realism.
Classification: LCC BX4827.N5 M66 2020 (print) |
LCC BX4827.N5 (ebook) | DDC 261.8/7092—dc23
LC record available at https://lccn.loc.gov/2019044897
LC ebook record available at https://lccn.loc.gov/2019044898

1 3 5 7 9 8 6 4 2

Printed by Integrated Books International, United States of America

Dedicated to Kenneth W. Thompson,

advisor, mentor, friend

November 2019

Reinhold Niebuhr, 1930

Contents

Acknowledgments

Acknowledgments are due to Kenneth W. Thompson and S. C. Leung, my former master's degree dissertation supervisors at the University of Virginia where this project was originally launched, and to Michael J. Smith, Jack Donnelly, Paul Viotti, Dean Curry, Chris Wood, Daniel Philpott, John Pella, Jared McKinney, anonymous Chinese academics who gave me feedback on the Niebuhr on China chapter, conference panel discussants where parts of this project were presented (including John Mearsheimer and Zhang Baohui), and anonymous reviewers, all of whom gave me helpful comments at various stages of this project. None of them should be held accountable for any of the shortcomings found herein, however. Thanks are due also to my parents and to my wonderful wife and kids for their love, patience, and support throughout this project, spanning more than 29 years.

1

Introduction*

Niebuhr's Enduring Relevance

*Man's capacity for justice makes democracy possible; but man's incli-
nation to injustice makes democracy necessary.*

—Reinhold Niebuhr[1]

*Perhaps the best that can be expected of nations is that they should jus-
tify their hypocrisies by a slight measure of real international achievement, and learn how to do justice to wider interests than their own,
while they pursue their own.*

—Reinhold Niebuhr[2]

Reinhold Niebuhr (1892–1971) may have been the most influential and insightful American thinker of the twentieth century. In dealing with matters
such as the intricacies of human nature, human society, politics, ethics, theology, racism, and international relations, Niebuhr, the teacher, preacher,
philosopher, social critic, and ethicist, brought the polemical criticisms
and revelations of his brand of human nature, Realism, to bear on utopian
idealists and overly cynical realists in the secular and religious worlds alike.
Whether or not one accepts Niebuhr's conclusions, his work was highly influential and difficult to ignore in the heyday of the Cold War because of his

---

* This book is a greatly expanded version of original research presented in Gregory J. Moore,
Human Nature, Collective Society and International Relations in the Thought of Reinhold Niebuhr,
Master's Thesis 1991.M66 (Charlottesville: University of Virginia, 1991).

[1] Reinhold Niebuhr (hereafter referred to in the footnotes as RN), "Foreword to the Original
Edition," *The Children of Light and the Children of Darkness: A Vindication of Democracy and a
Critique of Its Traditional Defense* (Chicago: University of Chicago Press, 2011[1944]), Kindle
Location 286.

[2] RN, *Moral Man and Immoral Society* (New York: Charles Scribner's Sons, 1932), p. 108.

Niebuhrian International Relations. Gregory J. Moore, Oxford University Press (2020).
© Oxford University Press.
DOI: 10.1093/oso/9780197500446.001.0001

intellectual heft and the novel manner in which he addressed the economic, spiritual, social, and political problems of his time.

> Niebuhr symbolizes the possibility of a prudent liberalism that takes the measure of every group's self-interest and is chastened by a realistic under-standing of the limits of power. . . . He is the most important thinker of the past century concerning the relation of Christianity to problems of social ethics and politics. And his great theme [is] the necessity of navigating be-tween sentimental idealism and cynical realism.[3]

During his day, Niebuhr had an audience with the world's leading academics, social thinkers, and policymakers, including America's foreign policy establishment. George Kennan, one of America's most prominent diplomats in the Cold War era, said of Niebuhr in 1971 upon his passing, "I regarded him during his lifetime, and continue to do so, as the greatest of my own teachers—as the man whose thought and example have exerted the greatest influence on my own view of life."[4] In a letter to Niebuhr's wife written on August 1, 1976, President Jimmy Carter (not as yet president) said,

> When I heard of your husband's death in 1971, mine was a selfish sorrow—because I had always wanted to meet him. He contributed to my private education more than you could know. In my acceptance speech at the con-vention [where Carter had been nominated by the Democratic Party as their candidate for president in 1976] I used one of Dr. Niebuhr's ideas, that love must be translated into justice in order to be effective.[5]

Niebuhr was so influential that in 1948 there was even a movement among prominent Democratic Party members (including Eleanor Roosevelt) to press Niebuhr to run for president of the United States, though he declined in the end.[66]

---

[3] Gary Dorrien, "Introduction," in RN, *The Children of Light and the Children of Darkness*, Kindle Location 217.

[4] George F. Kennan, "Reinhold Niebuhr: 1892–1971" (no further citation information is available about this small booklet), p. 79; as found in Box 49, Reinhold Niebuhr Papers, Manuscript Division, Library of Congress, Washington, DC.

[5] Letter from Jimmy Carter to Ursula Niebuhr, August 1, 1976, Box 46, Reinhold Niebuhr Papers, Manuscript Division, Library of Congress, Washington, DC.

[6] Richard Wightman Fox, *Reinhold Niebuhr: A Biography* (San Francisco: Harper & Row, 1985), p. 233.

Niebuhr has also provided the most important representation of what in international relations (IR) theory some have called classical Realism's "human nature Realism,"[7] a Realism that is driven not by structures and/or balance of power per se, but by what adherents see as the greed, fallibility, and "will to power" inherent in human nature itself. Diplomat and intellectual George F. Kennan, in speaking of Niebuhr's influence on the early classical Realists who arose after World War II, including Hans Morgenthau, Arnold Wolfers, Kenneth Thompson, Henry Kissinger, and Kennan himself, said of Niebuhr, "he is the father of all of us."[8]

Yet, having said all this and given the difficulty of sifting through all of Niebuhr's disparate (and largely obscure, hard to find, and/or out of print) writings on public policy issues, what exactly are Niebuhr's views on IR? Has Niebuhr left us with anything, any guidelines, that might be helpful as we navigate the future of IR? If so, what are they? Given his intellectual gravitas and the influence he wielded in the twentieth century, what words of wisdom might his work offer us as we consider the most intractable international problems thus far in the twenty-first century? This book seeks to answer these questions and others, though certainly Richard Fox is correct when he says, "Niebuhr's Christian realism . . . did not ordain specific positions on political issues. It demanded only that its adherents follow a middle path between the twin pitfalls of utopianism and resignation, sentimentality and cynicism."[9]

In recent years, David Brooks has helped rekindle the fire of interest in Niebuhr, or at least provided the most public reinvocation of Niebuhr when in an *Atlantic Monthly* piece in 2002 he asked why, in the wake of the September 11 attacks, Niebuhr's name and ideas were not being discussed more.[10] In 2005, following the election and reelection of the outspoken Christian president George W. Bush, the growing national divide over abortion and same-sex marriage, the growth of megachurches, and the waxing of evangelical Protestant churches as the mainline Protestant churches waned,

---

[7] I use capital R Realism to refer to the political Realism of international relations theory, and small r realism to refer to realism in the more conventional sense, in the sense of something being realistic.

[8] Kenneth W. Thompson recounts Kennan's words in a conversation with him. Kenneth W. Thompson, "Niebuhr and the Foreign Policy Realists," in Daniel F. Rice, ed., *Reinhold Niebuhr Revisited: Engagements with an American Original* (Grand Rapids, MI: Eerdmans, 2009), p. 139.

[9] Fox, *Reinhold Niebuhr*, p. 277.

[10] David Brooks, "A Man on a Gray Horse," *Atlantic Monthly* (September 2002). Having said this, it may in fact have been Wilfred McClay who was the first to bring Niebuhr back post–9/11, and Brooks references McClay's February 2002 *First Things* piece in his own 2002 article. See Wilfred McClay, "The Continuing Irony of American History," *First Things* (February 2002, accessed March 17, 2012 from http://www.firstthings.com/article/2007/06/001-the-continuing-irony-of-american-history-36).

the influential historian Arthur Schlesinger Jr. asked, "Why, in an age of religiosity, has Niebuhr, the supreme American theologian of the 20th century, dropped out of 21st-century religious discourse?"[11] Although this statement was perhaps apropos in 2005, it is less so today, for in recent years there *has indeed* been a marked resurgence of interest in Reinhold Niebuhr's work in the United States and even abroad,[12] as evidenced by many influential books,[13] radio programs,[14] a documentary,[15] essays,[16] and an oft-quoted statement in 2007 by then-candidate Barack Obama in response to journalist David Brooks's question as to whether he'd ever read Niebuhr, to which Obama replied, "I love him. He's one of my favorite philosophers."[17] Conservatives like David Brooks and John McCain[18] invoked Niebuhr's name following September 11, and others like Catholic neoconservative Michael Novak had been calling Niebuhr their intellectual "father" for some time. Novak once observed, "The fact is, neoconservatives cite Niebuhr at least as often as those

[11] Arthur Schlesinger Jr., "Forgetting Reinhold Niebuhr," *New York Times* (September 18, 2005), Section 7, Page 12.

[12] For example, see Liang Chen, *From a Christian Socialist to a Christian Realist: Reinhold Niebuhr and the Soviet Union, 1930–1945,* doctoral dissertation (National University of Singapore, 2007).

[13] See Rice, ed., *Reinhold Niebuhr Revisited;* Richard Crouter, *Reinhold Niebuhr: On Politics, Religion and Christian Faith* (Oxford: Oxford University Press, 2010); Richard Harries and Stephen Platten, eds., *Reinhold Niebuhr and Contemporary Politics: God and Power* (Oxford: Oxford University Press, 2010); Charles Lemert, *Why Niebuhr Matters* (New Haven, CT: Yale University Press, 2011); and John Patrick Diggins, *Why Niebuhr Now?* (Chicago: University of Chicago Press, 2011). Several of Niebuhr's classics have also been re-released, including *The Irony of American History* (Chicago: University of Chicago Press, 2008), with an excellent new introduction by Andrew Bacevich, who has played an important role, along with David Brooks, in spurring renewed interest in Niebuhr in the last decade.

[14] On American Public Media's National Public Radio program, "On Being," with host Krista Tippet, there have been two special radio programs on RN, one in 2009 with journalists David Brooks (*New York Times*) and E. J. Dionne (*Washington Post*), "Obama's Theologian: David Brooks and E. J. Dionne on Reinhold Niebuhr and the American Present" (February 12, 2009; accessed March 13, 2012 from http://being.publicradio.org/programs/2009/obamas-theologian); and another with Paul Ellie, Jean Bethke Elshtain, and Robin Lovin, "Moral Man and Immoral Society: The Public Theology of Reinhold Niebuhr" (October 25, 2007; accessed March 14, 2012 from http://being.publicradio.org/programs/niebuhr-rediscovered/index.shtml).

[15] Martin Doblmeier, "An American Conscience: The Reinhold Niebuhr Story," PBS Video, Journey Films (April 2, 2017) accessed from http://www.pbs.org/video/mpt-presents-american-conscience-reinhold-niebuhr-story.

[16] For examples, see David Brooks, "A Man on a Gray Horse," *Atlantic Monthly* (September 2002), accessed from https://www.theatlantic.com/magazine/archive/2002/09/a-man-on-a-gray-horse/302558/; Schlesinger, "Forgetting Reinhold Niebuhr," (September 18, 2005), Section 7, Page 12; David Brooks, "Obama, Gospel and Verse," *New York Times* (April 26, 2007): A25; and Paul Elie, "A Man for All Reasons," *The Atlantic* (November 2007), accessed from https://www.theatlantic.com/magazine/archive/2007/11/a-man-for-all-reasons/306337/.

[17] Brooks, "Obama, Gospel and Verse." For more on Obama and Niebuhr, see R. Ward Holder and Peter B. Josephson, *The Irony of Barack Obama: Barack Obama, Reinhold Niebuhr and the Problem of Christian Statecraft* (Surrey, UK: Ashgate, 2012).

[18] John McCain, with Stephen Salter, *Hard Calls: The Art of Great Decisions* (New York: Hachett Book Group, 2007), pp. 319–39.

on the Left do," calling Niebuhr "the father of neoconservatives."[19] It should be noted that from 1968 to 1975, neoconservative Novak served as contributing editor of *Christianity and Crisis*, the progressive magazine Niebuhr founded in 1941! It should also be noted, however, that Novak was expelled from the editorial board of the magazine in 1975 for having moved too far right, and thus out of step with the magazine's editorial slant.[20] In response to statements such as Novak's, liberals like Paul Elie, Niebuhr's daughter, Elizabeth Sifton, Barack Obama, and Mac McCorkle have fought to reclaim Niebuhr, a liberal himself (though one not easily categorized). The fact that both liberals *and* conservatives claim Niebuhr today would probably have made Niebuhr smile. The fact that present members of both sides of the political spectrum would find something in his work to appreciate is a good reflection of the nuances in his own thought, the lack of "black and whiteness" with which he viewed the world, and the dialectical reality of life and our social existence as he understood it.

In a post–Cold War era characterized by the United States' seemingly unchallenged preeminence until September 11, 2001, followed by the U.S. invasions of Afghanistan and Iraq, and then the global financial crisis that started in the United States in 2008 and spread around the world, followed by turns to a more robust foreign policy in Beijing and Moscow, it is clear that Niebuhr's prophetic voice should be heard again in the halls of power (particularly in Washington, D.C.) and in the halls of academe. As it regards the halls of power, during the Cold War era, Niebuhr was a voice crying in the wilderness, never afraid to speak truth to power, even when he knew it would be unpopular, as was the case with his opposition to the Vietnam War. In the years following September 11, 2001, the United States once again found itself in an unpopular war, overreaching politically, economically, and militarily in the eyes of many. Today, as the United States and its allies face global recession; as both challenges to democracy (e.g., Afghanistan, Iraq, Lebanon, Syria, and Iran) and surprising advances of democracy (e.g., the Arab Spring, Myanmar/Burma) take place; as a formerly democratic Russia is slipping back into authoritarianism while annexing parts of neighboring countries; and as China is rising to prominence in international affairs at an unprecedented speed while posing new challenges with

---

[19] Michael Novak, "Father of Neoconservatives," *National Review* (May 11, 1992): 39.
[20] Mark Hulsether, *Building a Protestant Left: Christianity and Crisis Magazine, 1941–1993* (Knoxville: University of Tennessee Press, 1999), p. 152.

its growing material power coupled to its alternative market–authoritarian style of government, Niebuhr's call for humility, prudence, and sober (but not pessimistic) realism in Washington is once again sorely needed.

With regard to the need for a rehearing of Niebuhr's voice in the halls of academe, IR theory and Realism in particular would benefit from a reconsideration of Niebuhr's work. While his contribution to IR theory is an important one, in many respects it has been forgotten. Kennan called Niebuhr the father of the IR Realists, and while Realism remains the most influential approach to IR in the world, in recent years Realism (structural Realism in particular) has come under attack and finds itself on the defensive in graduate seminars on IR around the world. Challengers such as neoliberal institutionalism, constructivism, the English School, critical theory, and the democratic peace theory have gained adherents at Realism's expense. A renewed look at the more nuanced Realism of Reinhold Niebuhr, and its basis in the realities of the depths of human nature, would be helpful to the Realist enterprise, which has arguably suffered under the post–1979 hegemony of the structural form of Realism promoted by Kenneth Waltz[21] and John Mearsheimer. A Niebuhrian approach to IR could also inform other forms of IR theory, including constructivism and new forms of human nature IR (Rosen 2009).

In this book, I collect and examine Niebuhr's thoughts on and contributions to IR, which are rooted in his views of human nature and the "Christian Realism" he came to personify. I then apply a Niebuhrian analysis to a number of important contemporary issues in IR, things Niebuhr did not live to see, such as the United States' decision in 2003 to invade Iraq, the rise of "the responsibility to protect" (R2P), and the twenty-first century rise of China. Whether or not the reader shares Niebuhr's faith, I believe any reader will benefit from his wisdom regarding the human condition and the problems we faced in decades past, as well as those that confront us today.

This study begins by briefly tracing Niebuhr's background as a thinker, followed by an examination of his conception of human nature and a look at his thoughts regarding collective society and IR, with an attempt at making very clear the logical thread that Niebuhr wove between his conception of human nature and his approach to IR. It then turns to Niebuhr's views of communism and U.S. policy in the Cold War in an attempt to examine Niebuhr's approach as it relates to a specific problem faced by

---

[21] See Kenneth Waltz, *Theory of International Politics* (Reading, MA: Addison-Wesley, 1979).

policymakers. This includes case studies of his analysis of the 1956 Suez Crisis and the U.S. war in Vietnam. I then discuss Niebuhr's views on national transcendence, or the likelihood that nations might agree to surrender their national sovereignty to a higher authority. My focus is on Niebuhr's writings on the role of the United Nations in IR and the potential and desirability of world government, including a brief consideration of what Niebuhr's views of globalization might have been had he lived long enough to see it. Although he died in 1971, forty years before the events of September 11, 2001, his thoughts are prescient as they regard American policy in the wake of those terrorist attacks. This study also includes an analysis of the U.S. invasion of Iraq from a Niebuhrian perspective, bringing to the table the notion of the just war tradition and Niebuhr's place therein. Given the importance in the late twentieth and early twenty-first centuries of humanitarian intervention and the recent notion of R2P, I provide an analysis of what I call "Niebuhrian take-aways" in this respect, or points taken from cases he wrote about during his own lifetime that are applicable or analogous to cases of humanitarian intervention or R2P discussions in our time.

Given the importance of China's rise and the apparent reality that it will be the primary great power challenger to U.S. preeminence in the twenty-first century, a chapter addresses the following questions about China. What would Niebuhr say about China today, especially its likelihood of getting along with its neighbors and the United States? What would he conclude about the particular type of government it has and the implications of that government type for its foreign policy, and ultimately for its neighbors and the United States? While the Chinese government is not "communist" in the traditional sense, its nominally "communist" authoritarian system coupled to its market-driven, state-owned corporation-dominant economy presents the West with new problems that are potentially far more challenging than those presented by the Soviet Union at its height. Niebuhrian wisdom seems particularly helpful as the world ponders the realities of the rise of modern China.

Following this discussion, I offer an analysis of Niebuhr's contribution to, and rightful place in, IR theory, in terms of historical influence (which is immense), as well as the potential of his more nuanced, classical Realist IR to serve as a needed alternative to the hegemony of structural Realism in IR in particular. The chapter on this subject also brings out the seldom appreciated existentialist undertones of Niebuhrian thought, while considering

Niebuhr's contributions to various traditions in IR theory, from democratic peace theory to constructivism to postmodernism.

Finally, in the conclusion and throughout this study, I discuss Niebuhr's use of dialectics as a common theme throughout his work, one that ties together his human nature-driven Christian Realism to the intricacies of U.S. foreign policy and IR in general. I will also take up the challenge of the new world of "post-truth" that has developed with the rise of the new nationalism and the new nationalists, with considerations of what Niebuhr might have to offer such a world.

This book is framed, as the sub-title suggests, in the language of ethics, the ethics of foreign policymaking. Niebuhr always denied he was a theologian.[22] He said his brother Richard was the real theologian in the family. He said this likely because he did not really teach much theology but taught mostly social ethics, Christian ethics, and other dimensions of ethics.[23] Surely he sells himself short, for he was an accomplished theologian by every indicator, and theologian John C. Bennett, close friend of RN, says so explicitly. "Niebuhr is basically a theologian who sees the implications of his theology for Christian ethics, but he has never addressed himself primarily to the Church as the Church."[24] Having said this, what Niebuhr was interested in more than anything else was ethics, social ethics to be precise, for he was first and foremost an ethicist who liked to bring his ideas to bear on the social, economic, religious and political problems of his day, not the least of which were foreign policy issues.[25] Almost everything Niebuhr ever wrote had an ethical dimension, an ethical conundrum he sought to address, to solve. He wrote much about international relations and foreign policy. He did so through a lens of ethics with an eye to influencing policy, to helping nudge foreign policy decision-making in the United States in particular in a more ethical and at the same time effective and prudent direction. To understand Reinhold Niebuhr's approach to IR and his contribution thereto, to understand his ethics and the way they drove his thinking, his writing, and his approach to international relations, we must begin with the man and the times in which he lived. To this we now turn.

---

[22] John C. Bennett, "Reinhold Niebuhr's Contribution to Christian Social Ethics," in Harold R. Landon, ed., *Reinhold Niebuhr: A Prophetic Voice in Our Time* (Greenwich, CT: Seabury Press, 1962), pp. 55–95.

[23] Ronald H. Stone, *Professor Reinhold Niebuhr: A Mentor to the Twentieth Century* (Louisville: Westminster, UK: John Knox Press, 1992), pp. 54–55.

[24] Bennett, "RN's Contribution," p. 61.

[25] For more on how Niebuhr saw ethics, see, RN, "The Ethic of Jesus and the Social Problem," *Religion in Life* (Spring, 1932), in D. B. Robertson (ed.), *Love and Justice* (Lousville, KY: Westminster/John Knox Press, 1957), pp. 29–40.

2

Contextualizing Niebuhr

A Biography and a Sketch of His Intellectual Development

Beginning this study with a biography of Reinhold Niebuhr and a brief sketch of his intellectual development is important for a number of reasons. First, Niebuhr was a creature of the times in which he lived, times that included World War I, the Great Depression, World War II, the Cold War, and the Vietnam War, among other important events. Each shaped him personally and intellectually. Moreover, Niebuhr's intellectual orientation and his policy positions evolved significantly over time, from Liberal pacifist to activist Marxist to Christian Realist. Therefore, placing his work/words in the specific context of the events of the time in which they were expressed is helpful, even vital, in understanding his perspectives on the issues and events of those times. In sum, this chapter seeks to contextualize the life, work, and arguments of Reinhold Niebuhr as he considered international relations.

The Early Years—German Americans in the American Heartland

Karl Paul Reinhold Niebuhr was born in 1892 in Wright City, Missouri. His father was a German Lutheran minister. When he was 10 years old, Reinhold moved with his family to Lincoln, Illinois. From an early age, he spoke of becoming a preacher like his father, Gustav.

> [My father] was probably more responsible than anybody else for the choice of my vocation and avocation. . . . I was thrilled by my father's sermons and regarded him as the most interesting man in town. So what else should I do but be a minister in his image?[1]

---

[1] William G. Chrystal, "A Man of the Hour and the Time: The Legacy of Gustav Niebuhr," in Chrystal, *Niebuhr Studies* (Reno, NV: Empire for Liberty LLC, 2012): Kindle Location 625.

Niebuhrian International Relations. Gregory J. Moore, Oxford University Press (2020).
© Oxford University Press.
DOI: 10.1093/oso/9780197500446.001.0001

Gustav was not only a preacher, but a missionary; a church planter; an intellectual writing for a denominational newspaper and a denominational theological journal while editing another periodical; the founder of a home for epileptics and the "feebleminded"; and the founder of a hospital, among other things.[2] Given that Gustav was a "biblical evangelical" with "a pietism which evinced a real sense of God's presence in his life" his father instilled in Reinhold and his siblings a love for God's word, a love for God's people, and a burning desire to take the love of God into the streets, into the economic realm, and into the political arena.[3] At 15, young Reinhold left home to attend Elmhurst College (Elmhurst, Illinois), and in 1910 he transferred to Eden Theological Seminary in Webster Groves, Missouri, where he worked toward finishing his Bachelor of Divinity degree. Though gifted academically and intellectually, he struggled because English was not his native language.

Weeks before graduation, in April 1913, his father died suddenly at 50, leaving Reinhold's 43-year-old mother potentially destitute. Reinhold put his studies on hold and moved home to take over his father's pastorate, fulfilling his dream to become a preacher, but in a fashion unlike any he had imagined. He still managed to graduate on time however, in May 1913, and was ordained while pastoring his father's church, St. John's Lutheran Church, of the German Evangelical Synod of North America. Having then fulfilled his dream to be a minister, Reinhold soon became restless, feeling called to further studies, and accepted an offer to attend Yale University that fall. On August 31, 1913, he gave his final sermon at St. John's (it was in German, Richard Fox notes),[4] before leaving for Yale Divinity School, where his true academic promise began to be realized.

Because the schools Niebuhr had attended in the Midwest were not accredited, he was admitted to Yale University but would be allowed to continue only if he received straight A's. He did fulfill this academic proviso, but Yale viewed his first year of studies as in essence remedial, and he was granted a Bachelor of Divinity degree in the spring of 1914. With no promise of formal admission to the graduate program, Niebuhr continued with his graduate coursework in the fall of 1914 and began working on his master's thesis. To support himself that year, he accepted an offer from the Congregational

---

[2] Chrystal, "A Man of the Hour and the Time."
[3] Chrystal, "A Man of the Hour and the Time," Kindle Location 944.
[4] Richard W. Fox, *Reinhold Niebuhr: A Biography* (New York: Pantheon, 1985), p. 24. Fox's biography is the definitive, exhaustive, magisterial work on Niebuhr, and I am much indebted to him in my presentation of biographical details throughout this book.

Church of Derby, Connecticut (10 miles from Yale), to serve as pastor, and commuted there from New Haven while working on his thesis.[5] He prevailed in his studies and in persuading his professors to recognize and formalize his candidacy as a graduate student, graduating from Yale with a Master of Divinity degree in June 1915.

World War I and the Detroit Pastorate

In 1915, Niebuhr was offered a pastorate at Bethel Evangelical (Lutheran) Church in Detroit, Michigan. While it was not his dream position, he accepted it in August of that year for family reasons. His older brother, Walter, a war correspondent in Europe during World War I, had run up a series of debts, and Reinhold was under pressure both to take care of their mother and help Walter recover financially. At $900 per year and without a parsonage, he eked out a living at Bethel, a member church in the German Evangelical Synod of North America, the church tradition in which he had grown up. Bethel was a church of but 65 parishioners when Niebuhr arrived, and three-fourths of them were German.[6] He conducted both English and German services to meet the needs of his flock.

Because Niebuhr had adopted a liberal American identity and a progressive political ethos, he found himself sometimes at odds with his German parishioners, many of whom were profoundly conservative and identified more with Germany in the new war in Europe than with the United States. Over the years, he had come to revile historical German autocratic traditions, in part under the influence of his father, Gustav, who had left Germany to escape his own father's autocratic tendencies.[7] With his mother's arrival in January 1916 to live with him and take over many of the church's organizational responsibilities, Reinhold was able to spend more time writing, and he began to find success making his views more widely available. His first publication, describing his life as a German American during the war era, appeared in *The Atlantic* in July 1916.[8] His article was a critique of German conservativism and a call for German Americans to be more liberal, more progressive. His second publication, which also appeared in *The Atlantic*, in

---

[5] Fox, *Reinhold Niebuhr*, p. 37.
[6] Fox, *Reinhold Niebuhr*, pp. 39–40.
[7] Chrystal, "A Man of the Hour and the Time," Kindle Location 643.
[8] RN, "The Failure of German Americanism," *The Atlantic*, July 1916.

November 1916,[9] critiqued modern nationalism and its stress on sacrificing all for the fatherland. He argued that nationalism was too often simply the state's attempt to coopt citizen support of the frivolous and vainglorious activities of national leaders exemplified by the tragedy and folly of World War I. Niebuhr argued that such nationalism came at the expense of the dignity of the individual. "The crime of the nation against the individual is not that it demands his sacrifices against his will, but that it claims a life of eternal significance for ends that have no eternal value."[10] He was supportive of President Wilson's efforts to keep America out of the war, but when, finally, in 1917 Wilson supported U.S. entry into World War I, he supported the war effort and its higher principle of "making the world safe for democracy," but again after the war he returned to the argument of his second *Atlantic* piece: that the nation was not sacred and could not offer anyone eternal significance. That could be found, according to Niebuhr, only in an individual's relationship to God and to principles of eternal truth found therein. He was offended by the modern state's inclination to appropriate religion to mobilize individuals for utilitarian national ends.

Having made this point, without doubt during this period in particular, in both his writings and oratory Niebuhr exhibited a tendency toward being a kind of "super patriot" with regard to his views of the United States and what it stood for, and his role as a German American in support of the U.S. war effort in Europe. Niebuhr worked hard to encourage pro-U.S. patriotism among German Americans, and he played a key role in de-Germanizing his Lutheran denomination. For example, he worked to persuade synod leaders to remove "published by the German Evangelical Synod of North America" from the cover of its periodical, the *Evangelical Herald*. In this way, the soldiers on the front lines in Europe receiving it could be encouraged by it and not be ostracized because of it.[11] Niebuhr's congregation voted in January 1919 to use English exclusively. In 1918, he wrote,

> If you have no appreciation for the American ideals of democracy, if you cannot see that in spite of some faults there is a potent strain of idealism in American life, you do not really love America. America is more than fields of grain or rich mines of ore or prosperous industries; it is an ideal not yet

[9] RN, "The Nation's Crime against the Individual," *The Atlantic*, November 1916; as found in Fox, *Reinhold Niebuhr*, p. 47.

[10] Niebuhr, "The Nation's Crime against the Individual," as found in Fox, *Reinhold Niebuhr*, p. 47.

[11] Fox, *Reinhold Niebuhr*, p. 52.

fully realized but in the process of realization. If you do not appreciate that you do not know and you cannot love America.[12]

While some might wonder whether Niebuhr wasn't just trying to convince himself and the world that he was a loyal German American during World War I when many in America doubted the loyalty of anyone in the United States with a name as Teutonic-sounding as his own, Richard Fox's own tireless perusal of Niebuhr's period writings, letters, and diary entries persuades him (and this author) that Niebuhr was sincere in his pro-Americanism here, for it pervades his writing at the time. Fox is convinced that Niebuhr found in the American nation, and its restrained approach to World War I as exemplar, a duty to a higher cause than parochial nationalism, something of true eternal value.[13] Niebuhr was an ardent supporter of Wilson and his idealism. In fact, by 1919 Niebuhr had announced his resignation from the pastorate at Bethel so that he could join the U.S. military and more directly support the war effort himself. Before the synod was able to find a replacement for him, however, the war was over, making his moves moot, except perhaps for the satisfaction it offered his own conscience.

With the war over, Niebuhr returned to church building in Detroit. His new parish, Bethel Evangelical Church, was located in the industrial heart of Detroit, the population of which was to expand from a half million people to one and a half million during his 13-year pastorate there. After the war, it was the fourth largest city in the United States. With Niebuhr at the helm, Bethel continued to grow, and by 1921 he oversaw the construction of a large, new church on prominent West Grand Avenue, funded in part with the help of a close friend of Henry Ford. Niebuhr was "a committed church builder throughout his thirteen years at Bethel," and it was "Niebuhr's preaching [that] was the chief magnet that drew people to Bethel. By the early 1920s he was an accomplished pulpit performer, the educated Protestant's Billy Sunday."[14] Although Niebuhr found evangelists like Billy Sunday a bit too populist in their appeal, he respected Sunday and took some of Sunday's strengths away with him, making the cross central to his preaching and not being afraid to appeal to the hearts and emotions of his listeners, while not neglecting their minds as some evangelists were wont to do.[15] Perhaps what

---

[12] RN, "Love of Country," *Evangelical Herald* (April 18, 1918), as found in Fox, *Reinhold Niebuhr*, p. 52.

[13] Fox, *Reinhold Niebuhr*, pp. 52–3.

[14] Fox, *Reinhold Niebuhr*, pp. 62 and 64, respectively.

[15] Fox, *Reinhold Niebuhr*, pp. 48, 64.

truly appealed to Niebuhr was Sunday's role as prophet: serving as the conscience of a nation like the prophets in the Old Testament, warning listeners
of social and spiritual dangers, and admonishing them to make changes so as
to avoid tragic pitfalls. It was a role Niebuhr relished throughout his career
and one that he played with zest until the end of his days.

Niebuhr's Early Liberalism, Pacifism, and Challenges Thereto

During his early academic years, Niebuhr confessed to entertaining what he
called a "liberal and highly moralistic creed."[16] The outbreak of World War
I in 1914 was cause for Niebuhr to reevaluate his idealism, but as he himself
said, "it wasn't the then distant war so much as the social realities in Detroit
which undermined my youthful optimism."[17] The Ford Motor Company was
the engine of the city's growth, and Niebuhr's parishioners the pistons and
cogs. There was no better place in the United States to observe the realities of
early twentieth-century industry–worker relations than Detroit. While some
members of his parish were in management, most of them were laborers at
the Ford plant, working at the mercy of "Fordism" and enduring the harsh
conditions typical of American industry prior to the formation of the nation's
labor unions. Niebuhr grew to become appalled at the effects of Fordism
and the "enforced vacations" (layoffs without pay for retooling or sales lulls)
that sometimes lasted as long as a year, leaving many members of his parish
penniless. Niebuhr was sobered with the realization that the idealism[18] of
the classical Christian faith seemed abstract for some of his parishioners in
light of the immense social problems of a modern industrial city.[19] He began
increasingly to publicly oppose Henry Ford and the methods of Fordism, a
stance not lightly taken by one living in the city that Ford built.

Yet Niebuhr's criticism went beyond Fordism to idealism in general and
the pacific effects of liberal Protestantism, the ideological camp from which

---

[16] RN in Charles W. Kegley, ed., *Reinhold Niebuhr, His Religious, Social and Political Thought*
(New York: Pilgrim Press, 1984), 5.

[17] RN in Kegley, *Reinhold Niebuhr*, p. 5.

[18] I refer here to what some would consider the idealism of biblical Christian notions such as "turn
the other cheek" when struck, or the call to "love your neighbor" and "love your enemy," or the sense
that Christians ought to entrust their hopes and dreams into the hands of a sovereign God, as encapsulated by the biblical phrase, "the battle belongs to the Lord."

[19] RN in Kegley, *Reinhold Niebuhr*, p. 6.

Niebuhr himself had risen. He believed that an idealistic, sentimental, pacifistic morality was inherent in the teachings of the liberal Protestant church,
which he believed encouraged unconditional submission to authority, even
when authority protected an unjust status quo. In other words, he believed
this idealistic moralism perpetuated social phenomena such as Fordism because it failed to acknowledge and/or confront injustice when doing so might
entail the overthrow of the status quo and/or the use of force. He was afraid
that this engendered naiveté, a naiveté that allowed the political exploiters
of the day to have their way as their idealistic flocks blindly accepted their
lot in life and naively failed to take precautions against the unscrupulous of
the world, particularly when the unscrupulous cloaked themselves in moral
pretension.

As he became more concerned about economic inequality, injustice, and
the blind spots of liberalism and liberal Protestantism, Niebuhr became yet
more politically active. He often spoke on social or political issues from the
pulpit, and in 1925 he initiated "The Bethel Forum," which focused on social, moral, economic, and political issues. The topics included were war,
race relations, divorce, and Prohibition.[20] By 1923, Niebuhr was moving in a
pro-labor direction, given his experiences with Ford in Detroit, and he began
to see the British Labour Party as the perfect mix of political and Christian
positions.

Niebuhr arrived at a pacifist position in 1923 when, after a study tour to
the UK, he went to France and Germany to better understand the postwar
situation there and to visit his ancestral home in Germany, Lippe Detmold.
The UK trip solidified his appreciation for the British Labour Party, but it
was his side-trip to the Ruhr Valley of Germany, then under occupation by
France in accordance with the provisions of the Versailles Treaty ending the
war, that drove him to embrace pacifism. Being fluent in German, he was
able to hear first-hand from German citizens there about the "horrible tales
of atrocities, deportations, sex crimes, etc.," as he recorded in his diary.[21] He
then visited other areas of Germany, where he found poverty and starvation.
The vindictiveness he saw in the postwar settlement led him to conclude that
the liberal ideals present in the stated war aims of the Allied powers rang
hollow, but rather were to him just another example of arrogant great power

---

[20] Fox, *Reinhold Niebuhry*, p. 66.
[21] From Niebuhr's diary, as found in Fox, *Reinhold Niebuhr*, p. 78.

politics, with war simply a tool to garner yet greater power and prestige for those with imperial ambitions.

By living and working in Detroit, Niebuhr, a white man who had grown up in a small town in the Midwest, also began to come to a deeper understanding of America's race problems. As Detroit became the industrial heart of America and the nation's fourth largest city, the need for low-cost labor burgeoned, and African Americans began to move to the Motor City in increasing numbers. As the number of black Americans increased in the city (along with Catholic workers and Jewish exiles from Europe), so did the activities of the hate group, the Ku Klux Klan (KKK), among white residents. During the 1925 mayoral contest, the KKK brought in outside support and a war chest of funds to support its favored candidate, Charles Bowles, who argued for the need for unity of Detroit's whites against the increasing numbers of black, Catholic, and Jewish residents.[22] On the Sunday prior to the election, for the first time in his career Niebuhr spoke from the pulpit about the problem of racism, and both major Detroit newspapers quoted Niebuhr in front-page stories.

> We fair-minded Protestants cannot deny that it was Protestantism that gave birth to the Ku Klux Klan, one of the worst specific social phenomena which the religious pride and prejudice of peoples has ever developed. . . . I do not deny that all religions are periodically corrupted by bigotry. But I hit Protestant bigotry the hardest at this time because it happens to be our sin and there is no use repenting for other people's sins. Let us repent of our own. . . We are admonished in Scripture to judge men by their fruits, not by their roots; and their fruits are their character, their deeds and accomplishments.[23]

Incumbent John Smith defeated Bowles narrowly and later named Niebuhr to a municipal Interracial Committee, set up to help improve relations between Detroit's races, a task Niebuhr embraced with gusto. On the committee, Niebuhr worked closely with a Jewish committee member named Fred Butzel, whom Niebuhr came to respect greatly. Richard Fox observes that "Butzel was the first Jew Niebuhr knew intimately," and Niebuhr came to have a lifelong respect and admiration for the Jewish people, in no small part

---

[22] Fox, *Reinhold Niebuhr*, p. 91.
[23] From Detroit *Free Press*, November 2, 1925, p. 1, as quoted in Fox, *Reinhold Niebuhr*, p. 91.

because of the friendship he shared with Butzel and Butzel's sensitivities to issues of justice and social ethics.[24] During his time in Detroit, Niebuhr also got involved in the Detroit mayor's efforts to better manage race relations, chairing the Mayor's Committee on Race Relations in Detroit in 1926. This resulted in a report that advocated practical measures to help address race relations and assist the African American community in Detroit.[25]

Niebuhr's Break with Liberalism and His Embrace of a Marxian Worldview

By the mid-1920s, as a result of his growing disillusionment with idealism in general and the liberal Protestant idealism so prevalent in America, together with his views of the harshness and injustice of Fordist industrial policies in Detroit, Niebuhr made a major change in his ideological orientation toward an embrace of some of the realist tenets of Marxist thought. Niebuhr was particularly attracted to Marx's critique of Western capitalism, and he found himself increasingly agreeing with Marx's notion of the exploitation of the proletariat by the capitalist classes, a phenomenon that particularly resonated with Niebuhr given his experiences in Detroit. He was not a communist of any stripe, for he saw communism as leading to unacceptable tyranny. Rather, he was primarily a progressive who saw in socialism a gradualist, progressive agenda for deep social, economic, and political reform. His brand of socialism might best be described as that of a modern European, Fabian variety. He found the ideal political, moral, economic, and social tonic for an ailing modern industrialism in a strong church, moral conservatism, social and political idealism, and a strong Christian political party embracing an activist labor movement.[26]

Richard Fox notes that by 1928, Niebuhr's energies were increasingly focused on social, economic, and political issues, and his mother (who still lived with him), his associate pastor and lay leaders in the church did most of the pastoring.[27] Consequently, it came as no great surprise when in 1928 Niebuhr announced his decision to leave Detroit and Bethel Evangelical

---

[24] Fox, *Reinhold Niebuhr*, p. 93.
[25] RN et al., "Report of the Mayor's Committee on Race Relations, Detroit, Michigan," The Mayor's Office, City of Detroit, 1926; as found in Box 16, Reinhold Niebuhr Papers, Manuscript Division, Library of Congress, Washington, DC.
[26] Fox, *Reinhold Niebuhr*, p. 83.
[27] Fox, *Reinhold Niebuhr*, p. 108.

Church to take a position at Union Theological Seminary in New York City, where he would remain a faculty member until his retirement. Union was by many accounts the best liberal seminary in the country at the time, and it provided Niebuhr a platform for his growing interest in the ethical and social issues of the day.

It was there in the 1930–1931 academic year that Niebuhr met his future wife, Ursula Keppel-Compton, the "British Fellow" at Union that year and an Oxford graduate. The inveterate bachelor, church builder, activist, and public intellectual had found in erudite and highly intellectual Ursula the perfect companion, and they announced their engagement at the end of that academic year and were married in England in December 1931. While Ursula found a faculty position at Barnard College and they settled down in a state of great joy, it was also a difficult time for Niebuhr: his mother—who had been living with him since his father's death in 1913—was now forced to live separately from him, as his wife did not want his mother to live with them following their marriage.[28] He was comforted somewhat in that his unmarried sister, Hulda, lived with his mother, so she was not alone, and they all lived near each other on New York's Upper West Side.

It was also during the 1930–1931 academic year that Niebuhr first encountered German theologian Dietrich Bonhoeffer (then only 24 years of age), who was "German Fellow" at Union for that year. Bonhoeffer, of course, was the well-known German pastor/theologian who stood up to Adolf Hitler as Hitler sought to pacify and coopt the German churches, later participated in an assassination attempt on the Führer's life, and was executed for it just weeks before the end of the war. Bonhoeffer took courses with Niebuhr at Union. Bonhoeffer and Niebuhr related well but disagreed on important points, particularly given that Bonhoeffer was a disciple of German theologian Karl Barth, whom liberals like Niebuhr at Union saw basically as an anachronistic, fundamentalist throwback. Of Union and its students, Bonhoeffer wrote,

They become intoxicated with liberal and humanistic phrases, laugh at the fundamentalists, and yet basically are not even up to their level. . . . In New York they preach about virtually everything; only one thing is not addressed, or is addressed so rarely that I have as yet been unable to hear

---

[28] See Ursula M. Niebuhr ed., *Remembering Reinhold Niebuhr: Letters of Reinhold and Ursula M. Niebuhr* (New York: Bloomsbury, 2001), p. 417 in particular.

it, namely, the gospel of Jesus Christ, the cross, sin and forgiveness, death and life.[29]

Although Niebuhr could not be found guilty of the latter charge (leaving out the cross, the gospel, etc.), Bonhoeffer found Niebuhr theologically shallow, and for his part, Niebuhr thought Bonhoeffer was politically naive. In the end, it seems that Niebuhr was influenced by Bonhoeffer to take theology more seriously, and Niebuhr influenced Bonhoeffer to take politics more seriously.[30] As Germany's politics became darker and darker, in 1939 Bonhoeffer asked Niebuhr to help him escape Germany (and his imminent draft into the German Army) by way of a lectureship in the United States. Niebuhr arranged it, having come to greatly respect Bonhoeffer's courageous stand, along with other German clergy who stood up against Hitler's increasing despotism. While Bonhoeffer's friends in America had arranged a stay for him in America that could have lasted two or three years or longer, after a few days in the United States Bonhoeffer felt guilt pangs, the sense that he'd abandoned his people in his nation's time of need. And so it was that he decided to return to Germany, where he became more political than either he or Niebuhr had ever imagined. After his return to Germany, Bonhoeffer continued his involvement in the "Confessing Church" there,[31] deepened his work with the resistance against the Nazis, even took part in an assassination attempt on Hitler's life, and was ultimately executed by the Third Reich. After the war, Niebuhr spent considerable energy helping to raise money for Bonhoeffer's family and the family of other clergy executed under Hitler. Most of them had become destitute, having suffered punishment and guilt by their association with clergy such as Bonhoeffer, as well as the general economic travails suffered by all German during and following the war.[32]

---

[29] Eric Metaxes, *Bonhoeffer: Pastor, Martyr, Prophet, Spy* (Nashville, TN: Thomas Nelson, 2010; Kindle Location 1955–62).

[30] Fox, *Reinhold Niebuhr: A Biography*, pp. 124–6. Eric Metaxes describes the impact of one aspect of Bonhoeffer's encounter with Niebuhr that did affect him deeply—Bonhoeffer's exposure to the book, *All Quiet on the Western Front* by Erich Remarque (a German soldier during World War I) which Metaxes concludes he read as part of a course with Niebuhr, and the subsequent viewing of the film with a French friend in New York thereafter. The French friend, Jean Lasserre, said he could barely console Bonhoeffer after viewing the film together and that he believed Bonhoeffer became a pacifist that day as a result, something that impacted Bonhoeffer deeply as his country moved deeper into the throes of Nazism in subsequent years. Metaxes, *Bonhoeffer*, Kindle Location 2172–208.

[31] The Confessing Church was a group of German Christian leaders who opposed Nazism's increasingly authoritarian ways, its domination of the church in Germany, and the regime's treatment of the Jews.

[32] For more, see letters between Niebuhr and Bonhoeffer's surviving twin sister, Sabine Leibholz, in Boxes 49 and 55 in the Reinhold Niebuhr Papers, Manuscript Division, Library of Congress, Washington, DC.

While Niebuhr listed 1926 as the year that he decided socialism had the answer to the problems associated with modern industrial society,[33] it was after his move to New York in 1928 that he became increasingly involved in socialist politics. His convictions about socialism's virtues and capitalism's shortcomings only deepened as the Great Depression began in October 1929, soon reaching around the world. In fact, in 1928, 1932, and 1936, he supported the Socialist Party's Norman Thomas for president of the United States, and he himself joined the Socialist Party in the summer of 1929.[34] He even ran as a socialist candidate for the New York State Senate in 1930 but lost badly. Taking his defeat in stride, he returned to his academic work and produced a highly acclaimed yet controversial (and now-classic) work, *Moral Man and Immoral Society*, published in late 1931.[35] *The New York Times* described the book in this way: "Doctrine of Christ and Marx Linked."[36] More recently, Gary Dorrien called it "the most important American theological work of the twentieth century," but noted that it got "terrible reviews." Leaders in the Protestant community denounced "its hard-edged Marxism, its condemnations of liberal stupidity, and the fact that Niebuhr ignored the teachings of Jesus, had no theology of the church,"[37] And so on. Niebuhr then ran for the U.S. Congress as a socialist candidate representing New York City and his home 19th District in 1932 but lost again, after which he returned to his academic pursuits. In 1935, Niebuhr said that "capitalistic society is destroying itself [and] must be destroyed, lest it reduce, in the delirium of its disintegration, our whole civilization to barbarism."[38] Such statements underline the point that Niebuhr's political radicalism during this period should not be understated, though neither should his aversion to Soviet totalitarianism[39] even prior to the worst of Stalin's purges. Despite his leftist

---

[33] See Daniel F. Rice, *Reinhold Niebuhr and His Circle of Influence* (Cambridge, UK: Cambridge University Press, 2012), (Kindle Location 2747–55). Rice cites "Interview with R. Niebuhr" (Oral History Research Office, Columbia University, 1954) as his source for this statement.

[34] For more on this topic, see Daniel Rice's discussion of Niebuhr's association with American socialist Norman Thomas (Rice, *Reinhold Niebuhr and His Circle*).

[35] RN, *Moral Man and Immoral Society* (New York: Charles Scribner's Sons, 1932)

[36] Fox, *Reinhold Niebuhr*, pp. 124–6.

[37] Gary Dorrien, "Introduction," in RN, *The Children of Light and the Children of Darkness: A Vindication of Democracy and a Critique of Its Traditional Defense* (Chicago: University of Chicago Press, 2011[1944]), Kindle Location 96.

[38] RN, "Radical Religion," in the inaugural issue of *Radical Religion*, 1 (Fall 1935), pp. 4–5; as quoted in Fox, *Reinhold Niebuhr*, p. 167.

[39] Having said this, it should be noted that Niebuhr had been sympathetic to and a defender of the Soviet experiment in socialism, at least prior to Stalin's 1930 purges and Niebuhr's turn away from socialism.

sensibilities, Niebuhr never abandoned his love and respect for the democracy he found in the United States and the UK.

Niebuhr's Break with Leftism and Pacifism

Yet, as his thinking developed in the 1930s at Union, Niebuhr began to believe Marxism had several fundamental flaws, and he slowly began moving away from it. He now parted ways with his socialist friends, including Norman Thomas, whom he increasingly came to see as being "in close proximity to those utopian romantics of whom he was most critical."[40] Because the socialism of his day was closely associated with pacifism, his alienation from socialism/Marxism grew as he began to find pacifism more and more problematic. The 1931 Japanese invasion of Manchuria (and the lack of Western willingness to respond to it with gusto) had already evoked in Niebuhr a growing aversion to pacifism.[41] He began to conclude that it was unloving and unrealistic for governments to simply disavow the tools of power on principle. As he listened to Christian pacifists charging Christian interventionists like himself with being traitors to the gospel, he said,

> The presupposition of all of this criticism is, of course, that there is a "gospel" political program, based on the Sermon on the Mount, and that anyone who engages in the rather dreadful but necessary business of resisting aggression and defying tyranny is untrue to his Christian faith.[42]

For Niebuhr, there was no "gospel political program," however. Rather, "there is no political program that stands in direct relation to the Sermon on the Mount, and . . . the only personal ethic that stands in such a relation is one that prompts the earnest believer to choose martyrdom rather than resistance to evil."[43] In other words, for Niebuhr "turning the other cheek" was an option for individuals, and that might well be what God might call individuals to do as it regarded their own safety and/or interests. As his thought

---

[40] Rice, *Reinhold Niebuhr and His Circle*, Kindle Location 2958–66.

[41] This movement away from pacifism is already evident in *Moral Man and Immoral Society*.

[42] RN, "Pacifism and 'America First,'" *Christianity in Crisis* (June 16, 1941); as found in D. B. Robertson, *Love and Justice: Selections from the Shorter Writings of RN* (Louisville, KY: Westminster/John Knox Press, 1957), p. 286.

[43] RN, "Pacifism and 'America First,'" *Christianity in Crisis* (June 16, 1941); as found in Robertson, *Love and Justice* (1957), p. 286.

later developed (and as will be discussed in the sections below), he found this cheek-turning ethic unsustainable as it regarded decisions made on behalf of others by political leaders.

So in addition to abandoning pacifism, Niebuhr started to move away from Marxism and his leftist proclivities as well. He began to see Marxist views of human nature as overly optimistic in their assumption that human beings could be perfected under the right social conditions. By 1937, he wrote that the world's crises were caused not by capitalism, but by humanity's penchant toward sin, which for Niebuhr was a return to a more traditional Christian understanding of social relations.[44] Niebuhr had come to the conclusion that Marxism was simply too idealistic, even utopian, in its supposition that the end of capitalism and the rise of the proletariat to power would bring about an end to class conflict and oppression, and would ultimately bring peace and prosperity to all. Niebuhr believed that the political manifestations of Marxism in Soviet Russia, particularly under Stalin with his ruthless purges in the 1930s, showed that the utopianism he came to see as inherent in Marxism created the justification for cruel oppression to ensure its mainte-nance as an economic and political system. Subsequently, Stalin and other Soviet leaders killed, imprisoned, or in other ways neutralized their oppo-sition and forced the people to work for the good of the state, perpetuating a system of government that was more oppressive and exploitative than any capitalist system it was thought to render obsolete.

For all of these reasons, by 1940 Niebuhr had come to the conclusion that he could no longer support socialism/Marxism. That year he resigned from the Socialist Party and voted for Democratic candidate Franklin Delano Roosevelt in that year's presidential election.[45] In addition to his changing views of socialism, his split with the Socialist Party in the United States was hastened by his growing identification with Roosevelt and his New Deal policies, and his agreement with the U.S. policy of entering World War II, a move that the pacifist socialists opposed in general and that they expressed to Niebuhr specifically in a pointed letter to him, criticizing his position.[46] In 1948, Niebuhr wrote, "the deepest tragedy of our age is that the alterna-tive to capitalism has turned out to be worse than the disease which it was meant to cure."[47] In 1965, in a retrospective statement about his former

---

[44] Fox, *Reinhold Niebuhr*, pp. 179–80.

[45] Rice 2012, Kindle Location 3128–36. Fox, however, argues that Niebuhr, while still a socialist, voted for Roosevelt already in the 1936 election. Fox, *Reinhold Niebuhr*, pp. 177–8.

[46] Rice 2012, Kindle Location 3128–43.

[47] RN, *Radical Religion*, XIII, no. 4 (Autumn 1948): 5.

leftism, Niebuhr opined, "I made so many mistakes that I now pathetically seek to claim credit for avoiding the cardinal mistake of many on the left," namely, that "I did succeed in escaping all the hallucinations of the left, who hailed the Russian Revolution as an emancipation for all mankind without noting that its annulment of freedom made the Stalinist despotism almost inevitable."[48] Niebuhr would always have a place in his heart for the plight of workers and the need for a progressive social ethic, but he would never return to the pacifism and socialism of his early intellectual life.

The Triumph of Christian Realism in Niebuhr's Thinking

With his alienation from Marxism/socialism complete, Niebuhr became theoretically grounded in Christian Realism, the plateau of his theoretical development—a plateau on which he remained encamped for the rest of his life. After his Gifford lectures at Edinburgh University in the autumn of 1939 as Nazi Germany launched its *blitzkrieg* in Europe, Niebuhr developed "a strong conviction that a realist conception of human nature should be made the servant of an ethic of progressive justice."[49] These ideas came to life most fully in his magnum opus, *Nature and Destiny of Man*, Volumes I and II (1941 and 1943), which were based on the Gifford Lectures. Robin Lovin notes that, while Christian Realism has been seen as Niebuhr's creation and he is most famously associated with it, Christian Realism per se was already a genre in theological circles (as distinct from the use of the term as applied to international relations [IR]) by the early 1930s, and it is from this that basis that Niebuhr developed his own iteration of the concept.[50] Niebuhr had already identified with Christian Realism (in the general sense) to some degree while he was a leftist. Of course, Marxism claims to be "realist" in the sense that it purports to describe social, economic, and political reality, so it should not come as a surprise that certain "realist" elements were already present in Niebuhr's worldview while he was still a leftist. Yet as he left behind his leftism, he moved more fully and completely into Christian Realism and famously applied it to IR and politics more generally, with great success.

---

[48] RN, *Man's Nature and His Communities* (New York: Charles Scribner's Sons, 1965), pp. 22 and 21, respectively.

[49] RN, *Man's Nature and His Communities*, pp. 24–25.

[50] Robin Lovin, *Reinhold Niebuhr and Christian Realism* (Cambridge, UK: Cambridge University Press, 1995), p. 2.

Christian Realism is driven by "a Christian view of human nature . . . involved in the paradox of claiming a higher stature for man and taking a more serious view of his evil than other anthropology,"[51] Niebuhr said. Christian Realism, while not claiming to reconcile the perennial differences between idealism and Realism, contains elements of both, and therefore a measure of dualism. Here idealism is seen as a relatively consistent approach to human thought and social life, focusing on what ought to be and/or what could be, as opposed to the realist approach which could be said to emphasize instead, what is. Idealism exists in philosophy, IR, and perhaps every field of study as a relatively consistent approach and no particular distinction is made here between general idealism and that which is found in IR, best characterized by the writings of Immanuel Kant (1991) or the policies of U.S. President Woodrow Wilson. Realism, however, has more than one usage, and so one should be a bit more cautious in how one uses it. In its most general sense, it is that which is realistic, sober, not idealistic, or overly optimistic. The second sense of the term is that which is used in Political Realism, or IR Realism.[52] Realism as used in IR is in this volume denoted with a capital "R" so as to differentiate it from the more common form of realism, which, like idealism, is found in nearly all academic disciplines. IR Realism is a school of thought or even a theory of IR elaborated by E. H. Carr, Hans Morgenthau, Kenneth Waltz, and many others, including Niebuhr himself. It stresses the assumptions of an anarchical, self-help international system characterized therefore by states seeking first and foremost their own national interests defined in terms of power so as to avoid the security dilemma that must come with the inherent uncertainty of other states' intentions. This Realism is truly the root of Niebuhr's IR thought, but the marriage of the Christian element to it introduces a sense of hope, in the idealist tradition, to a school of thought not known for its optimism. The element of hope suggested here is rooted in the Christian notions that God is good and God is sovereign, that "for those who love God all things work together for good" (Romans 8:28), and that with God there is the terrestrial potential (at least at times) for individual

---

[51] RN, *The Nature and Destiny of Man: Volume 1* (New York: Charles Scribner's Sons, 1941), p. 18; as cited in Lovin, *Reinhold Niebuhr and Christian Realism*, p. 2.

[52] There is another use of realism one might encounter in the IR literature, and that is that of scientific realism, as brought into IR discourse by Alexander Wendt in his discussion of the term in philosophy of science. I have come to use the term *scientific realism* (along with many others) as one of three epistemologies (along with positivism and interpretivism), scientific realism being the middle ground between the two. See Alexander Wendt, *Social Theory of International Politics* (Cambridge, UK: Cambridge University Press, 1999); David Marsh and Jerry Stoker, eds., *Theory and Methods in Political Science*, 2nd ed. (New York: Palgrave Macmillan, 2002).

transcendence of the sinful nature, and so on. While Niebuhr concluded that the self-interested realities of human nature made sincere altruism unlikely, he believed that through faith and God's grace human beings could transcend themselves and their own interests at the personal/individual level, at times, to an approximation of God's "agapé" (or unconditional) love.[53] Hence, Niebuhr's form of realism and/or Realism in the IR sense is decidedly more upbeat and less pessimistic than one might expect at times given his view of human nature. This view will be seen in the discussion in Chapter 5 regarding his view of the potential of the United Nations in particular.

Niebuhr's true realism showed itself, however, in the distinction he made between the potential for individual self-transcendence and collective or political "self"-transcendence, referring here to the notion that the "self" might be able to yield to or at least take into account the interests of other "selves." He was not speaking of two separate moralities, for as a Christian he believed in but one transcendent morality. Yet, Niebuhr recognized that a paradoxical distinction had to be made between the practical potential for manifestations of morality in the world at the individual level, versus that which one might expect to find at the collective level (for reasons to be discussed in greater depth later). While Niebuhr believed the transcendence of self-interest was possible (if not probable) at the personal level, he saw it as well nigh impossible at the collective or international level because of a phenomenon he called "collective self-interest"[54] Yet he was not a pessimist even in this respect. By recognizing both human potential (at least while in communion with its creator) and human limitations, he believed it was possible to reach a practicable, tolerable level of both prudence and morality. Still, it was inevitable, he felt, that the "love ethic"[55] associated with his Christian faith would have to be infringed upon to maintain justice at the social, governmental, and international levels. This will be discussed further below.

---

[53] RN, *Moral Man and Immoral Society* (New York: Charles Scribner's Sons, 1932), pp. XXII–XXIII.

[54] More on this notion of the distinction between individual versus collective/group moral potentialities in subsequent chapters.

[55] What is alluded to by "the Christian love ethic" is encapsulated in Christ's admonitions to "love your neighbor as yourself," (Mark 12:31), to "love your enemies and do good, expecting nothing in return" (Luke 6:35), to "not resist the one who is evil. But if anyone slaps you on the right cheek, turn to him the other also" (Matthew 5:39), and statements in the Bible's "love chapter," 1 Corinthians 13, especially verses 4–6: "Love is patient and kind; love does not envy or boast; it is not arrogant or rude. It does not insist on its own way; it is not irritable or resentful; it does not rejoice at wrongdoing, but rejoices with the truth." (All of these passages were taken from the English Standard Version of the Holy Bible.)

Christian Realism was the embodiment of Niebuhr's desire to create an alternative to both (what he saw as) morally bankrupt Machiavellian, purely self-interested power politics on the one hand and naive, utopian idealism on the other. He thus attempted to cast asunder the exaggerations of both without entirely surrendering the insights of either. Niebuhr once astutely observed that "a view more sober than that of either idealists or realists must persuade us that 'If hopes are dupes, fears may be liars.'"[56]

The Christian Realist Views World War II

World War II had a profound effect on Niebuhr's thinking. In the fall of 1939, he was at the University of Edinburgh giving the Gifford Lectures, which became the foundation for his most intellectually impressive work, *The Nature and Destiny of Man*. Niebuhr had no illusions about Adolph Hitler, given his views of human nature and his many German contacts, the likes of Dietrich Bonhoeffer being just one. He even experienced a German bombing raid on a Royal Navy base a few miles away from his location in Edinburgh during his time there.[57]

Niebuhr feared that Europe and America were too soft on Hitler and the Nazis, and he had been extremely worried even before the actual outbreak of the war in September 1939. It was precisely the kind of liberal pacifism he'd earlier espoused that he felt was responsible for the weak British, French, Russian, and American responses to Hitler's Germany. Niebuhr opposed Stalin's deal with Hitler in the Molotov–Ribbentrop Act, seeing it as Soviet capitulation to an untrustworthy Nazi German partner. He thought Chamberlain's meeting with Hitler in Munich led to an inexcusable British surrender to tyranny. Niebuhr wrote to his friend, Waldo Frank, "The world is continuing to go to hell. I have never seen anything so cynical as Chamberlain's policy. It has written the doom of European civilization. . . . Britain has practically advertised the fact [that] Germany can have her way in Prague."[58] Niebuhr's words were prophetic of course for, as we all know now,

---

[56] RN, *The Children of Light and the Children of Darkness* (New York: Charles Scribner's Sons, 1944), p. 176.
[57] Fox, *Reinhold Niebuhr*, p. 191.
[58] RN to Waldo Frank, June 1, 1939, Frank Papers, University of Pennsylvania; as quoted in Fox, *Reinhold Niebuhr*, p. 186.

after the Munich meeting the rest of Czechoslovakia was occupied and Hitler invaded Poland as well, followed by invasion of most of the rest of Europe.

Perhaps because of his many German contacts, coupled with his deep respect for the Jewish people, Niebuhr was aware of and concerned about what was happening to the Jews in Europe. This was another element in his shifting position on politics, the use of force in IR, and U.S. foreign policy. As Richard Fox recounts, the plight of the Jews was

> for him [Niebuhr] one of the key arguments for [Western] intervention. . . .
> By the early thirties, he had made the ethical leap to coercion [in interna-
> tional relations], and grasped that Hitler was bent on the cultural anni-
> hilation of the Jews. From that time on he was a firm, though sometimes
> qualified, backer of the Zionist cause.[59]

Niebuhr even made the case that U.S. and British power should be used after the war to establish a Jewish homeland in what was called Palestine.[60] After the war, indeed he was an ardent supporter of the establishment of the state of Israel.

As the crisis in Europe continued to develop, Niebuhr became so upset by the events in Europe and the lack of U.S. support of Great Britain and Europe's Jewish community that it impacted his health in a very negative way. "Niebuhr was so agitated he could not sleep; his exhaustion deepened."[61] It should be noted here that Niebuhr, an American citizen who saw clear evil in Hitler, was doing his Gifford Lectures in the UK, his wife was a British citizen, and the United States was at this point in the war doing little to help in the European crisis. Upon his return to the United States, he fell ill as a result of chronic exhaustion due to overwork, lack of rest, and anxiety. Unfortunately, this was not to be his first experience with serious illness. Health problems would remain with him for the rest of his life.

Britain's entrance into World War II with its declaration of war on Nazi Germany following the German invasion of Poland, and then British bravery at Dunkirk and the Battle of Britain, brought Niebuhr to do all he could to drum up support for the UK in its war effort against the Nazis. While Niebuhr had become increasingly supportive of President Roosevelt's

---

[59] Fox, *Reinhold Niebuhr*, pp. 209–10.
[60] Fox, *Reinhold Niebuhr*, pp. 209–10.
[61] Fox, *Reinhold Niebuhr*, p. 192.

policies, he thought the president too slow to join the war effort wholeheartedly. Writing in February 1941, prior to the Pearl Harbor attack that finally
brought American entry into the war, Niebuhr said,

> . . . .Nazi tyranny intends to annihilate the Jewish race, to subject the nations
> of Europe to the dominion of a "master" race, to extirpate the Christian reli-
> gion, to annul the liberties and legal standards that are the priceless heritage
> of ages of Christian and humanistic culture, to make truth the prostitute of
> political power, to seek world dominion through its straps and allies, and
> generally to destroy the very fabric of our Western civilization.[62]

Niebuhr was moving steadily away from his former pacifist stance. He became firm in his conviction that political pacifism was akin to complicity
with tyrants like Hitler, whom he believed represented evil too profound to
be ignored or appeased.

In 1940, the Socialist Party in the United States (which was pacifist)
took note of Niebuhr's stand and confronted him on it. Niebuhr replied by
resigning from the party—no small step considering he had been one of its
intellectual leaders and a New York State senatorial candidate running on its
ticket. Even as Niebuhr parted ways with the leftism of his earlier years and
was campaigning for a stronger foreign policy to protect Western civilization
from the dual threats of Nazi and Soviet communist tyranny, "the FBI was
working overtime to protect the nation from Reinhold Niebuhr."[63] Some on
the right had branded Niebuhr a dangerous leftist during the 1930s, not really understanding that, while he was a socialist, he was not a communist and
had always opposed the totalitarian form of communism that arose in the
Soviet Union, even before he disavowed his leftist ties altogether. After an in-
depth investigation (that became known to Niebuhr, to his amusement), the
FBI concluded that he was not a threat and dropped the matter.

During this time, Niebuhr's career continued to develop. He founded a
new journal, *Christianity and Crisis*,[64] which became extremely influential
in liberal Protestant circles and was in circulation from 1941 to 1993. He
also published what many consider his magnum opus, *Nature and Destiny*

---

[62] RN, "The Christian Faith and the World Crisis," *Christianity and Crisis* (inaugural issue,
February 10, 1941); in RN, *Love and Justice*, pp. 281–4.

[63] Fox, *Reinhold Niebuhr*, p. 207.

[64] For more, see Mark Hulsether, *Building a Protestant Left: Christianity and Crisis Magazine,
1941–1993* (Knoxville: University of Tennessee Press, 1999).

of Man, Volume I (1941) and *Volume II* (1943), to rave reviews.[65] It should be noted that in *Volume II* his thinking on the ability of groups/nations to cooperate exhibited an evolution from his earlier thinking in at least one important way. In *Moral Man and Immoral Society*, he famously argued that the possibility of love and cooperation between individuals was real (hence the possibility of "moral man") but much more difficult to be realized between groups/nations (hence the prevalence of "immoral society").[66] In *Nature and Destiny of Man, Volume II*, he argued that love and cooperation between groups was in fact possible because of the roles of institutions and customary law, for example, which could potentially channel and/or contain man's unrighteous proclivities, at least in democratic societies.

Despite this change in his thinking, Niebuhr had not become an idealist and Germany's and Japan's evils and expansionism only underlined to him the flaws of the post-World War I liberalism and the liberals' enlightenment assumptions about the rise of liberal values and scientism being able to make such wars obsolete. The very science that such liberals were arguing would draw the world together was being exploited in new ways to perpetrate new evils, from the Nazis' mass gassing of Jews to the deployment of flame throwers and mass air bombing campaigns, to the development and use of nuclear weapons. With the admission of the United States into the war following the attacks at Pearl Harbor, he did note the high level of cooperation and self-sacrifice among the Allies in their fight against Nazi Germany and Imperial Japan, underlining the virtues of democratic societies in his eyes, in stark opposition to their authoritarian and totalitarian counterparts.

As World War II progressed, Niebuhr witnessed the democratic allied nations commit gross violations of morality, underlining in his view of the fallenness or depravity of human beings, whether fascist, communist, or democratic. Niebuhr found bombing cities very problematic morally, and it was in World War II that the capacity to wreak untold havoc from the air became technically possible. "For the bombing of cities is a vivid revelation of the whole moral ambiguity of warfare. It is not possible to defeat a foe without causing innocent people to suffer with the guilty."[67] What the just war tradition[68] refers to as discrimination between combatants and noncombatants,

---

[65] Volume II was published in 1943.

[66] This will be discussed in greater depth in subsequent chapters.

[67] RN, "The Bombing of Germany," *Christianity and Society* (Summer, 1943); in RN, *Love and Justice*, p. 222.

[68] For more, see Michael Walzer, *Just and Unjust Wars: A Moral Argument with Historical Illustrations*, 3rd ed. (New York: Basic Books, [1977] 2000).

between targets of military necessity and surrounding structures, becomes exceedingly difficult, creating dilemmas of *jus in bello*, or justice in how war is waged. Moreover, once the cows were out of the barn, so to speak, it would be very difficult to put them back in again, Niebuhr feared. In other words, "Once bombing has been developed as an instrument of warfare, it is not possible to disavow its use without capitulating to the foe who refuses to disavow it."[69] Niebuhr was yet more troubled by the atomic bombing of Hiroshima and Nagasaki. He was a member of a special commission of the Federal Council of Churches which issued a statement (which he signed), declaring that the surprise atomic bombing of Hiroshima and Nagasaki was "morally indefensible" and in fact that "we [Americans] have sinned grievously against the law of God and against the people of Japan."[70]

Yet, despite these arguments, Niebuhr later argued that the use of atomic weapons against Japan was "justified," for it shortened the war.[71] He maintained that only the unconditional surrender of Japan was acceptable and, with most people in the United States, he believed that when surrender was not to be forthcoming, the atomic bombs were preferable to a long, bloody land war on Japan proper, which is what most observers (and President Truman himself) believed would have to happen otherwise. In a letter to James Conant explaining why he signed the Federal Council of Churches statement when the pragmatism of his *Children of Light, Children of Darkness* arguments might suggest otherwise, Niebuhr made this comment, starting out by saying that the report did not

> make sufficient[ly] clear what was the conviction of most of us—that the eventual use of the bomb for the shortening of the war would have been justified. I myself consistently took the position that failing in achieving a Japanese surrender, the bomb would have had to be used to save the lives of thousands of American soldiers who would otherwise have been perished on the beaches of Japan.[72]

---

[69] RN, "The Bombing of Germany," *Christianity and Society* (Summer 1943); in RN, *Love and Justice*, p. 223.

[70] Federal Council of Churches, "Atomic Warfare and the Christian Faith," excerpted in "Theology and the Bomb," *Christian Century*, April 10, 1946; as cited in Fox, *Reinhold Niebuhr*, p. 224.

[71] RN to James B. Conant, letter of March 12, 1946; as cited in Fox, *Reinhold Niebuhr*, p. 224.

[72] RN to James B. Conant, letter of March 12, 1946; as described and cited in Fox, *Reinhold Niebuhr*, pp. 224–5.

This statement highlights well the dialectical element in Niebuhr's work, acknowledging that fighting evil requires choices that themselves sometimes lead to evil. Niebuhr might say that, although Americans committed grievous sins against Japan, war itself unleashes evil, and it was Japan who in fact had unleashed this evil by its initial imperialism. To put it another way, Niebuhr believed that, while in the process "sin[ning] grievously" by resorting to the indiscriminate force of dropping a nuclear bomb, America was just in bringing the greater evil of war itself to an end and those who started the war to justice.

With the surrender of Nazi Germany and Imperial Japan, Niebuhr found a new cause—forgiveness toward the defeated powers and reconciliation with former combatant nations and their peoples. In the summer of 1946, he accompanied John Foster Dulles to Cambridge in the UK for a meeting that would lay the foundation for the World Council of Churches (founded in 1948). At that meeting, Niebuhr and Dulles pressed for a resolution that would in turn press the governments of the delegates for policies of forgiveness toward the defeated nations. Unfortunately, the resolution was defeated, but as Douglas Johnston and others have documented, the general notion of forgiveness did find a welcoming audience in some circles. Forgiveness and reconciliation between victors and vanquished ultimately did win the day in postwar Europe for the most part, as Germany and its Western European neighbors sought and found reconciliation.[73]

Niebuhr and the Cold War

Given that a chapter in this book is devoted to Niebuhr's experience of and commentary on the Cold War, this section will be brief, but important here from a biographical standpoint is the fact that the Cold War saw Niebuhr come into his own as a public intellectual of national stature. Having turned away from his earlier intellectual and political leftism, in the late 1940s he came to a position of ardently hawkish anticommunism. Like fellow Realist George Kennan, he saw the Soviet threat as being primarily ideological rather than military in nature. Early on in the Cold War, he feared that the West was too complacent about the dangers posed by the Soviet Union. Later

---

[73] Douglas M. Johnston, *Religion: The Missing Dimension in Statecraft* (Oxford: Oxford University Press, 1994).

in the Cold War, he feared that the West, the United States in particular, had come to exaggerate its own righteousness in the face of what he saw as the "evil" of communism, and began to overplay its hand in the Cold War drama. He saw Europe and the contest between Soviet totalitarianism and Western liberalism as being the core of the conflict. He did not regard the Asian theater of the Cold War as fundamental a challenge to the West as was Europe. The Asian theater (China, Korea, and Vietnam) was primarily a question of national self-determination versus imperialism, with communism playing a junior role in his view.

The Vietnam War, of course, became the defining military conflict for the United States during the Cold War. It is therefore worth considering briefly here Niebuhr's position on U.S. policy in Vietnam, for the themes inherent therein are indicative of the most fundamental Niebuhrian themes during the Cold War. While Niebuhr was, again, a hawk on Soviet communism and an advocate of containment of communism in Europe, Niebuhr praised Eisenhower's decision to avoid helping the French in Vietnam in 1953–1954, arguing that the United States should not get involved in military affairs in the Asian continent, which Niebuhr felt were doomed to fail and which, in his view, were peripheral to U.S. interests. Again, he believed that Europe was the crux of the conflict and that communism in Asia was not of a pure type but was a rallying cry and/or vehicle for anti-imperialist Asian nationalists rather than a true ideological type of communism that was a threat to the world, as was that of the USSR. As the United States became more deeply involved in Vietnam in the 1960s, Niebuhr became increasingly critical of U.S. policy there, arguing that hubris and not strategic interests were driving U.S. policy. While he supported Lyndon Johnson's presidency, as Johnson escalated U.S. involvement in the region, Niebuhr became increasingly disillusioned. He disagreed with Johnson that Vietnamese communism needed to be contained because he saw Vietnamese communism as being a Vietnamese nationalist movement, not a major new front in international communism. With other Realists of his era, he came to be highly critical of U.S. policymakers during the Vietnam era, arguing that the United States had gone overboard in Vietnam and that the U.S. war there was counterproductive and morally unjust. As a result, he lost favor with much of the Washington establishment, a fact that didn't seem to bother him much at his age. In fact, he always relished speaking truth to power, challenging the status quo, and in his perspectives on the Vietnam War he made no exception.

Niebuhr's Final Years

Niebuhr's final years were characterized by severe health challenges and a bit of depression. Starting in the spring of 1952, at age 60, Niebuhr's health began to fail him, and, as noted earlier, health problems plagued him for the rest of his life. That spring he began to experience spasms and paralysis on one side of his body, and much to his dismay, he had to cancel that spring's courses. He experienced a stroke due primarily to overwork and exhaustion. Just as his father, who died at 50, did, Niebuhr had always driven himself and had given himself little rest. It was now finally catching up with him. Accompanying the inactivity that his physical incapacitation brought him came clinical depression, most likely driven by his inability to meet his work commitments and the fact that all of this took him off the playing field and put him on the sidelines when he was yet near the peak of his influence socially, academically, theologically, and politically. He still managed to write, however, and by any human standard of activity, he was quite productive.[74] He managed to recover to some degree and continue teaching at Union Theological Seminary, though with a lighter course load and reduced duties at the behest of his seminary president. He finished *The Structure of Nations and Empires* in 1959, to mixed reviews. But 1959–1960 brought even more difficult events for Niebuhr, especially his sister Hulda's death in April 1959 and his mother's death in 1960. In 1960, too, Niebuhr retired from Union Seminary, at the age of 68, and this was particularly hard for him. As Richard Fox notes, "Niebuhr was more at home with his students than with anyone else.... Retirement for him was not just the end of a teaching career, but the disruption of a primary bond.... At the final dinner in his honor, in May, 1960, he wept openly."[75]

After his stroke, and increasingly as he faced further health challenges, Niebuhr came to depend on his very capable wife, Ursula, not only for physical care, but for professional support as well. Rebekah Miles argues that Ursula Niebuhr was at minimum an editor of much of her husband's work and more likely a co-author.[76] I think this is even more likely after Niebuhr's physical condition worsened and his energy began to wane. Yet it is clear that Ursula was an important part of his intellectual activity at a number of different levels and from an early stage in his career. As early as in the dedication

[74] Fox, *Reinhold Niebuhr*, p. 261.
[75] Fox, *Reinhold Niebuhr*, p. 270.
[76] Rebekah Miles, "Was Ursula Niebuhr Reinhold's Coauthor?" *The Christian Century* (January 19, 2012; https://www.christiancentury.org/article/2012-01/uncredited, accessed August 11, 2018).

to his 1941 magnum opus, *The Nature and Destiny of Man, Volume I: Human Nature*, Niebuhr wrote this:

> *To my wife*
> URSULA
> *who helped, and*
> *To my children*
> CHRISTOPHER *and* ELIZABETH
> *who frequently interrupted me*
> *in the writing of these pages*[77]

With this dedication he seems to indicate that his wife helped him with the work, though he does not say in what manner. In her own edited volume, *Remembering Reinhold Niebuhr*, she said as much, noting that when Reinhold typed away while working on *Nature and Destiny of Man Volume II*, "characteristically he would emerge for a break and for me to look at some pages."[78] My own research suggests that he trusted his wife's intellectual gifts (she was an Oxford graduate and an academic in her own right, having been the first chair of the Religion Department at Barnard College in 1940),[79] as well as trusting her English skills more than his own. Having grown up in a German-speaking home in a small town in Missouri and then Illinois, he was insecure in his early career about his own English, and it seems likely that he felt more confident allowing his Oxford-educated English wife to check his writing before sending it off to the publisher. He is more explicit about Ursula's contribution, as Miles points out, in the introduction of his 1965 book, *Man's Nature and His Communities*, where he says,

> I will not elaborate an already too intimate, autobiographical detail of a happy marriage except to say that this volume is published under my name, and the joint authorship is not acknowledged except in this confession. I will leave the reader to judge whether male arrogance or complete mutuality is the cause of this solution.[80]

[77] RN, *The Nature and Destiny of Man, Volume I: Human Nature* (Scribner's, 1941).

[78] Ursula M. Niebuhr, ed., *Remembering Reinhold Niebuhr: Letters of Reinhold and Ursula M. Niebuhr* (New York: Bloomsbury, 2001), p. 154.

[79] I take this detail from Niebuhr's daughter, Elisabeth Sifton, in her own book, *The Serenity Prayer: Faith and Politics in Times of Peace and War* (New York: W. W. Norton, 2005).

[80] RN, *Man's Nature and His Communities* (1965), as cited in Miles, "Was Ursula Niebuhr Reinhold's Coauthor?" (2012).

Here he concedes joint authorship. It's less striking here because we know that by 1965 his health was truly fragile and the degree to which his wife helped him was undoubtedly higher. Neither Ursula nor Elisabeth, in their respective books, suggests that this bothered Ursula, though Miles's article suggests that it may (I think understandably) have bothered her a bit. In any event, it is clear that Ursula played an important role in Niebuhr's intellectual and professional pursuits. As someone has said, "Behind every great man stands a great woman." Perhaps in this case it was, "*Alongside* every great man stands a great woman."

After retirement, Niebuhr continued to remain academically and politically active, as much as his health struggles would allow him. He took visiting lectureships and research positions at Columbia and Harvard universities, and he continued to write and to be an active observer and commentator on American and international political affairs. With the rise of the Kennedys in Washington in 1960, though a Democrat, Niebuhr felt highly uncomfortable. He disliked John F. Kennedy's marital infidelities and what he saw as the family's dynastic, bourgeois ways. In the end, he did vote for Kennedy, for he disliked Richard Nixon even more. Yet Niebuhr thought Kennedy's Cuba policy was too aggressive, even reckless in reference to the Bay of Pigs operation. Niebuhr *did* heartily approve of Kennedy's egalitarian policies, calling them "brilliant," and slowly he came to have respect for the young senator turned president, so much so that the assassination in 1963 deeply impacted Niebuhr and he mourned the president's death.[81]

Niebuhr's views of the 1960 Supreme Court decision to ban school prayer and his position on Martin Luther King Jr.'s civil rights movement provide some additional insights into Niebuhr's political ethos. When the Supreme Court banned school prayer, Niebuhr was critical, siding with the conservatives who opposed it, saying that it was in effect the endorsement, even the establishment, of secular religion and that it violated "the establishment clause" of the First Amendment of the Constitution. In an earlier letter to his friend, Supreme Court Justice Felix Frankfurter, he explained his position. "The prevailing philosophy which is pumped into our schools day after day is itself a religion . . . [which] preaches the redemption of man by historical development . . . and scientific objectivity."[82] While surely conservative

---

[81] Fox, *Reinhold Niebuhr*, pp. 272, 281.
[82] RN to Felix Frankfurter, March 31, 1948. Frankfurter Papers, Library of Congress; as found in Fox, *Reinhold Niebuhr*, p. 296.

Christians will approve of the stand he took on this issue, again Niebuhr is hard to categorize, for he was uncomfortable with Christian conversion narratives and fundamentalist interpretations of the Bible. He was more comfortable with what might be called Jamesian Christianity, the notion that, rather than discussing their faith, Christians should show their faith by what they do and how they live.[83]

With regard to Martin Luther King Jr., Niebuhr knew of and had great respect for him and wholeheartedly supported MLK's strategy of civil disobedience and campaign for equality. Niebuhr recognized the problem of racism and linked it to human nature and what Christians call "original sin." He called racial hatred "the most vicious of all human vices," and, comparing racism in the United States to South African apartheid said,

> We may be grateful that our situation is several levels above that of the dismal South African situation. But we can not deny that we are dealing with the various facets of a single historical development. That is the rise to political consciousness of the Negro of the world, and their justified rebellion against any custom or law which [sic] denies or obscures their common humanity with the rest of us. Thus the negro is in the process of validating a common humanity which many white men on all continents have arrogantly and futilely denied.[84]

He added this explanation. "The Christian knows that the ideal of racial brotherhood is the 'law of God' in which we delight 'after the inward man'; but he ought also to understand that racial arrogance is 'the law in our members which wars against the law that is in our mind' "[85] (referring here to Romans 7:22–23). Following the "Montgomery savagery," the beatings of black Freedom Riders in Montgomery, Alabama in 1961, Niebuhr wrote, "The question is simply whether we are prepared to treat our fellow man with the respect that his innate dignity as a human being requires and deserves."[86] Niebuhr was greatly bothered by "white pride" and worked in his own church and his own city while in Detroit to do what he could to address the

---

[83] For more, see James 2:18, the Holy Bible.

[84] RN, "The Rising Tide of Color," p. 2, original manuscript found in Box 17, Reinhold Niebuhr Papers, Manuscript Division, Library of Congress, Washington, DC. No further information on date or whether it was published is available in the box/folder.

[85] RN, *The Children of Light and the Children of Darkness*, p. 14.

[86] RN, "Montgomery Savagery," *Christianity in Crisis* (June 12, 1961): 103; as found in Fox, *Reinhold Niebuhr*, p. 282.

problem of racism. Consequently, Niebuhr had great respect for King and his movement. At the same time, King knew of Niebuhr, had read his work, and had great respect for Niebuhr, one who, like him, was a minister, a scholar, and a public figure. Niebuhr's work had a profound impact on King. King's aide, Andrew Young, who explained that King always said that his (King's) approach to social justice was "much more influenced" by Niebuhr than by Ghandi, and that King viewed his own approach, using nonviolent civil disobedience, to be "a Niebuhrian stratagem of power."[87]

As Niebuhr's age advanced and his career slowed further in the late 1960s, he came to be at peace with who he was, with his life's work, and with all he had accomplished. He noted in particular that he was thankful to have been a minister, to have taken up his father's calling.[88] When in 1961 June Bingham's biography[89] of Niebuhr appeared to warm reviews from critics and fans alike, while Niebuhr was somewhat overwhelmed, he was also a bit embarrassed and somewhat uncomfortable. For Niebuhr had always considered himself a prophet, and the warmth with which the book was received, and the kind and celebratory words it had for him and his life of service, may have made him wonder if perhaps he had sold out to success, to pride, to worldly ambition. Surely, he thought, true prophets live in opposition to mainstream trends and rarely receive such kudos, at least in their own lifetimes.[90]

The kudos continued to come, however. In 1964, for example, President Lyndon Johnson awarded Niebuhr the Presidential Medal of Freedom, the highest honor the U.S. government can bestow on a civilian. This must have come as a great blessing to the German American who lived through two American wars against Germany, and to the former radical leftist turned ardent anticommunist, investigated for loyalty several times by the FBI during the Cold War even as he served his country and hoped and prayed fervently for its success, for its very heart and soul. On June 1, 1971, Reinhold Niebuhr the Christian, intellectual, Liberal, conservative, prophet, polemicist, peacemaker, moralist, pragmatist American, left this world for the next.

To Richard Fox all students of Niebuhr owe a great debt, for his biography of Niebuhr stands unequaled for its depth, breadth, intelligence, and

---

[87] *Christianity and Crisis* editor Wayne Cowan to RN, April 13, 1970, RN Papers; as found in Fox, *Reinhold Niebuhr*, p. 283.

[88] Fox, *Reinhold Niebuhr*, p. 287.

[89] June Bingham, *Courage to Change* (New York: Scribner's, 1961).

[90] I thank Richard Fox for this insightful observation. Fox, *Reinhold Niebuhr*, p. 273.

insights. It seems fitting to close this biographical section with one of Fox's observations about Niebuhr.

> The uniqueness of Reinhold Niebuhr lay in the energy and zeal with which he pursued paradox and irony in both life and thought. The prophet-priest seeking influence and humility. The German-American Anglophile. The religious-secular preacher chastising the pious and chiding the worldly. The teacher-academic who distrusted the scholars and hoped for their respect. The liberal crusader against liberalism. The Jamesian relativist who embraced the God of Abraham and the revelation of Jesus. The booming polemicist beset with hidden anxieties. Truth could be expressed only in paradox, he believed, and life lived as a succession of pregnant contradictions.[91]

It is exactly these paradoxes and contradictions that Niebuhr found so important in his scholarship and polemics, things from which he urged us all not to run, uncomfortable though they might make us. These paradoxes, contradictions, ironies, and dualisms are the source of Niebuhr's decision in his work, ministry, and ideational orientation to marry idealism with realism. Niebuhr's analysis of the relation of the Christian love ethic to a world based on pragmatic self-interest was the central theme of his work and thus, by its very nature, an exercise in dialectics, or the attempt to find the point of convergence between two opposing forces. The dialectical element in Niebuhr's work stems from a deeper source, however—his conception of human nature—a discussion we turn to next.

---

[91] Fox, *Reinhold Niebuhr*, p. 291.

3

Niebuhr on Human Nature

The basis of Reinhold Niebuhr's social and political thought is found in his conception of human nature. William John Wolf called this conception "the basis of his whole thought."[1] In like manner, Kenneth Thompson said, "Niebuhr explicitly assumes that an understanding of political phenomena, whether international or domestic, is inseparable from a clear picture of human nature."[2] After all, societies and political institutions *are* made up of individuals—powerful individuals who shape and direct them. Though still controversial in many quarters, more recent research on human nature in the social sciences affirms the place given to human nature in Niebuhr's work, suggesting that human nature indeed exists and that it is universal across humanity. In an important edited volume by John Tooby and Leda Cosmides, the starting point of the project is the notion that "there is a universal human nature, but that this universality exists at the level of evolved psychological mechanisms, not of expressed cultural behaviors."[3] Some of IR's most cutting-edge research also has returned to human nature. For example, Harvard's Stephen Rosen takes human nature seriously, potentially launching a whole new subfield of IR with his work on war and human nature.[4] In his most recent work on the mind, neuroscience, quantum physics, and IR, Alexander Wendt, too, considers the role of human nature.

With the human body as our starting point, the first question to ask is of its nature: what essential properties and dispositions do we have that might enable and constrain social possibilities? Some may doubt whether

---

[1] William John Wolf, "RN's Doctrine of Man," in Charles W. Kegley, ed., *Reinhold Niebuhr, His Religious, Social and Political Thought* (New York: Pilgrim Press, 1984), p. 306.

[2] Kenneth W Thompson, "The Political Philosophy of RN," in Charles W. Kegley, *Reinhold Niebuhr*, p. 235.

[3] John Tooby and Leda Cosmides, "Introduction," in Jerome Barkow, Leda Cosmides, and John Tooby, eds., *The Adapted Mind: Evolutionary Psychology and the Generation of Culture*, Revised Ed. (Oxford: Oxford University Press, 1995), p. 5; also cited by Stephen Rosen, *War and Human Nature* (Princeton, NJ: Princeton University Press, 2009).

[4] Rosen, *War and Human Nature*.

Niebuhrian International Relations. Gregory J. Moore, Oxford University Press (2020).
© Oxford University Press.
DOI: 10.1093/oso/9780197500446.001.0001

a human nature exists, but in my view, there is no less reason to think that humans have a nature than horses or honeybees do. We all come from the same evolutionary process and in each case our behavior is differentially empowered by its material and mental gifts.[5]

Wendt goes on to define human nature in a way that is not inconsistent with Niebuhr's use of the term.

By the content of human nature I mean what most of the debate is about, namely fundamental behavioral dispositions: the extent to which, compared to animals or each other (men vs. women), people are naturally selfish, altruistic, aggressive, sociable, and so on.[6]

While I would not say Niebuhr would agree with every aspect of where the current human nature research is going in IR, nor would these scholars agree with all that Niebuhr said about human nature or human ontology,[7] it may be that Reinhold Niebuhr was ahead of his time regarding the role of human nature and IR. Modern neuroscience seems to provide strong evidence that Niebuhr was right about much that he said about human behavior, as I will argue later. In any event, because Niebuhr's particular insights into human nature are what set his social, political, and international thought apart, a thorough understanding of his views of human nature is necessary as a basis for understanding his social and political theories. For this reason, this chapter focuses on Niebuhr's views on human nature.

---

[5] Alexander Wendt, *Quantum Mind and Social Science: Unifying Physical and Social Ontology* (Cambridge, UK: Cambridge University Press, 2015), p. 150. Wendt goes on to define human nature in a way that is not inconsistent with Niebuhr's use of the term: "By the content of human nature I mean what most of the debate is about, namely fundamental behavioral dispositions: the extent to which, compared to animals or each other (men vs. women), people are naturally selfish, altruistic, aggressive, sociable, and so on."

[6] Wendt, *Quantum Mind and Social Science*, p. 150.

[7] Niebuhr was of course not an evolutionary psychologist but a Christian ethicist and clergyman. He held a traditional Christian view of humanity and human nature. For more, see RN, "Christianity and Darwin's Revolution," written for a 100-year anniversary symposium on Darwin at the University of Pittsburgh, convened by Prof. Ralph Buchsbaum (submitted by RN on February 28, 1957), as found in Box 15, Reinhold Niebuhr Papers, Manuscript Division, Library of Congress, Washington, DC.

Niebuhr's View of Human Nature: Christian Realism

Niebuhr embraced the biblical, realist view of human nature. He saw human nature as dialectical,[8] consisting of two elements—one spiritual, one physical. In Niebuhr's view human beings are earthly creatures, yet through spiritual union with God they can transcend their earthly bounds and limitations. Biblically speaking, God created human beings in his image, but in their post-Adamic birth and existence, they were creatures of the earth. For Niebuhr, what separated them from the beasts was their capacity to reason, to will, and to create, but most importantly God gave human beings the capacity to know himself. Through this fruitful union of earthly and divine (humanity honoring God by seeking his favor/will, and God loving/blessing humanity), Niebuhr believed human beings have the capacity for virtue and fulfillment. The human being is creature yet creator—creature because of his or her biological composition, yet creator because of the God-given rational capacities that allow human beings to act and to create.

Consequently, Niebuhr concluded that human nature is dual in nature from birth. While "created in the image of God," our creatureliness, our weaknesses to the desires of a physical, material world, place great limitations on our spiritual and rational potentialities. He saw God, on the one hand, as a fully spiritual being, unlimited by the bounds of flesh or earthly existence, but rather holy and wholly good.[9] Niebuhr viewed animals, on the other hand, as fully limited by their physical constitution and lack of spiritual nature, regulated by a series of self-preservation-driven biological mechanisms.[10]

For Niebuhr human beings are a fusion of the spiritual potentialities inherent in the notion of *imago dei* (that humans are created in God's image as per Genesis 1:27) and the material limitations of the flesh and this material world. Like animals, they are bound by the constituency of their flesh, placing on them the taxing and distracting demands of biological needs and desires. Yet, like God, they are spiritual, rational beings with the God-given potential

[8] Wolf, "RN's Doctrine of Man," p. 307.

[9] I do not believe Niebuhr is arguing for a simple Manichaean "flesh = evil," "spirit = good" position, though some may take him that way. Surely Niebuhr recognized that the person of Satan, purely spirit, is purely evil from a Christian perspective, and Niebuhr's writings on these subjects are more nuanced than any such black-and-white Manichaean characterization of him would suggest.

[10] Despite what some might see as a low view of animals presented here, we know that certainly some animals can be trained in a Pavlovian manner and some may even have higher powers of cognition and even conscience. Niebuhr would undoubtedly agree in light of data on such things but would maintain the distinction between human and animal, as would most Christians and other monotheists holding to their traditional positions.

in conjunction with their creator to transcend themselves and the visible, physical realm, at least on occasion. "Man is a child of nature," Niebuhr once wrote, yet "a spirit who stands outside of nature, life, himself, his reason and the world."[11] The human being is thus a being at odds with himself.

Niebuhr did not fully embrace the doctrine of Natural Law, held by most Catholics (and some Protestants), yet he did not fully reject it. Natural Law is the doctrine, most famously articulated by Saint Thomas Aquinas (and based on scriptures such as Romans 2: 14–15), arguing that human beings have in their nature the basic programming or software of God's law written on their hearts, such that in a very basic way all humans know "right" from "wrong." In a 1940 essay,[12] Niebuhr addressed the question of natural law, saying that neither the Catholic, Thomist understanding of the human condition as "natural order from God" nor the Lutheran and Calvinist Protestant position of human condition as "natural disorder" and "total depravity" got it quite right. Rather, "the facts of human history are more complex than either the traditional Catholic or Protestant doctrines of natural order and natural law suggest."[13] Here Niebuhr argued that the Protestants were closer to the truth in that the fall brought humanity low and sin reigned in human beings after the fall, and so "human history is consequently more tragic than Catholic theology assumes."[14] And yet, Niebuhr conceded that perhaps Luther and Calvin went too far with their notions of the "total depravity" of man, and that "man is [not] completely bereft of 'original justice.' "[15] Niebuhr concludes that

> men are not completely blinded by self-interest or lost in this maze of historical relativity. What always remains with them is not some uncorrupted bit of reason, which gives them universally valid standards of justice. What remains with them is something higher —namely, the law of love, which they dimly recognize as the law of their being, as the structure of human freedom, and which, in Christian faith, Christ clarifies and redefines, which is why he is called the "second Adam."[16]

---

[11] RN, *The Nature and Destiny of Man: Volume 1* (New York: Charles Scribner's Sons, 1941), p. 3.

[12] RN, "Christian Faith and Natural Law," in D. B. Robertson, ed., *Love and Justice: Selections from the Shorter Writings of RN* (Louisville, KY: Westminster/John Knox Press, 1957).

[13] Niebuhr, *Love and Justice* (1957), pp. 46–7.

[14] Niebuhr, *Love and Justice* (1957), p. 47.

[15] Niebuhr, *Love and Justice* (1957), p. 50.

[16] Niebuhr, *Love and Justice* (1957), p. 53.

Niebuhr's nuance here should not, however, be read as any backtracking on his conclusions that human nature is most fundamentally predisposed toward self-interested behavior with great potential for evil.

He takes this dark view of human nature because the historical human dilemma, according to Niebuhr (and the Bible), centers on the propensity of human beings to pursue their own agendas according to their own perceived best interests, as opposed to God's agenda, his justice, and his perception of what is best for humanity. According to Christian tradition, the human being was created in the image of a divine, perfect God, to live in peace and willing, happy servitude to that God. However, because of their rational capacities and the freedom of their wills, humans quickly exploited their physical separation from God and sought their own ends. This pattern was established with the biblical fall of humanity, which came to signify it.

The biblical view of the human condition Niebuhr advocates is that, by effectively declaring their independence from God, humans have alienated themselves from God because of their sin and consequent guilt. Sin, or doing that which is opposed to God's will, creates a barrier that separates humanity from God. Yet, according to Christian tradition, this alienation is unnecessary because of the redemption that Christ brought to humanity as described in the New Testament. According to the Bible, the repentant Christian need not feel alienated from God because Christ grants forgiveness and maintains (and in fact is himself) an open gate transcending the separating wall of sin that lies between God and humanity. Niebuhr agreed and believed that the difficulty with humanity was that most of its members failed to acknowledge their sin or their dependence on a sovereign God. Niebuhr said in his Gifford Lectures of 1939,

> The Christian view of man . . . affirms that the evil in man is a consequence of his inevitable though not necessary unwillingness to acknowledge his dependence, to accept his finiteness and to admit his insecurity, an unwillingness which involves him in the vicious circle of accentuating the insecurity from which he seeks to escape.[17]

Human insecurity and the need to escape it were important forces in Niebuhr's conception of human nature and social problems.

[17] RN, *Nature and Destiny 1*, p. 150.

Niebuhr believed human insecurity arose from the ambiguity of humanity's dual nature—being in and yet above nature, weak yet strong, and so on. He believed this struggle to escape insecurity culminated in the "will-to-power." In seeking to escape insecurity, humans overestimate their own abilities and virtues as a source of additional security (creating egoism as a defense mechanism) and seek to advance their ends, seek power, and strive to impose their wills on others to protect their own egos and interests. In this situation, humans continue to alienate themselves not only from God, but from each other as they seek security via power at each other's expense, further elevating the collective level of insecurity, in turn extending to perpetuity the whole process.

Ideally, from Niebuhr's Christian perspective, all this security-seeking would be unnecessary if everyone were to live as Christ suggested; by faith, hope, and love. "Without faith in the providence of God man cannot be freed of the anxiety that drives him to sin; without hope he cannot face the future unafraid; without love he cannot relate himself creatively to his fellow men."[18] Thus, because sin makes insecurity latent in human nature, the struggle goes on, alienating the strugglers further and further from the source of their salvation and from each other. In other words, God created the need for security (or a need to be loved) in human beings, planning that they would turn to him for that security and find it in loving one another. In rejecting God, they leave more of their security need unfulfilled, creating a greater need for security from other sources. In rejecting God's principles, they find it more difficult to love one another. When they fail to love one another as one means to fill their security needs, they extenuate their insecurity and hence tend to seek security by isolating themselves from one another, building up stores of material goods to ensure safety or bring pleasure, seeking power in its myriad forms[19] so that others might respect them, or by dominating their fellows.

In sum, Niebuhr saw in the process described above a causal chain of sin creating a descending spiral. He believed that the failure to acknowledge and to know God, his sovereignty, and his word, prevents human beings from enjoying his consequent security (accompanied by "the peace that passes all understanding," Philippians 4:7), thereby creating an insecurity that they seek to transcend largely by the will-to-power, egoism, materialism and/or greed (all of which, for Niebuhr, are symptoms of individuals seeking

---

[18] Wolf, "RN's Doctrine of Man," p. 318.
[19] For a good definition of power, see Joseph Nye, *The Future of Power* (New York: Public Affairs, 2011).

power over the insecurities of their places in nature). Once people turn from God and from each other, their security-seeking actions only lead them to act *against* God and each other, alienating them further from both, making their insecurity yet more acute. At the point where one's only sense of security or satisfaction comes from ruthlessly seeking power over others to build up one's self esteem or in dominating others, one's self-servient, security-seeking actions can actually serve to undermine one's security, creating a more insecure world.

> The will-to-power is thus inevitably involved in the vicious circle of accentuating the insecurity which it intends to eliminate . . . the more man establishes himself in power and glory, the greater is the fear of tumbling from his eminence or losing his treasure, or being discovered in his pretension.[20]

Herein lays the ultimate paradox or irony of the human predicament according to Niebuhr, that, in lieu of seeking that which they need—security (found in God and God-inspired peaceful relations with others for Niebuhr)—humans tend to seek ends that take them further away from the very source of true security.

Niebuhr pinpointed pride as the root of all human sin/folly.[21] In some cases, pride might be the factor that initiates the vicious cycle (actually more of a downward spiral) initiated by humanity's rebellion from God (if not done out of ignorance—pointing to the importance of wisdom, to be discussed later); in others, it could simply be the factor that maintains it. Often it is both. Pride in the Niebuhrian context is basically the failure to acknowledge God's sovereign status and the personal relevance of biblical teachings, but it also includes egoism or delusions of grandeur. Niebuhr believed that by one's failure to acknowledge God or one's own propensity to sin against God, others, and oneself, an individual in effect makes him or herself God. This is a gross insult to the God of the Judeo-Christian tradition, viewed as the true creator and Lord of all.

---

[20] RN, *Nature and Destiny 1*, pp. 192–3.

[21] Daphne Hampson argues that Niebuhr's conception of pride as the root of all sin is uniquely a male reality, contending with Kierkegaard that, for women, failure to take responsibility for self-actualization (i.e., losing self in others) is the root of all sin. For more, see Daphne Hampson, "Reinhold Niebuhr on Sin: A Critique," in Richard Harries, ed., *Reinhold Niebuhr and the Issues of Our Time* (Grand Rapids, MI: Eerdmans, 1986), pp. 50–1.

Niebuhr identified three different categories of pride: the pride of know-ledge, or intellectual pride; the pride of virtue, or moral pride, of which spir-itual pride is an offshoot; and the pride of power.[22] None of the three are mutually exclusive. Niebuhr said they are, in fact, "never completely distinct in actual life."[23] The first, the pride of knowledge, or intellectual pride, is characterized by the conviction that one or one's group is wiser than others and "the inability of the agent to recognize the same or similar limitations of perspective in himself which he has detected in others."[24] One who harbors intellectual pride is convinced of one's own intellectual superiority or even infallibility relative to others and denies one's own biases, claiming to be guided by pure, rational objectivity. The self here fails to see the limits of its own knowledge, intellectual ability, and potential for true objectivity.

The second form of pride Niebuhr discussed, pride of virtue or moral pride, assumes the characteristics of intellectual pride but stretches it a little further to moral self-righteousness. This pride assumes its own virtue, whether or not based on God-knowledge (the former even more irksome to Niebuhr as we will discuss next), projecting an image of itself as a just, some-times even holy, alternative to "the rest of the corrupt lot." The self judges itself by its own standards and reaches a verdict of self-approval, claiming, as above, that it is objective and rational. "Moral pride is the pretension of finite man that his highly conditioned virtue is the final righteousness and that his very relative moral standards are absolute. Moral pride thus makes virtue the very vehicle of sin."[25] By assuming one's own general righteousness or absolute virtue, one also assumes one's own verdict on a specific issue to be similarly just. This may mean that an "enforcement of justice" taking place outside of mutually acceptable channels of justice is simply an imposition of one's own standards of justice on another because of finite man's "highly con-ditioned virtue" and his "very relative moral standards."

Moral pride has caused many to feel obligated to correct someone else's "injustice," "state of savagery" or "backwardness," as has been the case histor-ically in many patronizing, often self-serving acts of injustice under imperi-alism and colonialism. Niebuhr's observation that "moral pride thus makes virtue the very vehicle of sin" was troubling to him, and it bothered him even

[22] RN, *Nature and Destiny 1*, pp. 188–200.
[23] RN, *Nature and Destiny 1*, p. 188.
[24] RN, *Nature and Destiny 1*, p. 196.
[25] RN, *Nature and Destiny 1*, p. 199.

more when it manifested itself in individuals, or religious or other orders, through self-deification or claims of divine sanction.

This Niebuhr called spiritual pride, which he saw as an outgrowth (and subset) of moral pride. In some cases, the self may claim divine sanction for itself because of perceived spiritual righteousness—possessing a special communion with God that puts the self in a unique position to receive God's revelation, giving it a responsibility to see that God's will is carried out. In other cases, spiritual pride leads to the usurpation of God's supremacy through self-deification. In other words, spiritual pride may or may not explicitly take religious form. As Niebuhr pointed out, while religious leaders have suffered spiritual pride by taking their claim to divine sanction too seriously, other historical figures, such as Caesar or Stalin, have succumbed to it by basking in the delusion of self-deification. Niebuhr called spiritual pride the "ultimate sin" because it was the ultimate form of pride. Not only did it fail to recognize human fallibility, it justified its failure to do so, literally assigning God-like qualities to an individual or group.

The third form of pride Niebuhr discussed, the pride of power, manifests itself in two ways. The first is a delusionary pride of power, in which case one sees oneself or one's group as being stronger and more secure than could realistically be possible. Here, "the human ego assumes its self-sufficiency and self-mastery and imagines itself secure against all vicissitudes."[26] It fails to see the reality of its own weaknesses, for Niebuhr believed that security and strength are relative, not absolute. This pride is most likely to occur in situations in which an individual or group is relatively strong or relatively secure. With the second form of the pride of power, on the other hand, the self recognizes its weaknesses and seeks power to overcome them. This form of pride is more likely to affect those who are not in an ostensible position of power but would like to be. "It is the sin of those, who knowing themselves to be insecure, seek sufficient power to guarantee their security, inevitably of course at the expense of other life."[27]

Niebuhr believed that insecurity, whether recognized consciously or not, is a base motivation for the pride of power. While the second form of the pride of power (manifested in the would-be power) *consciously* reacts to insecurity, Niebuhr felt the first (the established power) *unconsciously* reacts to insecurity. The second strives for power to rise above insecurity, while the

---

[26] RN, *Nature and Destiny 1*, p. 188.
[27] RN, *Nature and Destiny 1*, p. 190.

first clings to power to stay above insecurity. In either case, the pride of power is a common attempt to bolster the ego as a defense against the insecurities of a threatening world. Whether rooted in knowledge, virtue, or power, pride's sin is, in the end, essentially the same—it assigns the self unrealistically high estimates of its capabilities and unrealistically low estimates of its limitations. This is a key Niebuhrian insight/emphasis.

The realism in Niebuhr's Christian doctrine of human nature strove to offset this fault by finding a balance between the simultaneous recognition of human limitations and human potentialities. To deny either would be equally ludicrous in his mind. Yet Niebuhr felt that this was precisely what the other two historically prevailing doctrines of human nature, the classical and the modern, had done.

Alternative View of Human Nature 1:
The Classical View of Human Nature

Niebuhr held that the first of these, the classical doctrine of human nature, was put forward by the Greek rationalists. Their basic position was that the mind was opposed to the body as good was opposed to evil. For them, the body represented physical desires and by overcoming the desires of the flesh with the purity of rationality, one could achieve the ultimate good. Niebuhr greatly respected the work of the ancient Greek thinkers, seeing in their thinking the dualism that he himself proclaimed in human nature. Greek thinking juxtaposed the realism of the Greek tragedy and its expression of the limitations of the human character, with the quest for wisdom and the untapped human potential envisioned in the Platonic and Aristotelian discourses in particular, but in the work of other ancient Greek thinkers as well.

According to Niebuhr, the classical doctrine held that human shortcomings were a result of a lack of contemplation. All the problems one might face or all the transgressions one might commit against others could subsequently be resolved or overcome by analyzing the situation intellectually, thereby finding the error in one's logic or one's action that caused the mishap to occur. Rationality therefore embodied the potential to overcome all human shortcomings, including evil. "Evil" was simply the illogical.[28]

---

[28] Wolf, "RN's Doctrine of Man," p. 315.

The classical doctrine supposed wisdom (or rational contemplation) was the greatest good. For Niebuhr, however, this was problematic, and in effect it was akin to equating human rationality with God.

One cannot, and certainly Niebuhr would not, deny the importance of reason or wisdom, for indeed King Solomon said, "Blessed is the one who finds wisdom, and the one who gets understanding. . . . She is more precious than jewels, and nothing you desire can compare with her" (Proverbs 3:13, 15).[29] But the Apostle Paul said, "And if I have prophetic powers, and understand all mysteries and all knowledge, and if I have all faith, so as to remove mountains, but have not love, I am nothing." (1 Corinthians 13:2) What I think Paul is saying is that wisdom alone is not a final end or supreme good for human beings. Wisdom alone cannot replace the individual's need for love, or the need for compassion, at any level. Wisdom is also prey to being tainted by human partiality—and therefore, as a tool in human hands, it is imperfect and could not be a supreme good, no matter how great its virtue. Solomon, perhaps one of history's wisest men, also said, "If you seek it [wisdom] like silver and search for it as for hidden treasures, then you will understand the fear of the LORD and find the knowledge of God. For the LORD gives wisdom; from his mouth come knowledge and understanding" (Proverbs 2:4–6). Niebuhr, like Solomon, believed that true wisdom came with fear of/respect for the Lord and the recognition that wisdom was given by God, not generated by humans. With "fear of the LORD" and "the knowledge of God," an individual would see virtue in the recognition of the limits of the human creature and human rationality in relation to God. From the Christian perspective, wisdom truly is one of the greatest virtues, but it is only a tool and not above being used unwisely by fallible human beings.

Niebuhr said that because humans so commonly use reason to rationalize or justify their own interests, reason, like anything else, was corruptible and could not therefore be equated with good. Reason could not triumph over evil in and of itself because reason was a human action or characteristic (even though given by God) and was therefore as corruptible as any other human action or characteristic. While reason certainly was capable of producing virtue, it was equally capable of leading to evil as humans contemplated better ways to rationalize their actions to coincide with their interests.

---

[29] All Bible references are taken from the English Standard Version of the Holy Bible (Wheaton, IL: Crossway Publishers, 2001).

While Niebuhr had great respect for the Greeks, he felt the classic doctrine of human nature missed this important point.

Alternative View of Human Nature 2: The Modern View of Human Nature

Skipping over the Christian conception of human nature, which we have already discussed and which followed the classical conception chronologically, Niebuhr argued that the modern conception of human nature that emerged during the eighteenth-century Enlightenment prevails in the world today. Niebuhr saw the modern conception of human nature as a marriage of classical, Christian, Renaissance, and Enlightenment-era idealist conceptions.[30] He called it a "modern naturalism," which finds some concurrence with the Christian conception of the human as "creature" but does not see this creatureliness as necessarily limiting or as the cause of human shortcomings as does the Christian conception.

Niebuhr held that the modern view of human nature evolved from the thoughts of Renaissance thinkers, who emphasized anew the fact that human beings were in fact created in the image of God, but played down the limitations placed on humans by what they thought was an overly pessimistic view of human nature.[31] The new idealism Renaissance thinkers espoused maintained that medieval pessimism unjustly and unnecessarily stunted human development during the Dark Ages by doubting the possibility of human virtue and by consequently placing limits on human freedom.[32] Following the Renaissance, Niebuhr argues that thinkers such as Montaigne (known for skepticism) and Bacon (known for empiricism) paved the way for Enlightenment thinkers such as Descartes and Spinoza, who moved further in the direction of modernist rationalist idealism, paving the way for yet more radical modern thought.[33] Unlike the deists of the seventeenth, eighteenth, and nineteenth centuries, with whom they otherwise shared much in common, the adherents of the modern view of

---

[30] RN, *Nature and Destiny 1*, p. 18.
[31] Niebuhr mentions specifically the influence of Bruno, Copernicus, Leonardo, and Petrarch (RN, *Nature and Destiny 1*, p. 19).
[32] RN, *Nature and Destiny 1*, pp. 299–300.
[33] RN, *Nature and Destiny 1*, p. 19.

human nature have for the most part done away with the notion of a sovereign God, or "humans created in God's image." They have, however, retained the Renaissance idealists' optimistic view of human nature, which claimed that humans were capable of and responsible for their own perfectibility. This view in turn gave birth to modern individualism and faith in the potential of the individual and science. In short, modern views acknowledge human potential as do Christian views, but without the restraints of the Christian recognition of the human propensity for sin and the pursuit of self-interest. Niebuhr found this problematic.

Niebuhr believed that, like the classicists, modernist thought portrays human shortcomings as being largely a result of underdeveloped human potential. Through education, institutional reform, and science, the modernists envision the "rationality of human beings" as eventually being able to triumph over nature and over the shortcomings of human nature itself. Various forms of the modern view of human nature have, like the classical view, also identified the flesh and its desires as a source of weakness and therefore the necessity of rationalism's prevalence over sensuality or emotionalism. Others simply stressed rationality and the *prudent* pursuit of physical desires, in other words, maintaining that they do not impinge on others' rights or are otherwise injurious to others.

In a more uniquely modern sense, however, those who have embraced the modern notion of human nature have tended to identify or equate "evil" with external factors such as capitalism/wealth, inequality, tyranny, unjust human institutions, and/or ignorance (lack of education). According to Niebuhr, the modernists consequently suggest that evil, as an external factor, can in fact be removed from human society through the advance of science and human intellectual development, coupled with the eradication of injustice, tyranny, poverty, capitalism, or whatever else is identified as inherently evil at a given point in time. The Marxist variation of the liberal mainstream of modern thought shared liberal modernism's reverence for science and human intellectual development and its hope for the eradication of injustice (particularly "economic injustice"), but differed from the liberal mainstream in that it focused on material wealth and capitalism as the great "evils" in need of eradication from society. In either case, the modern view of human nature rejects original sin or the notion that human beings are evil unto themselves, as Christian doctrine presupposes. The modern view thus entertains a decidedly optimistic view of human nature, presupposing that the discord among humans can be overcome eventually by the advance of science and the full development of the human potential.[34]

Niebuhr found fault with the modern conception of human nature for several reasons. In his words, "the modern mind fails to find a secure foundation for the individuality which it ostensibly cherishes so highly . . . its estimates of human virtue are too generous and optimistic to accord with the known facts of human history."[35] Niebuhr did not, of course, entertain so optimistic a conception of human virtue. Evil may be aided and abetted by external factors, but in his opinion evil had been and always would be an indwelling presence in human nature. History appears to support him, given that crime is committed by paupers as well as by white-collar criminals, injustice occurs in societies with high levels of education and development, and in nations low in both senses, atrocities have been committed by democratic and/or "civilized" political decision makers as well as by authoritarian and/or "barbarian" persons. While avoiding the error of equivalency here (i.e., suggesting that development levels, education levels, or regime type do not matter), Niebuhr is clearly right in the sense that human beings have not been able to root out injustice, crime, inequality, and suffering, no matter how well developed, well educated, well policed, or how egalitarian or democratic their societies have been. Throughout history, when corrupt monarchies or political regimes have been removed from power, corruption has to some degree always remained. Similarly, when capitalism and any emphasis on material wealth was supposed to have been eliminated from Soviet Russian society after 1917, corruption and unscrupulous behavior remained. Nor have the lifting of the yoke of feudal oppression placed on humans in Western civilization during the Middle Ages, nor the end of the eras of slavery or colonialism, the advent of modern science, pure rationality or the birth of democracy and other freedoms been able to eradicate (or significantly reduce the amount of) evil or corruption as the progenitors of these movements suggested should have been the case.

A fair amount of recent scientific evidence shows that Niebuhr's early views of human nature, the relationship between truth/reason and emotions, and the sociology of group dynamics are true and right on target. More specifically, in his recent book, Christopher Beem provides data and

---

[34] RN, *Nature and Destiny 1*, p. 23.
[35] RN, *Nature and Destiny 1*, p. 123.

arguments to support each of these contentions, concluding that "whatever you believe, there are good scientific grounds for taking Niebuhr's analysis seriously."[36] Providing evidence against the classical and modern views of human nature with its trust in rationality, Beem says, "We want what we want, and the more the information is associated with what we want, the less likely our reasoning will operate in a wholly rational way."[37] Rationalists believe that people make the most rational choice based on available information and that emotions or gut feelings are not salient as it regards decision-making outcomes. Beem cites the work of psychologist Peter Wason, who found that "confirmation bias" shapes people's assessments of ostensibly objective factors, that "we seek out information that confirms what we already believe, and we ignore or actively disparage evidence that does not."[38] In another experiment Beem cites, Lord, Ross, and Lepper sampled 48 undergraduate students half of whom supported capital punishment coming into the study and half opposed it. When presented with the results of fake scientific experiments, some showing the benefits of capital punishment (that it deterred crime) and others showing that capital punishment did not deter crime, the authors reported that students found the studies that supported their preconceived views extremely persuasive, whereas they found the studies that drew conclusions different from their own views as flawed, and so on. These findings were in spite of the fact that the studies were carefully constructed to be equally persuasive and well conceived. Lord, Ross, and Lepper concluded that "the same study can elicit entirely opposite evaluations from people who hold different initial beliefs about a complex social issue."[39] In these studies, the authors also found that those subjects who had no opinion (i.e., those who knew the least) in such studies were more likely to make an unbiased judgment. In other words, the more subjects were knowledgeable or cared about something, the less likely they were able to make an unbiased judgment about that subject. Classical and modern versions of human nature tell us that better educated, more

---

[36] Christopher Beem, *Democratic Humility: Reinhold Niebuhr, Neuroscience, and America's Political Crisis* (Lanham, MD: Lexington Books, 2015), p. xv.

[37] Beem, *Democratic Humility*, p. 34.

[38] P. E. Wason, "On the Failure to Eliminate Hypotheses in a Conceptual Task," *Quarterly Journal of Experimental Psychology* 12 (1960), as found in Beem, *Democratic Humility*, p. 38.

[39] Charles Lord, Lee Ross, and Mark Lepper, "Biased Assimilation and Attitude Polarization: The Effects of Prior Theories on Subsequently Considered Evidence," *Journal of Personality and Social Psychology* 37/11 (1979): 2102; as found in Beem, *Democratic Humility*, p. 39.

informed individuals make more rational, unbiased choices. This is not necessarily what the science shows us, however.

> Smart people are *not* more likely to consider the issue in all its complexity. In fact, they are no less likely than anybody else to have their emotions direct their reason. That is to say, their reasoning is not less motivated than anyone else's. The only difference is that they are better at it. The smarter we are, the better we are at coming up with strategies that allow us to dismiss the threatening information and preserve our well-being.[40]

The science tells us that rationalization rather than rationality is more often the rule, as it regards human behavior, and neuroscience explains this. These are defense mechanisms in the human brain, giving us confidence that we are wise, right, and okay, while others are more likely biased and inferior in their abilities.[41] All of this is just as Niebuhr argued it was. While he didn't have the science at the time to support his claims, subsequent scientific work has supported his claims, which he would have argued were derived from biblical truth and historical evidence. What he described as human nature has been generally vindicated in subsequent behavioral studies as being an accurate portrayal of the human condition.

Consequently, Niebuhr saw folly in putting too much faith in "rationality," human institutions, human virtue, the objectivist claims of science, or anything else outside of God, though certainly he recognized how each of these forces could be used to reduce the effects of evil in the world. Niebuhr believed that because of the shortcomings of human nature and humanity's subordinate position to God (coupled with its general willingness to rationalize its own flaws and its unwillingness to admit its flaws or its subordinate status to God), the potential for human freedom could not be unbounded as Renaissance thinkers and modernists proposed. Rather, it must exist within the practical bounds and concomitant humility that ultimately comes with the recognition of human fallibility and the human tendency toward pride and folly. In other words, for Niebuhr, proper understanding of the nature and importance of human nature is fundamental to any analysis of human endeavors.

---

[40] Beem, *Democratic Humility*, p. 42.
[41] Beem, *Democratic Humility*, pp. 46–7.

4

Niebuhr on Collective Society, Nations, and International Relations

Moving from human nature to Reinhold Niebuhr's analysis of relations between nations, one must first come to an understanding of Niebuhr's views on group dynamics as manifested in collective society and political tendencies at the national level. In Niebuhr's approach to society, politics, and international relations, one central idea effects his entire line of thought—that is, his assertion that a distinction must be made between the potential for moral behavior between individuals and the potential for moral behavior between groups. He once wrote:

> Our contemporary culture fails to realize the power, extent and persistence of group egoism in human relations. It may be possible, though it is never easy, to establish just relations between individuals within a group purely by moral and rational suasion and accommodation. In inter-group relations this is practically an impossibility. The relations between groups must therefore always be predominantly political rather than ethical, that is, they will be determined by the proportion of power which each group possesses at least as much as by any rational and moral appraisal of the comparative needs and claims of each group.[1]

In other words, in Niebuhr's opinion morality, though always checked by the human propensity for the pursuit of self-interest, *is* quite possible in interpersonal relations, giving credence to the Christian love ethic. However, morality as expressed among classes, ethnic groups and nations, is much more difficult to realize because self-interest is so much more persistent in intergroup relations than it is in intragroup relations.[2]

---

[1] RN, *Moral Man and Immoral Society* (New York: Charles Scribner's Sons, 1932), pp. XXII–XXIII.
[2] RN, *Man's Nature and His Communities* (New York: Charles Scribner's Sons, 1965), p. 22.

Niebuhrian International Relations. Gregory J. Moore, Oxford University Press (2020).
© Oxford University Press.
DOI: 10.1093/oso/9780197500446.001.0001

The Nature of Group Unity: Groupism

Niebuhr explained this phenomenon by referring to the nature of group unity. Nations and other social groupings form an identity revolving around common goals, interests, and/or common physical, religious, geographical, or other characteristics. These groupings may be organized along vocational, social, ethnic, religious, racial, national, or other lines. Niebuhr felt that membership in them inevitably creates a "we/they" situation—we being members, they being nonmembers. Individual interests then compete to become the interests of the group, with a broader base of support and seemingly greater justification or "collective legitimization." Here interest, transferred from individual to group, becomes much more pronounced, and group identity becomes groupism or nationalism, giving a new, collectivized force toward self-interest. Niebuhr said "collective self-concern is a compound of individual egotism, collectively expressed, and the spirit of loyalty and self-sacrifice of the individual which the community easily appropriates for its own ends."[3]Niebuhr felt that, while self-interest was only *likely* to guide action in interpersonal affairs, in intergroup or international affairs the interests of the collective "self" were certain to dominate. He believed that

> society . . . merely cumulates the egoism of the individual and transmutes their individual altruism into collective-egoism so that the egoism of the group has double force. For this reason no group acts from purely unselfish motives or even mutual intent and politics is therefore bound to be a contest of power.[4]

Hence the distinction Niebuhr made between interpersonal and collective ethics. Any propensity for moral or rational self-righteousness in the individual is, in his estimation, bound to be multiplied to the nth degree at the collective level, making concurrence or conflict resolution between different factions much more difficult than that of individuals at odds.

Because a group is such only by virtue of unity as a consequence of shared interests, Niebuhr believed that this sort of groupism was inevitable. He argued that moral action by a group requires group transcendence. That is, its members must be able to see interests other than those of their own group.

---

[3] RN, *World Crisis and American Responsibility; Nine Essays,* Ernest W. Lefever, ed. (New York: Association Press, 1958), pp. 38–9.

[4] RN, "Human Nature and Social Change," *Christian Century* 50 (1933): p. 363.

This may necessitate the questioning or criticism of the group's leaders and their motives. Such introspection, humility, willingness to entertain self-criticism in a group, as Niebuhr pointed out, is dangerous for group cohesion because it can threaten unity, the cement that bonds and maintains group solidarity, "for self-criticism is a kind of inner disunity, which the feeble mind of a nation finds difficulty in distinguishing from dangerous forms of inner conflict."[5] Thus, moral rebels and hardened criminals are often crucified on the same Golgotha.

The Consequence of Group Unity: Collective Pride

Consequently, group pride is even more dangerous to justice and morality than individual pride, for it is more difficult to challenge as a result of the "if you're not for us, you're against us" mentality that so often prevails within groups, particularly groups under duress. More recent psychological and sociological studies have underlined the wisdom of Niebuhr's conclusions. We join groups as a defense mechanism to increase security, creating in-group bonds and narratives supporting our own goodness, all of which are necessary to maintain that in-group unity. We disparage other groups for the same reason. Studies show that much of this groupism is irrational or, in other words, based on emotional investments and perceived vested interests rather than objective assessments.[6] In an analysis of Niebuhr's political philosophy, Kenneth Thompson called group pride "the corruption of individual loyalty and group consciousness,"[7] which I think is accurately and perhaps best personified by the case of Hitler's Nazi Germany.

The Case of Nazi Germany

By the early 1930s, the German people had grown weary of the weight of the Versailles Treaty and its postwar reparations. More and more Germans began to feel their nation had made its penance and justly deserved to be

---

[5] RN, *Moral Man*, p. 88.

[6] Christopher Beem, *Democratic Humility: Reinhold Niebuhr, Neuroscience, and America's Political Crisis* (Lanham, MD: Lexington Books, 2015), pp. 49–62.

[7] Kenneth W. Thompson, "The Political Philosophy of Reinhold Niebuhr," in Charles W. Kegley, ed., *Reinhold Niebuhr, His Religious, Social and Political Thought* (New York: Pilgrim Press, 1984), p. 238.

allowed to rejoin the community of nations as a member of equal standing. Rising to power in 1933, for many in Germany Hitler was the right man with the right message in the right place at the right time. Many Germans believed that Germany, a once proud, strong nation, had been treated unfairly and had been stripped of its dignity following World War I and that the Weimar Republic was not meeting the German people's needs, performing to their expectations. Hitler rooted the Nazi Party in nationalism, the appeal of strong leadership, ethnic pride, and ultimately racism. In essence, this was an appeal to collective pride—an appeal to the damaged egos of individual Germans brought together by a common identity and a common cause. Hans Morgenthau, a German Jew who fled Nazi Germany in 1939, had this to say about the relationship between individuals and the brilliant machinations of the Nazi state to mobilize individual aspirations.

> Thus National Socialism was able to identify in a truly totalitarian fashion the aspirations of the individual German with the power objective of the German nation. Nowhere in modern history has that identification been more complete. Nowhere has that sphere in which the individual pursues his aspirations for power for their own sake been smaller. Nor has the force of the emotional impetus with which that identification transformed itself into aggressiveness on the international scene been equaled in modern civilization.[8]

Drawing on that mass support and appealing to the hopes and dreams of his people, Hitler pledged to rebuild Germany economically and militarily, so that it could once again assert itself as one of the world's truly great nations. This appeal was extremely attractive to a very capable but oppressed people.

However, it later became apparent that Hitler was using his nationalistic appeal to the German people to garner their support for ends much beyond the scope of the national goals the people themselves expected initially. With what Niebuhr viewed as a twisted will-to-power motive, Hitler sought to establish himself as the leader of a race of German "supermen" following the expulsion (later extermination) of the Jews and the occupation of Europe. By the time Hitler's true agenda became apparent, his political machine had become so well entrenched that it became impossible to challenge from within

---

[8] Hans J. Morgenthau, *Politics Among Nations*, 4th edition (New York: Knopf, 1967), p. 108, as cited in Michael C. Williams, *The Realist Tradition and the Limits of International Relations* (Cambridge, UK: Cambridge University Press, 2005), p. 122.

Germany by the few who truly understood him. Hitler's charismatic appeal to the collective pride of the German people, his rationalization of German expansion (explained as a sort of German Manifest Destiny), and the nation-bonding effects of a long war all served to keep the majority of the Germans united and supportive of him to the end, despite the atrocities the regime committed, the rampant violation of the human rights of the people the regime governed in and out of Germany, and the general suffering the people had endured. At the international level, Nazi Germany might be a useful illustration of another phenomenon, one that Niebuhr called "tribalism," discussed next.

The Consequence of Collective Pride:
Conflict via Tribalism

Niebuhr believed that the conflict of interests among competing groups was doomed to bring overt conflict because of groupism and what Niebuhr referred to as "the tribal limits of his (man's) sense of obligation to other men."[9] Niebuhr grouped state nationalism, ethnic nationalism, racism, economic classism, forms of religious jihadism, and other such "isms" together into a category he called tribalism. Tribalism in this context is "the chief source of man's inhumanity to man,"[10] Niebuhr believed. In it he saw the "we/them" distinction taken to extremes of alienation, insecurity, and defensive reactionism. For Niebuhr, tribalism was the primary reason intergroup cooperation was so much more difficult to overcome than interpersonal cooperation. It was also the reason that decision makers could not escape moral dualism at the group/national level.

The Discomfiting Necessity of Individual/Collective
Moral Dualism

Niebuhr took such great pains to promote the distinction between individual and group morality, and likewise, between the "we-group" and the "they-group," because he found fault with Woodrow Wilson and other idealists

---

[9] RN, *Man's Nature*, pp. 84–5.
[10] RN, *Man's Nature*, pp. 84–5.

who, he thought, failed to see the true, self-interested nature of nations and collective entities and tended to analogize and confuse the potential for fruitful interpersonal relations with the potential for fruitful group, societal, and international relations. Religious idealists received much of the brunt of his criticism because he felt their moral, often "overly idealistic" teachings propagated the "myth" that if everyone loved each other and followed the Golden Rule, peace would descend on the earth like a dove. Niebuhr believed that coming to terms with the notion "that collective self-regard of class, race, and nation is more stubborn and persistent than the egoism of individuals" was profoundly important because modern "secular and religious idealists hoped to change the social situation by beguiling the egoism of individuals, either by adequate education or by pious benevolence."[11] Niebuhr believed this was unrealistic because human self-regard was too strong.

Niebuhr strongly advocated and stood behind the efficacy of the biblical love ethic and the Golden Rule at the interpersonal level (after all, he was a pastor), but—and this must be emphasized—he saw it as potentially misleading vis-à-vis collective society. This was a remarkable statement for a Christian clergyman to make. In 1932, he said,

> Whenever religious idealism brings forth its purest fruits and places the strongest check upon selfish desire, it results in policies, which, from the political perspective, are quite impossible. There is, in other words, no possibility of harmonizing the two strategists designed to bring the strongest inner and the most effective social restraint upon egoistic impulse. It would therefore seem better to accept a frank <u>dualism</u> in morals than to attempt a harmony between the two methods which threatens [*sic*] the effectiveness of both. Such a dualism would have two aspects. It would make a distinction between the moral judgments applied to the self and others; and it would distinguish between what we expect of individuals and groups.[12]

This notion of moral dualism may be Niebuhr's most important interjection regarding morality and its place in politics and the interrelations of collective entities.

Niebuhr believed we can hope for and in some cases even expect moral behavior from individuals, but with regard to nations and other social

---

[11] RN, *Man's Nature*, p. 22.
[12] RN, *Moral Man*, pp. 270–1.

groupings, we must expect action based purely on self-interested motives. It is not difficult to argue that even when nations or groups act morally or make concessions, there lays beneath such actions a bedrock of pragmatic self-interest. Of this tendency Niebuhr wrote, "man is a curious creature with so strong a sense of obligation to his fellows that he cannot pursue his own interests without pretending to serve his fellow men."[13]

Niebuhr argued that reason is no more a panacea for bringing about greater moral conduct among collective human groupings than it is among individuals. He stated that reason is to some extent always the servant of interest, and therefore social injustice cannot be alleviated simply by moral reasoning, as he believed liberal educators and moralists have traditionally emphasized for the most part.[14] Therefore, conflict is inevitable.[15] It would appear that justice will not be served without violence or a serious enough challenge to the status quo to affect a threat to the best interests of the established power, thereby making it in the interest of the established power to peaceably change its stance. Reason or common sense might suggest one measure, but interest will likely dictate its own, according to Niebuhr. Exuberant decision makers are found when reason and interest dictate the same end. Rationalization appears if and when they do not.

The Case of South African Apartheid

Although any one of hundreds of examples would suffice to illustrate this point, the situation in apartheid-era South Africa comes first to mind. Niebuhr recognized South Africa's policy of apartheid as something "which approaches the consistent evil of Nazism."[16] I believe Niebuhr would think it foolish to believe that the white South African government loosened the bounds of apartheid there strictly for moral reasons. Niebuhr would agree that the white establishment made concessions to black South Africans in the early 1990s only because it became increasingly in their interest to do so. Not only were white South Africans grossly outnumbered and faced imminent

---

[13] RN, as cited by Don Winter, "The Carter-Niebuhr Connection—The Politician as Philosopher," *National Journal* (February 4, 1978): 189.

[14] RN, *Moral Man*, pp. XXIV–XV.

[15] RN, *Moral Man*, p. XV.

[16] RN, "The Rising Tide of Color," p. 4, original manuscript found in Box 17, Reinhold Niebuhr Papers, Manuscript Division, Library of Congress, Washington, DC. No further information on date or whether it was published is available in the box/folder.

danger if black South Africans ever united effectively, but South Africa had been practically excommunicated from the world system. The pressures of world criticism coupled with crippling economic sanctions changed their perceived interests. While in the past it was in the white establishment's best interest to keep black South Africans under their thumbs for economic and political reasons, it came to be perceived as being in their best interest to loosen things up.

Niebuhr once wrote, "The world of history, particularly in man's collective behavior, will never be conquered by reason, unless reason uses tools, and is itself driven by forces which are not rational."[17] I believe the tools Niebuhr referred to here are individual or collective self-interest. History, like the above example, shows that to effect change, one must work to change established interests. Black South Africans, in conjunction with international pressures, had to work to show white South Africans that it was in their interest to allow black South Africans political, social, and economic freedom. They were unlikely to change because of moral platitudes. Their interests dictated against it. Only when held accountable and squeezed by domestic and international pressures did they change their policies.

One might also look at self-interest as it relates to economic motivation. A comparative examination of the economic vitality of workers, innovation, and economic dynamism in capitalist versus communist command economies would support the relevance of self-interest to economic motivation. Reason might suggest a patriotic worker should work hard for the good of the whole, but reality shows that in general workers are unlikely to work hard unless it is in their immediate perceived interest to do so.

Without reason of course, or with faulty reasoning, one may not realize what one's own interests or the interests of one's groups truly are, or one may misinterpret other players' interests, possibly leading to inappropriate actions and the subsequent failure to attain one's goals. Reason is the means by which one pinpoints interests and determines what one perceives to be just. It is also the means by which one determines the best way to change the environment so as to affect actors whose interests bar or threaten to bar justice, in this way causing their perceived interests to shift in order to enable justice to be served. Reason is a valuable tool and wisdom is precious, but because of the limits of human nature, Niebuhr stressed we must remember that reason can at any time fall prey to and become a servant of interest.

[17] RN, *Moral Man*, p. XVI.

Thus, while the virtues of reason can be celebrated, the limits of reason must be respected as well, in Niebuhr's estimation, and this is as true at the collective level as it is at the individual level. While collective or democratic decision making can be more objective than individual thinking in the intragroup context, because of the convergence of more divergent points of view this intragroup decision-making process still remains limited in objectivity when formulating intergroup relations because of tribalism and the limits of human nature vis-à-vis reason. Consequently, because of the shortcomings of human nature and its effects on pure reason, reason is no more apt to be truly objective and free of interest as a by-product of group thought than it is as a by-product of individual thought. While a group, society, or nation may resemble a machine in its functioning in some ways, given all the coordination of its working parts, Niebuhr would have us remember that it is composed of and driven by human beings, and ultimately by human nature and the paradoxes contained therein.

Nations and Their Interrelations and the Role of Power

While continuing this discussion of Niebuhr and his views of collective human life, I would like to shift focus now from his discussion of collective human interaction in general to his specific discussions of nations and their interrelations. While all that has been discussed thus far vis-à-vis collective human existence pertains directly to the discussion of the state and international relations, one element of collective human existence manifests itself commonly in this context in particular. Although this element might be found anywhere humans interrelate, from the family unit to the corporate business world, I would now like to discuss it as it relates to nations and their interrelations, as Niebuhr himself spent much energy doing so. The element alluded to here is, of course, power.

Throughout the history of communities, kingdoms, and states, power has been the traditional means of having one's way or gaining or maintaining advantage for one's people over another (Niebuhr's will-to-power). Niebuhr believed that nationalistic will-to-power is a result of individual human insecurity multiplied to the nth degree at the national level, n being perhaps the number of nationalists in a country or coalition supporting the tenets of a particular leader or regime, and perhaps the degree of power they control over the instruments of coercion and the media. This creates a collective will-to-power that is much more tenacious, resilient, and self-righteous than individual will-to-power.[18] Again we see Niebuhr's linking of the characteristics of human nature to both interpersonal and sociopolitical interaction as they are manifested in human society. Discussing Niebuhr's political philosophy, Kenneth Thompson stated, "the human predicament has roots primarily in the security–power dilemma. Weak men and nations assume that if they had more power they would be more secure."[19] Niebuhr believed this was true on both interpersonal and international strata.

Therefore, because nations act on human imperatives, like human nature itself Niebuhr believed the nature of the world order would never change. War and other forms of international conflict are, in Niebuhr's estimation, the collective manifestations of human insecurity and the base human sin of pride and are therefore inevitable. Because sin, defined as human pride, could not be eradicated from human nature, and international conflict is the result of collective pride, conflict, in Niebuhr's estimation, could not be eradicated from group and national interaction.

The Lack of International Moral and Ideological Consensus in International Relations

While we know humans are capable of astounding demonstrations of loyalty, charity, and self-sacrifice, why is it so difficult for their loyalties to transcend themselves, their family, friends, and countrymen? "Enlightened men in all nations have some sense of obligation to their fellow men, beyond the limits of their nation-state . . ." but "political cohesion requires common convictions on particular issues of justice and these are lacking."[20] As is readily apparent to any observer of world events, there is a great disparity of opinion on morality and other value judgments. Even the most basic of human rights, agreed to and ratified by the nations of the world in the United Nations' Universal Declaration on Human Rights, are regularly violated because of claims of the preeminence of security concerns over human rights, a lack of international accountability of rights violating states, and/or a lack of conviction and agreement among the nations over how to address such

---

[18] RN, *The Nature and Destiny of Man: Volume 1* (New York: Charles Scribner's Sons, 1941), pp. 193–4.
[19] Kenneth W Thompson, "The Political Philosophy of Reinhold Niebuhr," p. 238.
[20] RN, *World Crisis*, p. 101.

offenses and offenders. Here the question of legitimacy arises: -who or what is a legitimate enough authority in the eyes of all concerned to demand or enforce compliance to any established international mores, such as the Universal Declaration on Human Rights?

The Lack of International Accountability in International Relations

At present there is still insufficient international accountability (though the consensus of the world community regarding the aggressions of Iraq in August 1990, for example, suggest this may be changing), and there is yet no pervasive agreement regarding legitimate international structures of authority or values. Consequently, there exists the inevitability of conflict among nation-states in an international community lacking order. As Niebuhr said in his Gifford Lectures of 1941, "There is no possibility of making history completely safe against either occasional conflicts of vital interests (war) or against the misuse of the power which is intended to prevent such conflicts of interests (tyranny)."[21] Similarly, he stated, "Conflict is inevitable (in a social situation), and in this conflict power must be challenged by power."[22] Niebuhr could not be considered a hawk as it regarded international relations, but he embraced a firm, realistic approach to politics and international affairs that supported the use of force to maintain justice, recognizing that, on occasion, "for peace we must risk war."

Love and Justice: The Christian Love Ethic in a World of Power Politics

Yet, how does Niebuhr as a Christian relate the love ethic, the key to Christian morality, to a world such as this? To do so. he relies on the dialectic and distinguishing of the possibilities of ethical action between interpersonal relations on the one hand and those of groups and nations on the other, as discussed earlier. While Niebuhr skillfully attempts to relate the love ethic or morality to power and the realm of politics, he does not reconcile them. Niebuhr uses

---

[21] RN, *Nature and Destiny* 2, p. 284.
[22] RN, *Moral Man*, p. XV.

biblical morality or love as a moral gauge against which to measure actions at the societal and international levels. However, in his calculus nonviolent love, as it is presented in the Bible, may have to be carefully laid aside from time to time when one is confronted with conflicts in which the peaceful existence of a people is threatened by tyranny—domestic or foreign. Of the ultimate incompatibility of the love ethic and political reality, Niebuhr, theologian and political realist, said,

> I have spent a good deal of my life validating the love ethic as final on the one hand, and trying to prove on the other hand that it must and can include all the discriminate judgments and commitments which we may broadly define as commitments in the cause of justice. That these commitments may involve us at times in moral ambiguity must be recognized if an ethic of justice is not to degenerate into a merely political ethic. On the other hand, I am certain that an ethic of love which dispenses with the structures and commitments of justice is ultimately irrelevant to the collective life of man.[23]

In other words, a social group's or nation's actions should be directed by the love ethic whenever realistically possible, but when interaction degenerates into conflict, force may have to be used to defend a way of life that attempts to honor the love ethic or justice as final within its societal or group bounds.

Some might say that love and justice are dichotomous terms, that the two involve a trade-off. For Niebuhr this is a false dichotomy. For justice is a part of the fulfillment of love, as he says clearly in the preceding quotation.

> There is something rather ironic in the fact that we must be on our guard lest those who regard the peace of the Kingdom of God as a simple alternative to the difficult justice and precarious peace of the world deliver us into a peace of slavery. They would not do it willingly; but they willingly nourish illusions that obscure the difficulties of achieving justice and the sorry realities of a peace without justice.[24]

John Bennett, in addressing the relationship between love and justice in Niebuhr's work said the following.

---

[23] RN in Kegley, *Reinhold Niebuhr*, p. 526.

[24] RN, "A Negotiated Peace," *Christianity and Crisis* (April 7, 1941); as cited in RN, *Love and Justice*, edited by D. B. Robertson (Westminster, UK: John Knox Press, 1957), p. 174.

Niebuhr rejects the idea that love can take the place of justice, if those who love only become more loving. No, there must be structures of justice to enable people to defend themselves against the loving who are so sure that they know best what is good for others.[25]

For Niebuhr, love without justice is in the end not love at all. Love requires the pursuit of justice, which sometimes necessitates moral or even physical confrontation with those committing or standing on the side of injustice. I have three sons. If, in the name of love, I choose not to discipline my older son if he beats or otherwise bullies his younger brothers (because I love him), I become complicit then with injustice, and this indicates that I am not acting in love, either to him or to his younger brothers. Regarding his younger brothers, as a parent who loves them, both justice and love require that I defend them from any unjust actions from their older brother (or anyone else). That seems clear enough. Yet, regarding the older brother, my decision not to hold him accountable for injustice toward his brothers (his injustice in this example also indicates a lack of love toward them) is indicative of a lack of love toward him as well because love requires accountability and clear lines of communication so as to maintain harmony and peace. At one level, his breach of discipline and his misconduct in this example would have untoward implications for my relations with him. At another level, if I love him (and I do!), I would want to show him his error, to help him to be his best, for continued such behavior (whether in our home or in public or private with others later in his life) could have profoundly disadvantageous consequences for him personally, socially, and professionally. Because I love him, I have a responsibility to hold him accountable for these reasons. I also have a responsibility to defend the weak, those less able to defend themselves (in this case the younger brothers). In both situations, this is love and what love requires of those who seek love and justice. So in conclusion, again, the construction of a dichotomy between love and justice is a false dichotomy from a Niebuhrian perspective.

[25] John C. Bennett, "Reinhold Niebuhr's Contribution to Social Ethics," in Harold Landon, ed., *Reinhold Niebuhr: A Prophetic Voice in Our Time* (Greenwich, CT: Seabury Press, 1962).

Moral Ambiguity in International Relations

These discussions about the relationship between love and justice entail the existence of moral ambiguity, and these might make theologians, ethicists, and even policymakers uncomfortable. Yet one might argue that such can be seen as analogous to the biblical conception of the Judeo-Christian God as being at once the God of love and forgiveness and yet a God who must be respected and one whom is capable of great wrath (Exodus 34:6–7). As Niebuhr would remind us, while love and forgiveness are clearly the dominating currents in the message of the New Testament, the Bible as a whole has many examples of God's wrath as a consequence of injustice to himself or his people. From the Christian perspective (and Niebuhr's), Christ's sacrifice enables God to fully forgive human sin, but still His wrath is apt to be revealed in the presence of repeated hypocritical, pride-filled disobedience, so that a greater justice (and love) may be served in the interest of what the Bible would deem God's sovereign, unfolding plan for humanity. The Bible reveals a God of love, mercy, and tolerance, but also a God who represents justice, divine judgment, and moral universalism. This in itself may seem morally ambiguous or dichotomous at first glance, but the Bible's depiction of history reveals a pattern for God's justice, discipline, and wrath. While human beings have historically sought to replicate this divine justice on earth, a consistent pattern has been noticeably absent in the human interpretation and implementation of justice, something Niebuhr often noted.

For instance, to determine when force is necessary to defend the maintenance of justice, one must wonder exactly how and by what standards one defines justice. It would seem that justice is a relative term, as is morality, at least as it regards any sense of international consensus. When is it "just" to use force? At what point is force deemed appropriate or to be used "just" to counter "injustice?" How does one prioritize different forms of injustice so that one form of injustice may be justified in removing a "greater" form of injustice?

Unfortunately, Niebuhr has had no more success in satisfactorily answering these questions systematically than anyone else in international relations discourse. Niebuhr acknowledged this point in the quotation above when he stated that "these commitments (in the cause of justice) may involve us at times in war and that *at all times they involve us in moral ambiguity*"[26]

---

[26] RN in Kegley, *Reinhold Niebuhr*, p. 526.

(emphasis added). This "moral ambiguity" has been a point of some criticism from those scholars who suggest that Niebuhr's theories are perhaps too general, lacking the specificity to direct foreign policy measures, and so forth. It seems there may be some credence to these criticisms.

However, I think this moral ambiguity is a consequence of the nature of the realities of the social milieu that is the international system rather than a result of any shortcomings in Niebuhr's thinking. A great deal less moral ambiguity is found within cultures, societies, and nations that share common religious, philosophical, and/or political value systems than in the larger world society because within this society there are more firmly established common value systems. Moral behavior and justice are more likely when all parties involved can agree on what exactly is "just" and what exactly is "moral." Morality and justice are also more likely when all parties involved can agree on what authority is legitimate to enforce "justice," and can stand as judge over infractions of that justice. When all of this is in place, actors become accountable for their actions, and "moral, just behavior" becomes more likely or at least possible.

Niebuhr observed that in the larger global society that comprises all the diversity of the world's social, religious, philosophical, and political value systems, there is no clear universal consensus on what behavior is moral or just. Therefore, no acceptable legitimate authority exists to enforce what little might be agreed upon, and consequently there is little accountability among international actors. Ultimately, this leads to international moral ambiguity, which allows nations to do more or less as they please. Because of the relativity of morality as it pertains to international relations, those nations or policymakers who do try to mix their foreign policies with what they consider to be ethical actions or motives inevitably become parents of a certain degree of moral ambiguity. This is the case because their moral actions are, from the international perspective, at best *relatively* moral and at worst *"morally rationalized"* to suit their respective national interests. As Niebuhr once wrote, "Perhaps the best that can be expected of nations is that they should justify their hypocrisies by a slight measure of real international achievement, and learn how to do justice to wider interests than their own, while they pursue their own."[27]

This is not to suggest that Niebuhr felt morality was to be divorced from the social or political arena. In fact, as I hope I have shown, he was dedicated

[27] RN, *Moral Man,* p. 108.

to the advocacy of its realistic implementation in the sociopolitical sphere where it would not lead to naiveté or moral crusades. As I mentioned earlier, he believed "a realist conception of human nature should be made the servant of an ethic of progressive justice."[28] Writing on morality and foreign policy, George Weigel quoted Niebuhr: "The dream of perpetual peace and brotherhood for human society will never be fully realized," but then went on to say in his own words,

> That did not mean, as many have misinterpreted, that society and politics were somehow outside the boundaries within which moral reason could operate (according to Niebuhr). It did mean that social ethics was a distinctive enterprise, which ought not [to] be confused with the ethics of interpersonal relationships. One did not deal with Hitler in precisely the same way that one reasoned morally about dealing with Aunt Mary.[29]

This is a point well taken because taking at the collective level Jesus' command to turn the other cheek, which was given at the personal level, could suggest inviting the Japanese to bomb San Francisco after they had finished with Pearl Harbor. Would it be "just" for a Christian president to say such a thing? Can a willingness to lay aside one's own personal security to turn the other cheek, which may only put oneself in danger, be compared to a willingness to lay the security of one's child, one's spouse, or one's country aside? For Niebuhr the answer to these questions must be, "No." Niebuhr's argument would be that, while it might be admirable to turn the other cheek in one's own personal conduct with another human being, such conduct for a parent regarding the security of his or her vulnerable children or for a president regarding national security issues would be irresponsible. It would not be conducive to national security or the protection of the lives of innocents, and it would also invite tyrants around the world to rape and pillage wherever they pleased.

Though perhaps no one but true pacifists would take such "cheek-turning" at the national policy level seriously, Niebuhr attacked such moralism nevertheless, reminding such moralists that the avoidance of conflict in this way will not necessarily resolve dilemmas in human society where force is brought to bear. Perhaps the most discussed example of this principle is the

---

[28] RN, *Man's Nature*, pp. 24–5.
[29] George Weigel, "Exorcising Wilson's Ghost: Morality and Foreign Policy in America's Third Century," *Washington Quarterly* 10 (Autumn, 1987): 31–40.

failure of the West, and particularly the British under Neville Chamberlain, to confront Hitler prior to 1939. Of this sort of moralism and to the Neville Chamberlains of the world, Niebuhr said,

> They do not recognize to what degree justice in a sinful world is actually maintained by a tension of competitive forces, which is always in danger of degenerating into overt conflict, but without which there would only be the despotic peace of the subordination of the will of the weak to the strong.[30]

Niebuhr and others have argued that by appeasing Hitler and avoiding confrontation in the short term, Chamberlain and others contributed to the likelihood of the more serious long-term conflict that followed. When writing about the lack of strong response by the Western nations and League of Nations to Japan's invasion of Manchuria, Niebuhr gave us a premonition he had of a larger war to come, in part because of the world's failure to stand up to Japan, and the further aggression he feared this would incite from Japan and others. Writing in 1932, Niebuhr said,

> For the time being, the Japanese are in Manchuria to stay. They have gained concrete advantage by the use of force, and should they remain in possession of them, their success will invite every other nation with grievances and ambitions to resort to the old method once more. In that case we may as well resign ourselves to the inevitability of another world war. The depreciated prestige of peace machinery and the clash of rival imperialistic interests will make such a struggle a certainty.[31]

Niebuhr turned out to be correct. Japan was not held accountable for its aggression in any meaningful way at the time, and in 1937 it expanded and renewed its invasion of the rest of China. As Niebuhr predicted, Japan's invasions of China were followed by further aggression from nations such as Italy, who invaded Abyssinia (Ethiopia) in 1935 (with little opposition from the international community), and Germany, which in 1939 launched its attack on Czechoslovakia and Poland, and eventually much of the rest of Europe, leading to World War II.

---

[30] RN, *Nature and Destiny 1*, pp. 297–8.
[31] RN, "Peace Lessons from the Orient," *The Christian Advocate* (May 19, 1932), p. 524, as found in Box 56, Reinhold Niebuhr Papers, Manuscript Division, Library of Congress, Washington, DC.

Three Ways of Harnessing Self- and/or National Interest

Returning to our more general discussion of international relations, Niebuhr believed there were three ways to harness the "egoistic passions" of humans in society. One way was the balance of power, as manifested in nineteenth-century Europe, the Cold War, or the checks and balances of modern constitutional systems with separate executive and judicial power structures. The second was deterrence, or "mutual defenses against its (humans' egoistic passions, or the will-to-power's) inordinate expression," as exemplified by police or legal structures, or military deterrents to aggression. The third was the harnessing of these egoistic passions to social outlets, such as the competition of international business or team sports.[32] Niebuhr did not envision social groups or nation-states as ever unselfishly surrendering their interests unless structures were in place to make "good behavior" in their interests. Only then were peace and justice possible.

Peace is a biblical imperative[33] and is one that Niebuhr cherished throughout his career, whether as a pacifist or as a Realist. I hope thus far I have not left this point for granted. I feel I must stress that Niebuhr spent most of his life trying to "validate the love ethic," and the whole point of the love ethic's implementation is peace. Yet he believed that peace could not be maintained without justice. He realized that peace had to be defended or ensured by force from time to time in international relations, in ways that might make a Christian blush. Ronald Stone said of him, "With Augustine, he believed peace to be among the highest achievements, but to preserve it required a mixture of means including political authority which relied both on agreement and force."[34] Dialogue and diplomacy aimed at international conflict avoidance and resolution should always remain at the top of the national foreign policy agenda, as must appear obvious, for through these means war can often be avoided. Yet, averse to the ideals of the more pacifistic moralists and idealists, when force is brought to bear in such a way as to threaten one's nation's interests or security, force may be required to counter force and maintain or ensure peace.

---

[32] Thompson, "The Political Philosophy," p. 241.

[33] Of course, Jesus (called "the Prince of Peace" by Christians, Isaiah 9:6) said things such as "blessed are the peacemakers" (Matthew 5:9), turn the other cheek (Matthew 5:39), and "I have said these things to you, that in me you may have peace" (John 16:33, all from the English Standard Version of the Bible).

[34] Thompson, "The Political Philosophy," p. 73.

Niebuhr once said, "political values are highly relative" in time and across social, political, religious, and ideological boundaries. Moreover, each confrontational scenario has its own variables that carry their own hierarchical weight vis-à-vis the interests, justice, history, values, and world opinion of those involved and that are consequently too complex to realistically fall into a simple categorical breakdown or flowchart leading to decision A or B. However, some conclusions can be drawn in applying Niebuhrian thought to specific cases. What follows is one such consideration of Niebuhr's views of international relations and foreign policy issues—in this case, the United Nations and the potential for national transcendence in a Niebuhrian approach to international relations.

5

Niebuhr on the UN, Globalization, and the Potential for National Transcendence

Following World War II and the founding of the United Nations, there was much talk of the need for a greater degree of centralized international cooperation—some way to create a system of international justice that would serve, and yet possibly transcend, the interests of states. Many saw the need for a world federation or world government as an answer to the complexities of international relations. Many viewed the United Nations (UN) as the means to this end. Some even regarded the UN *as* this end. What were Niebuhr's views of the UN? How did his Christian Realism contend with the notion or potential of national transcendence? Although Niebuhr did not live to see globalization in the modern sense, how would he have likely viewed it and its impact on the freedom of states to act and the likelihood of their cooperation? What possibility, in Niebuhr's estimation, was there that nation-states could ever serve or yield to interests beyond their own?

World Community and the UN

Niebuhr saw a great gap between the level of international interdependence brought about by international trade, instantaneous communication, the jet age, and other factors on the one hand, and the level of international integration at the sociopolitical level on the other. This, he explained, was the heart of the dilemma among nations and peoples in the modern era. For example, modern international trade brings peoples of different cultures and their wares to all corners of the globe; modern aircraft allows an individual to eat breakfast in Nairobi, lunch in Cairo, and dinner in London; communications satellites or the Internet permit Koreans to watch an American television news team's live broadcast of a military operation in the desert of Iraq, thousands of miles away. Yet, in Niebuhr's words, "Our problem is that techniques [or the trappings of technology] have established a rudimentary world community

Niebuhrian International Relations. Gregory J. Moore, Oxford University Press (2020).
© Oxford University Press.
DOI: 10.1093/oso/9780197500446.001.0001

but have not integrated it organically, morally, or politically."[1] More and more of the peoples of the world, many of whom in the past have managed to remain isolated, are being thrust together by modernity and the forces of globalization all the time. Yet our abilities to work together effectively have failed to grow at the same rate as have our needs and opportunities to work together. Add to this the difficulties created by differences among the world's peoples regarding religion, language, views of morality and justice, historical and cultural heritage, the socioeconomic and physical environments in which they live, ideologies, and the different perceptions and worldviews all of these factors create, and it is no wonder the world suffers from so much conflict. At the same time, given all these differences, one might also conclude that it is amazing that the world runs as well as it does.

Of course, these difficulties were not born in the twenty-first century. They have been with us as long as one people group has interacted with another. From Thucydides to Hobbes to Kant to twentieth-century thinkers, many have expressed ideas on the management of international affairs. Since Kant, and especially since the world wars and the inauguration of international organizations such as the League of Nations and the UN, the notion of "peace through social contract," such as a world federation or world government, has remained popular. Yet even Kant, the originator of the notion of "perpetual peace," admitted the difficulties of his dream, a "pacific federation" of world states.[2] Nonetheless, following the horrors of two world wars, the advent of the nuclear age, and the onset of the Cold War, Niebuhr's realism about human nature and the ability of states to cooperate did not prevent him from saying, it is both necessary and laudable that men of good will should, in this situation, seek to strengthen every moral and political force which might give a rudimentary world community a higher degree of integration."[3] He stood firmly behind this idea, yet he did not agree with the world federalists who, after World War II, sought to draw up a constitution and erect a world government of one form or another. He believed world government in our age was impossible.

---

[1] RN, *World Crisis and American Responsibility; Nine Essays,* Ernest W. Lefever, ed. (New York: Association Press, 1958), p. 85.

[2] Immanuel Kant, *Kant: Political Writings,* Hans Reiss, ed. (New York: Cambridge University Press, 1991).

[3] RN, *World Crisis,* p. 86.

Niebuhr considered the actions of the world federalists unrealistic for two reasons in particular.

The fallacy of world government can be stated in two simple propositions. The first is that governments are not created by fiat (though sometimes they can be imposed by tyranny). The second is that governments have only limited efficacy in integrating a community.[4]

Regarding the first proposition, Niebuhr did not believe a world government was possible in our time because he did not believe it possible that anyone could create and implement a constitution that would be amenable to the values and perceived interests of all nation-states. He did not believe national leaders could agree to put in writing, let alone decide, at what point their states were willing to surrender their national interests to the interests of the world community, if indeed they could be defined. Drawing up a constitution for a world government would require the signatory approbation of all the governments of the world's nation-states. For in no other way could it be a world government. Unfortunately, however,

> if there *is* a "natural law" which is "self-evident" to all men, it certainly does not contain very much specific content beyond such minimal rules as the prohibition of murder and theft and such general principles of justice as the dictum that each man is to have his due.[5]

The multiplicity of different value systems and worldviews evident in our world, coupled with the tenacity of groupism and collective pride, brought Niebuhr to conclude that a true world government would not be realized in the near future, if ever. In Niebuhr's opinion, talk of constructing a world government presupposed a highly integrated world community that he believed simply did not exist. Therefore, any talk of drafting a world constitution was much ado about nothing unless or until such a community existed. For until then world government was impossible—unless, of course, such a world government was imposed by force.

The imposition of force was the only way government could precede community in Niebuhr's estimation. There certainly are many examples of this phenomenon in history, but history also reveals that the common results of

---

[4] RN, *World Crisis*, p. 88.
[5] RN, *World Crisis*, p. 102.

such fiat are tyranny, and this is consistent with Niebuhr's views on human nature and the will-to-power. When government imposes itself on a people by force, it lacks true legitimacy and ultimately must maintain itself by force.[6] As we can see with the example of the former Soviet Union, tyranny cannot suppress the people indefinitely. The only model for such an imposition of government by force on the international system which Niebuhr could possibly have envisioned would have been an imperial bid by either the United States or the Soviet Union for world domination. This was not a means of bringing about world unity that Niebuhr thought likely or attractive, for "though the perils of international anarchy are very great, they may still be preferable to international tyranny."[7]

Case Study: The United States

Many world federalists and advocates of a binding "social contract" of world government point to the United States as a possible model for the "birth by contract" phenomenon of world government. Niebuhr believed this analogy was problematic for two reasons. First, he referred to the preamble of the U.S. Constitution, which states that its purpose is to help create "a more perfect union." This of course suggests that there already was a union—it had come through the common experience of the people and the common cause of liberty and was forged on the battlefield. As Niebuhr pointed out, the "union" needed only to be made "more perfect." Therefore, the analogy between the United States and the world federalist movement failed because the 13 American colonies already shared a common language, similar histories and traditions, a common cause, a common purpose, and a common moral and religious background. The world community of nations as a whole does not enjoy these commonalities. The problems facing the more limited European Union suggest that Niebuhr was right, for the global economic crisis that began in 2008 has put severe strains on the ability of the European Union (EU) to remain united even around a single currency.

---

[6] There is much in this discussion of the problems of outside imposition of government and/or democracy that lend themselves to the discussion of the U.S./allied invasion of Iraq in 2003 and the difficulties the United States and its allies faced in trying to impose democracy on Iraq that is joined in chapter 7. This discussion provides more reasons that Niebuhr would likely have opposed the invasion of Iraq and the state-building project that followed.

[7] RN, *World Crisis,* p. 97.

Niebuhr's criticism of the world/America analogy also pointed out that, despite all the things the 13 colonies had in common, and despite the joys of victory and independence, one must not forget how the 13 new states bickered and feuded following their liberation from Great Britain. Niebuhr noted that the Civil War came and went before it became evident that all the reservations about federalism and the surrender of state sovereignty had passed. The lessons of groupism and collective pride are as relevant here as they have been anywhere.

The second primary reason Niebuhr believed the notion of world government in the present age was a fallacy was that even if, by some sort of "*coup de monde,*" a world government could be installed, the mere existence of such a government did not guarantee that the world community would become integrated and ordered, or function as a well-oiled machine of global governance. Niebuhr once said,

> Governments cannot create communities for the simple reason that the authority of government is not primarily the authority of law nor the authority of force, but the authority of the community itself. Laws are obeyed because the community accepts them as corresponding, on the whole, to its conception of justice.[8]

A common conception of justice is the key to legitimate governance; without it one sees deviance and rebellion. With it, and with acceptable leadership, one is generally much more likely to see submission to authority, cooperation, and justice within a given jurisdiction. As we have discussed, this common conception of justice is necessary for political cohesion, yet it is noticeably lacking at the international level.

Case Study: India

Niebuhr considered India as an illustration of this point at the national level.[9] India's Muslim and Hindu populations have quarreled and fought for centuries. When India became independent in 1947, it became one nation under

---

[8] RN, *World Crisis*, p. 94.
[9] For a good discussion of India and Britain, Gandhi and the Muslim-Hindu divide, see RN, "What Chance Has Gandhi?" *Christian Century* (October 14, 1931): 1274–76; as found in Box 17, Reinhold Niebuhr Papers, Manuscript Division, Library of Congress, Washington, DC.

a democratic constitution. Yet after independence the conflict between Hindus and Muslims threatened to derail the fledgling Indian democracy. As Niebuhr observed, "political cohesion requires common convictions on particular issues of justice," and these were not something one could take for granted in the Indian case (then or now), given the disparate Hindu and Islamic civilizations that underlay the two people groups and the differing pulls of regional politics on them. Considering the attempts of a government to unite its people by constitution, Niebuhr said, "The fact is that even the wisest statecraft cannot create social tissue. It can cut, sew and redesign social fabric to a limited degree. But the social fabric upon which it works must be a given."[10] The Indian government was attempting to take two similar but separate social fabrics and unite them by constitution. "Common convictions on justice" are a part of the "social tissue" Niebuhr spoke of, but seem to be truly even more basic to the functioning of legitimate governance than the rest of the "social tissue." With different convictions about justice resulting from different religious and cultural perspectives, the common social fabric needed for political and social cohesion has been very difficult to weave to this day in India. It must grow out of the common practices of living together in the same community in a spirit of mutual toleration. Linking this to what we discussed earlier, for peace to exist between Hindus and Muslims in India, or between rival groups anywhere, it must be attained (1) by the mutual transcendence of collective pride and groupism, (2) through a balance of power between the parties, (3) through the careful management and channeling of group interests into socially acceptable outcomes, or (4) through deterrence or enforcement.

Niebuhr believed that of these four mechanisms, the first (the mutual transcendence of collective pride and groupism) was the most ideal, but ultimately impossible, alternative. He saw the second, third, and fourth as the historical possibilities. Because the fourth could not be maintained indefinitely without the second and third (except by tyranny), he viewed the second and third as being the most practical and realistic. This was because a government can help facilitate these matters, but it cannot force groups to balance their power or to manage or redirect their interests as a long-term policy without the threat of crossing the abyss into tyranny. The respective groups can accomplish these tasks only for themselves as a result of their own convictions. These are just the sorts of convictions Niebuhr spoke of when

[10] RN, *World Crisis*, p. 99.

he said, "political cohesion requires common convictions on particular is-sues of justice." Toward facilitating this end government is imperative. Yet the community must want the government and agree to abide by its code. So again, only a fairly cohesive community can guarantee government. Niebuhr offered no easy solution to this dilemma because he did not believe there was one. He simply recommended that both India and the world do whatever was possible, given the realities of their situations, to build up community on a functional, case-by-case basis. Though still divided by Hindu–Muslim inequalities and differing worldviews, among other things, and though examples of Hindu–Muslim violence are still observed in India today, India has for the most part done as Niebuhr suggested, and the nation has come together as a democracy in ways that Niebuhr did not live to see. Despite its challenges, India, of course, has two advantages that our world community does not have—a recognized legitimate, democratic government with police powers to enforce the national unity; and an international community that holds the Indian government accountable for its actions toward Indian citi-zens of all stripes.

If it is so difficult to achieve in a democracy like India, with its relatively stable democratic government, what then are the prospects of democratic or "perpetual peace" via a world state? Even if a world state were to achieve the former(a legitimate, democratic government with policy power to en-force national unity), there is no way for it to enjoy the latter (an international community that holds the government accountable for its actions toward Indian citizens of all stripes), because such a state would ultimately stand above the political authority of the member states, if indeed it is worthy of being called a state and not simply something analogous to today's United Nations, which lacks governing authority and power. As we have discussed, Niebuhr believed that world government was impossible in his day.

Yet, while his attitude was decidedly cynical about the prospect of world government, he did not expressly appear to rule it out as a long-term possi-bility. In 1961, he said, "I think we will get some universal government partly by building up the United Nations and partly through Russian and American partnership."[11] This perspective illustrates an idealism that Niebuhr did not often reveal, but that explains his lack of rhetoric completely excluding the idea of world government and cooperative international organization as being within the realm of possibility. On another occasion he said, "We shall

---

[11] RN, "Universal Government," *The Center Magazine* 18 (November/December 1985).

have constant opportunity to perfect instruments of peace and justice *if* we succeed in creating some communal foundation upon which constitutional structures can rest."[12] The key, according to this statement, lay in building up this "communal foundation," this "social tissue." If we could succeed in weaving the world into a common social tapestry, in laying a communal foundation, Niebuhr said, "we shall have constant opportunity to perfect instruments of peace and justice." Unfortunately, this does not appear to be an easy task or a shortly forthcoming reality. In our quest to move toward strengthening the instruments of peace and justice, Niebuhr said,

> We shall exploit our opportunities the more successfully. . . if we have knowledge of the limits of the will in creating government, and in the limits of government in creating community. We may have pity upon, but can have no sympathy with, those who flee to the illusory security of the impossible from the insecurities and ambiguities of the possible.[13]

If something akin to Kant's "pacific federation" is "the impossible," let us return to "the insecurities and ambiguities of the possible."

Niebuhr believed strongly in the potential of the United Nations as a tool for moving the nations toward the ideal of a stronger, better integrated, more cooperative world community. However, as Ronald Stone put it, "Niebuhr's polemics against the illusions of world government often obscured his hopes for the United Nations and the work of its specialized agencies, particularly UNESCO."[14] Niebuhr's cynicism was not directed toward the United Nations, but rather toward the idealists who were so dedicated to it and, he felt, expected too much from it. He thought many of them were the same idealists who believed the world was ready for and needed a world constitution and subsequently were disappointed at the UN's lack of binding, constitutional structure. In Niebuhr's opinion, their lofty expectations actually worsened the situation for the UN because they caused many of these idealists to "irresponsibly" criticize the "necessary minimal constitutional structure" embodied in the UN, which Niebuhr said was as bad as its critics suggested only if something better were possible at the moment.[15] He believed there was not.

---

[12] RN, *World Crisis*, p. 104.
[13] RN, *World Crisis*, p. 104.
[14] Ronald H. Stone, *Prophet to Politicians* (Nashville, TN: Abingdon Press, 1972), p. 217.
[15] RN, *World Crisis*, p. 87.

Niebuhr saw the UN as a pragmatic, functional approach to international relations, which sought to make the world a better place by dealing with the world as it is, not as we would like it to be. "We can deflect, harness, and beguile the historical forces of our age but we cannot ignore, defy or annul them," he said.[16] He believed the idealists failed to face this reality of international life. A close reading of Niebuhr's reflections on the United Nations reveals a marked sense of optimism regarding the organization.

> [T]he United Nations fulfilled more than was expected of it because it was less than an ideal system. It was a system of co-operation among the nations designed not for ideal possibilities but for the actualities of the present. . . . The United Nations has become one (and the chief) of many devices by which we are going to organize our world.[17]

Niebuhr felt that the provision for the veto in the UN Security Council was the strongest expression of this realism.[18] While many idealists criticized the veto as an unnecessary hindrance to the work of the organization, Niebuhr saw it as recognition of the power conflict that might (and did) erupt between the Great Powers within the Security Council. The veto acted as a circuit breaker, designed to stop the organization from enacting a resolution over the head of a dissenting power that might embroil the organization in a conflict more dangerous than the conflict it was responding to. The founders believed, and Niebuhr agreed, that it was better for the organization to do nothing, than to act in defiance of one of the Security Council powers and risk the collapse of the organization, or worse, World War III. During the Cold War there could be little doubt that the veto was important in this capacity.

Niebuhr believed the UN was an effective tool for the expression of what William James once said were two things basic to any moral task: "A.) Resoluteness in the original commitment to the cause or discipline, and B.) a whole series of specific acts of loyalty to give historical body to the commitment."[19] Regarding the first consideration, Niebuhr compared the UN (representing "the broadest and highest of all human communities, the

---

[16] RN, *World Crisis*, p. 81.

[17] RN, *World Crisis*, pp. 71, 73.

[18] Davis, Harry R. and Robert C. Good, eds., *Reinhold Niebuhr on Politics* (New York: Charles Scribner's Sons, 1960).p. 256.

[19] RN, *World Crisis*, p. 69.

global community") to the family unit ("the smallest and most primordial community"). He felt that resoluteness to the original commitment was imperative; whether between nation and nation in light of the UN Charter, or between husband and wife in light of their marriage vows. In either case, "if the partnership is presumed to be tentative, there will not be enough resolution to overcome the hazards to its success which the vicissitudes of life always present."[20]

However, because of the doubts that arise about nations' commitments to the Charter, as well as the doubts that often arise regarding spouses' marriage vows in times of duress, Niebuhr believed it was the second of James's considerations which carried more weight in the real world. "An original covenant soon fades if it is not given substance by those daily acts of fidelity and forbearance through which lives are wedded and amalgamated."[21] This is the task in which the UN has been and continues to be actively engaging itself. Were Niebuhr alive today, I think he would be pleased to observe that the UN has slowly built up sufficient legitimacy among the nations by its past successes to engender respect for the organization and greater accountability between those nations, so as to become what its founders intended: a viable international forum for the discussion and even management of peace and security issues, as well as many other issues of global importance.

Case Study: The 1956 Suez Crisis

I must add, however, that Niebuhr, realist that he was, understood that though the UN was very useful, it was not a world government. Niebuhr's critique of U.S. policy in response to the 1956 Suez Crisis well illustrates this point. After Egyptian President Gamal Abdel Nasser nationalized the Suez Canal, three of America's allies, Israel, Britain, and France attacked and occupied the Suez Canal zone, the United States responded with condemnation and stood, ironically, with the Soviet Union behind a UN resolution demanding the immediate withdrawal of all invading troops. Niebuhr joined other realists by attacking the U.S. stance. Stone cited three reasons for Niebuhr's opposition to U.S. policy. First, he said because the UN was not, as many imagined, a world government, but rather a channel for international

---

[20] RN, *World Crisis,* pp. 71–2.
[21] RN, *World Crisis,* p. 72.

diplomacy, its resolutions carried no special moral sanction. Second, the U.S. response was pacifistic. It denied its allies the right to use force in a situation in which many (including the British and French) believed the United States would not have hesitated to use force (as it *has* done in the Panama Canal zone and elsewhere on many occasions). "Niebuhr's third criticism of United States foreign policy," as Stone put it, "was that it substituted legalistic platitudes for the diplomacy which the Western alliance needed at a time of crisis in the Middle East and eruption in the Soviet empire."[22]

Niebuhr was editor of *Christianity and Crisis* during the Suez Crisis, and a large debate that split the influential publication's editorial staff ensued surrounding an article by Kenneth Thompson in the January 7, 1957 issue. Thompson, along with Niebuhr, Morgenthau, and other prominent Realists, condemned the Eisenhower/Dulles policy of retribution against America's allies. Thompson explained their opposition,

> We might have firmly and deliberately disassociated ourselves from their [the British, French, and Israeli] action. Instead we conducted a crusade against their mistakes while closing our eyes to the wholly evil Russian aggression in the Middle East.[23]

Niebuhr responded to Thompson's article, agreeing with Thompson in his belief that

> the alliance between Europe and the USA, commonly called the "Atlantic Community," is in the process of disintegration and that among the reasons which he [Thompson] gives for this disintegration is the tendency of our nation to think in terms of broad principles, such as the "loyalty to the United Nations" and "anti-colonialism" instead of in terms of detailed strategy.[24]

Explaining why he and Thompson, who were by no means opposed to loyalty to the United Nations or anticolonialism, believed that the United States should not have lashed out against and humiliated its allies, Niebuhr stated,

> [W]e are in general favor of "self-determination for nations." But when one of the newly emancipated nations develops imperialistic ambitions of its

---

[22] Stone, *Reinhold Niebuhr*, p. 187.
[23] RN, "Can We Organize the World?" *Christianity and Crisis*, 13 (February 2, 1953): 186.
[24] RN, "Can We Organize the World," p. 186.

own, seeks to dominate the Islamic world and gets its hand on the life-line of European economy, we are not dealing with a "justified nationalism," but with a dangerous dynamism, which becomes the more dangerous to us because it has become an instrument of Russian policy just at a time when Russian power is in the process of decay in eastern Europe.[25]

Essentially, Niebuhr, Thompson, and others felt there was more at stake here than the ideal scenario of being able to appeal to the rules of "fair play" as established by the UN Charter. For them the threat of a crumbling Western alliance, which they believed stood between freedom and communist subjugation, took precedence.

Taking a closer look at this debate will allow us greater insight into Niebuhr's thought processes and will also permit an interesting look into the heart of the differences between the idealist and Realist approaches. John Stoessinger, outlining the conflict between Secretary of State Dulles and the realists on this issue, noted that "personal behavior is judged by an ethic of intention, while that of the statesman is essentially one of consequence."[26] Herein lies the statesperson's dilemma: when the would-be "moral statesperson," looking to the greater long-term moral good, is convinced on a given occasion that the greatest moral good can be served by sanctioning an ostensibly immoral action, how does he convince his constituency or other nations that his intentions are for the greater moral good and not for immediate political gain? Stoessinger refers us to Hans Morgenthau's oft-quoted illustration:

Neville Chamberlain's policies of appeasement were, as far as we can judge, inspired by good motives; he was probably less motivated by considerations of personal power than were many other British prime ministers, and he sought to preserve peace and to assure the happiness of all concerned. Yet his policies helped to make the Second World War inevitable, and to bring untold miseries to millions of men. Sir Winston Churchill's motives, on the other hand, have been much less universal in scope and much more narrowly directed toward personal and national power, yet the foreign policies that sprang from these inferior motives were certainly superior in moral and political quality to those pursued by his predecessor.[27]

---

[25] RN, "Can We Organize the World," p. 186.

[26] John Stoessinger, *Crusaders and Pragmatists* (New York: W.W. Norton, 1985), p. 126.

[27] Hans Morgenthau, *Politics among Nations*, 3rd ed. (New York: Knopf, 1960), p. 6.

I do not believe that we should take this statement to suggest that the states-person with superior motives is consistently doomed to bring greater hard-ship on his or her country through his or her policies than the statesperson with inferior motives. Rather, I believe it illustrates the need for policymakers to be well versed in the ways of both "the children of light and the children of darkness," as Niebuhr suggested in his book of the same title. In other words, in statecraft, consequentialist considerations must be part of the calculus, for policymakers cannot afford purely abstract deontological reasoning, but rather must root their policy choices in the realities of the morally broken world in which we all live.

Returning to our discussion of the Suez Crisis, Niebuhr thought it was extremely foolish to jeopardize the Western alliance, which he believed protected the free world from the free rein of communist tyranny, by alien-ating one's closest allies in an appeal to moralism that suggested the UN represented a higher level of international legal integration than could pos-sibly be the case. While Niebuhr believed it might be nice to think the UN Charter represented an irrevocable, universal code of international conduct, he reminded us that most nations were still playing by their own rules, in-cluding the Security Council's permanent five members. Therefore, he felt it was foolish of the Eisenhower administration to go so far out of its way in its appeal to the legal codes of the UN Charter and in support of a question-able regime like Nasser's, when doing so threatened the alienation of its allies and the potential fall of the Western alliance. In the end, the U.S. rebuttal of British and French policy *did* contribute to the eventual fall of the Eden and Mollet governments, respectively. He felt Washington's lack of support for their actions, coupled with a U.S. position of neutrality in the UN Security Council, would have said more than enough.

Once again we must be careful not to go too far by assuming that Niebuhr's stance on the Suez Crisis suggested that the United States should do entirely as it pleased, forsaking the UN for other, more immediate concerns. Niebuhr placed a high priority on the advocacy of U.S. support for and cooperation with the UN. He simply believed the UN did not yet have enough moral au-thority, given its youth and the general lack of international compliance with UN regulations, to give UN resolutions precedence to U.S. foreign policy in situations such as the Suez Crisis where he believed Cold War issues that were more immediately threatening to world security were at stake. This holds es-pecially true considering his view at the time of the United States as the pro-tector of the free world and the possibility that the actions of Britain, France, and Israel gave the Soviet Union sufficient cover to crush the 1956 Hungarian uprising soon thereafter with little reproach from the West, sheepish as a result of its own folly in the Suez.

Niebuhr did not write as extensively on the United Nations as we might have hoped and he died when the organization was still young (1971), so it is difficult to ascertain at what point, if ever, Niebuhr believed the UN would have enough moral and legal credibility and international adherence to deserve the willful deference of any nation's foreign policy to the Security Council. From what Niebuhr has said about the shortcomings of human nature, collective pride, groupism, and the prevalence of self-interest, as well as by his own analysis of the Suez Crisis, this sort of national transcendence would seem highly unlikely from the United States or other powerful nations and would lead him to conclude, likewise, that the UN itself was not above corruption and vainglory. Although the world's peoples might eventually be able to better organize themselves internationally, the perspective Niebuhr has laid out as it regards human nature and the prevalence of self- and/or national interest must lead one to conclude that he believed interstate conflict and violence would never be entirely eradicated.

The Potential for National Transcendence in a Globalized World

Let us reconsider several of Niebuhr's observations on the potential of national transcendence, linking these intentionally with his views of the UN, globalization, and the importance of world community. He said that all far-seeing observers see a world community taking shape, but that a functional approach would be more useful toward this end than "any abstract commitments to ideal and impossible world constitutions which some idealistic Americans regard as important."[28] Such a world community must precede any higher level of effective international organization, not the other way around. Niebuhr concluded one discussion on the UN and its role in the free world as follows. "Undoubtedly the constitutional instruments of world power must be perfected in time. But the more perfect instruments must grow out of the more perfect mutualities of daily living together."[29]

[28] RN, *World Crisis*, p. 80.
[29] RN, *World Crisis*, p. 84.

Mastering the art of daily living together via the functional approach was Niebuhr's hope for improving our world community, but he understood that this would undoubtedly take time and a lot of patience. The key to mastering daily living together at any level of human interaction, as Niebuhr stressed again and again, is to acknowledge, not undermine, the interests of all parties and to seek the highest point of convergence between the best interests of the individual units and the best interests of the whole.

Niebuhr viewed the United Nations as a tool that has been and can continue to be used at the international level toward these ends in the following ways: as a channel for international diplomacy; as a forum for international dialogue and conflict resolution; as a way of helping to bridge the gap between east and west, north and south; as a way to coordinate the interests of states; and as a means of encouraging resoluteness to the cause of international peace and security. The ultimate challenge to the collective life of humankind, the challenge that requires all the wisdom, sensitivity, prudence, and cooperation we can muster, is to constantly seek the highest point of convergence between the interests of the one and the many, while not sacrificing the freedom, hopes, and dreams of any. Any possibility for international justice and greater international cooperation will depend on our successes or failures in these endeavors.

Although Niebuhr did not live to see modern globalization of the twentieth century variety, I believe he would have concluded two things about globalization as it regards its impact on the potential of peoples and states to better cooperate. First, while the late nineteenth century and the entire twentieth century saw remarkable expansions in the ability of human beings to travel, to trade, and to interact, none of this has apparently led to the ability of human beings to lay down their parochial proclivities or self-serving sensibilities, for the twentieth century may have been the bloodiest century in human history. Nor has human nature and its tendency toward insecurity and the will-to-power changed, nor has modern education been able to reform it. Second, what Niebuhr would certainly recognize, however, is the functional advances globalization has brought about in how humans live on a daily basis, and the level and volume of interaction globalization has engendered. Based on his writings, it seems that he would see globalization as a functional means toward the slow process of constructing the world community he saw as the necessary underpinning to any greater level of international cooperation or potential national transcendence. This is how he saw the economic and technological advances of his own age. Globalization is a deepening and thickening of this process. Quoting Niebuhr from his *Children of Light and Children of Darkness* (1944), Larry Rasmussen puts it this way,

> Niebuhr names "the new technical-natural fact of a global economy" as one of the looming historical forces driving the world toward world community. The global economy is, in fact, a "force of universality," a contingent factor that presents new historical perils and opportunities, now on a planetary scale.[30]

In keeping with the dialectical view he held of so many things, Niebuhr would have seen globalization as a force for cooperation and greater world community, while at the same time he would have recognized both the limits of its transformative power and the ability of organizations like Al Qaeda to exploit it for evil.

In answer to the question of whether or not Niebuhr thought nations might ever submit their national interests to the overarching authority of a world body, I think he would say yes, and no. We may in fact arrive at a day when every nation agrees to submit itself to the overarching authority of a world body of some kind. Whether or not this is itself a positive good is another matter altogether, but given all that Niebuhr said about the dark side of human nature and the need for political and power-based checks on governmental power, I can only imagine that he would have grave reservations about a single global political entity, perhaps agreeing with the perspective of C. S. Lewis in his description of such potential evil and despotism in Lewis's *That Hideous Strength*, or with George Orwell in his futurist narrative of state abuse of power in *1984*, or Ayn Rand in her dystopian tale, *Atlas Shrugged*.[31] In any event, such an undertaking would depend not only on how successful humans are at weaving the "social tissue" of global community, but on how successful we are at engendering an atmosphere of mutual accountability. For no matter how sincere nations are about the ideal of international harmony and no matter how just and legitimate a potential world government may be, mutual accountability, which may necessitate the threat of force, will always be a necessary component of any international system. Niebuhr's

---

[30] Larry Rasmussen, "Empire of Global Community?" in Daniel F. Rice, ed., *Reinhold Niebuhr Revisited: Engagements with an American Original* (Grand Rapids, MI: Eerdmans, 2009).

[31] C. S. Lewis, *That Hideous Strength* (New York: Scribner, 2003[1945]); George Orwell, *1984* (New York: Plume, 2003[1949]); Ayn Rand, *Atlas Shrugged* (New York: Plume, 1999[1957]).

Christian Realist message emphasized this point—that although we may find peace, we must never forget the realities of human nature and the need for structures of accountability. Because of human nature's dualism, which matches its potential to find justice with its propensity to pursue self-interest, Reinhold Niebuhr believed the realization of a peaceful, mutually tolerable global community was the "final possibility and impossibility of human life," and "will be in actuality the perpetual problem as well as the constant ful-fillment of human hopes."[32] Niebuhr would say we must work for perpetual peace and never give up when we fail to find it; yet at the same time we must not get lost in utopian schemes nor forget the dark side of human nature or the need for checks on authority. This is what Niebuhr demanded of himself, and this is what he would ask of us.

[32] RN, *The Children of Light and the Children of Darkness* (New York: Charles Scribner's Sons, 1944), p. 187.

6

Niebuhr on U.S. Policy in the Cold War

During 1946 and 1947, Niebuhr took several trips to Europe, including Germany, and he was shocked to learn that even his old leftist friends there had developed extremely hawkish views of the Soviet Union and its intentions. He in turn wrote a number of pieces during that season warning his audience of the dangers of Soviet totalitarianism, even comparing the USSR to Hitler's Germany. Back in the United States he helped form a new organization of anticommunist but progressive activists, called the Americans for Democratic Action. The organizational charter ruled that neither communists nor communist sympathizers were welcome to join.[1] As detailed in greater detail in the biographical chapter of this book, it is clear that in this season of his life Niebuhr's break with leftism had brought him full circle, from leftist activist to progressive anticommunist campaigner.

Niebuhr, Communism, and the Cold War

The basis of Niebuhr's conception of the nature of the Cold War was that it was a conflict between the forces of freedom, embodied in the Western democratic tradition, and the forces of tyranny, as found in communism. The two forces were set at odds by their very natures and could not, Niebuhr believed, coexist except by a balance of power based on reciprocal deterrence which kept each other at bay. In Niebuhr's opinion, the United States rightfully accepted the role of "primary defender of the free world" in this conflict due to its hegemonic status. Though his views shifted over time as to the immediacy of the threat the Soviet Union presented, Niebuhr remained staunchly anticommunist owing to his own personal intellectual rejection of Marxism and to the extreme Stalin-era manifestations of the creed as witnessed in post-evolutionary Soviet communism.

---

[1] Richard Wightman Fox, *Reinhold Niebuhr: A Biography* (San Francisco: Harper & Row, 1985), p. 230.

Niebuhrian International Relations. Gregory J. Moore, Oxford University Press (2020).
© Oxford University Press.
DOI: 10.1093/oso/9780197500446.001.0001

Niebuhr came to believe that communism was "the most dynamic and demonic world politico-religious movement in history."[2] He wrote,

> Its [communism's] fury of self-righteousness and its vast monopolies of
> power against whose pretensions and aggression there are no checks,
> are directly derived from Marx's utopian vision of an innocent mankind,
> to be realized once the corruption due to the institution of property was
> removed.[3]

Niebuhr cited six reasons why he believed communism was so "evil."[4] The
first reason was the freedom-limiting monopoly of power enjoyed by the
central Communist Party in the various nations ruled by such parties, which
left no checks or balances to the "will-to-power" instinct. The second was
the "utopian Marxist illusions" of this "secular religion," misleading the
masses and preaching to them the long-term goals and sanctifying effects
of the elusive classless society. Because its message claimed to speak for the
long-term good of society, a) its shortcomings could be rationalized; b) suffering could be endured for the long-term "good" it preached; and c) its disciples' allegiance could be sustained indefinitely. The third reason Niebuhr
cited for communism's evil was that, unlike Nazism, which was based on a
particular brand of racism and nationalism, communism knew no boundaries, giving it a broader appeal and consequently making it ultimately more
dangerous. It could be adapted to fit the cause of virtually any oppressed
people. Communism was an ideology based on revolution, one that might
threaten the status quo of any establishment, just or unjust, because of its
broadly based proletarian appeal and its promises of salvation in a classless society. Fourth, it was deterministic in its underestimation of the potential of human beings to embrace freedom while accepting responsibility.
Fifth, because of Marxist dogma, and the pretenses of scientific rationality
and human perfectibility combined with the authority of the state, Niebuhr
saw communism as an ideologically subjective, inflexible monolith, incapable of accepting or benefiting from objective criticism, as is the norm in
free societies. Lastly, Niebuhr believed communism was evil because of its
inherent self-righteousness, subjectivity, authoritarian patterns of power

---

[2] RN, *World Crisis and American Responsibility; Nine Essays,* Ernest W. Lefever, ed. (New York:
Association Press, 1958), p. 16.

[3] RN, *World Crisis,* p. 17.

[4] RN, *World Crisis,* p. 50.

centralization, intolerance of dissenting opinions, and an almost missionary zeal to evangelize the world with its political creed.

Niebuhr believed the threat of communist subversion was greatest in the then newly free, developing countries. He feared communism would appeal to the people of the developing nations because of their general distaste for colonialism, which Marx of course believed was the expected and very natural outcome of the capitalist "evil." Niebuhr also feared communism's appeal because with its adoption of the Marxist error of equating egotism with economic-materialist motives, leaders corrupted and driven by the will-to-power could seek power while appearing innocent to the community because of their espoused disavowal of reaping ostensible material benefits.[5]

> The modern Marxist form of this compound of universalism and imperialism is particularly dangerous, partly because of the spuriousness of the utopian claims and partly because a monopoly of power has been built upon the basis of the ideological claims.[6]

History in Cuba and other Latin American, African, and Asian countries seems to have proven Niebuhr correct in this sense.

Niebuhr recognized that, on the contrary, in the modern democracies governments had been secure enough to allow organized labor unions to form, subsequently checking the potential tyranny of early industrial capitalism.[7] Ultimately, it has been the flexibilities of the free society which have saved the people of Western democracies from tyranny. Communism has historically failed to appreciate the practical efficacies of these freedoms, as well as the motivations of self-interest in production (perhaps with the sector-specific exceptions of Chinese and Vietnamese economic reforms in recent decades). Again, with the recent Chinese and Vietnamese exceptions (after all, Deng Xiaoping said, "to get rich is glorious"), it idealistically assumed everyone would work hard for the good of all, while capitalism, recognizing the persistence of self-interest, harnessed it by basing worker benefits and promotion on output and hours worked. Communism also failed to appreciate the political and economic flexibility, ingenuity, and ultimate potential of the free society. Ultimately and paradoxically, as Niebuhr

---

[5] RN, *World Crisis*, p. 56.
[6] RN, *The Structure of Nations and Empires* (New York: Charles Scribner's Sons, 1959), p. 27.
[7] RN, *Faith and Politics* (New York: George Braziller, 1968), p. 224

noted, "communism, designed to redeem the poor, became in fact an effi-
cient instrument for rapid industrialization at the expense of the poor."[8]

Containment and Nuclear Deterrence as a Response to Communism

For all of these reasons, Niebuhr advocated containment of this malignant
communist "evil" and a strong national defense, including a robust nuclear
deterrent. While the Christian faith professed tolerance, Niebuhr believed
the expansion of the communist threat could not be tolerated at the expense
of U.S. interests, particularly when it threatened to subvert much of what
America and Christianity purported to stand for. As did many during the
Cold War era, Niebuhr firmly believed that communism was inherently con-
spiratorial and expansionist, and that consequently it had the potential to
threaten the security and freedom of the entire free world.

The paradox of Niebuhr's Realism was once again evident as he rationalized the necessity of maintaining nuclear weapons in the face of such a threat.
He believed nuclear weapons were a dilemma because their use would bring
such cataclysm upon humanity that it could hardly be considered moral. He
rejected flat-out nuclear war as being "out of proportion to any ends,"[9] even
saying, "If the bomb were ever used, I would hope that it would kill me, because the moral situation would be something that I could not contemplate."[10]
The very presence of nuclear weapons as part of America's arsenal, he feared,
might tempt U.S. policymakers to resort to their use too easily without due
weight of consideration. He was against reliance on nuclear weapons as a first
line of defense because he felt this stance was morally unjustifiable. He also
labeled a preemptive first strike out of the question. He supported nuclear
weapons primarily for nuclear defense and deterrence purposes. Niebuhr
did add, however, that first-use response, though not at all desirable, could
not be ruled out.[11] This was a curious thought given the consequences of

---

[8] RN, *Faith and Politics*, p. 228.

[9] RN and Hans Morgenthau, "The Ethics of War and Peace in a Nuclear Age" (informal discus-
sion), *War/Peace Report* (February 1967), p. 5, as cited in James Childress, "Reinhold Niebuhr's
Realistic-Pragmatic Approach to War and 'The Nuclear Dilemma,'" in Richard Harries, ed., *Reinhold
Niebuhr and the Issues of Our Time* (Grand Rapids, MI: Eerdmans, 1986), p. 142.

[10] As quoted in June Bingham, *Courage to Change* (New York: Scribner's, 1961), p. 386, as cited in
Childress, "Reinhold Niebuhr's Realistic-Pragmatic Approach to War," p. 142.

[11] Fox, *Reinhold Niebuhr*, p. 240.

even a last-stand use in terms of world ecological safety or longevity. I would surmise that the conditions surrounding such a first-use nuclear response would have to be quite severe for Niebuhr to have supported such an action' where Niebuhr would draw the line, giving his blessing to first-use response, I am unsure. In any case, I believe Niebuhr saw this kind of rhetoric as a necessary evil for the maintenance of a credible deterrent.

While Niebuhr was uncomfortable with the prospect of nuclear exchange, he reasoned that America's abolition or disavowal of nuclear weapons and their use "would merely give modern despotism a simple victory over us."[12] He believed that public disavowal of the use of nuclear weapons could have morally unpalatable consequences for a nuclear state, in effect risking the sacrifice of both justice and order (peace).[13] However, he argued that the United States could not rely solely on nuclear weapons for its defense but must maintain a strong conventional defense as well, given that nuclear weapons were almost unusable. More specifically, Niebuhr said,

[W]e have the tremendous task of reversing the tactical tendencies which economic motives have gradually forced upon us. That is, the undue reliance on atomic weapons because they are cheaper than armies. We can not afford to dispense with the dread [atomic] weapons, but neither can we afford to put our sole reliance in them. Such a strategy will finally force the terrible alternative upon us of either capitulation or atomic warfare.[14]

For Niebuhr, the realities of the international order necessitated the maintenance of a horrible and immoral means of violence as a means of sustaining and/or guaranteeing a tolerable peace. So once again the irony of the human predicament revealed itself in the Niebuhrian dialectic.

Still, as anti-Soviet as Niebuhr had become, his familiar themes of the dangers of hubris, whether American, British, or Soviet, were ever present. He believed Americans and Western Europeans had to remain vigilant and must remain firm in their resistance to the spread of communism, but he did

---

[12] Harry R. Davis and Robert C. Good, eds., *Reinhold Niebuhr on Politics* (New York: Charles Scribner's Sons, 1960), pp. 326–7.

[13] Childress, "Reinhold Niebuhr's Realistic-Pragmatic Approach to War," p. 143.

[14] RN, "The Problem of Nuclear Warfare," an original manuscript submitted to Rev. Angus Dun, Bishop of the Diocese of Washington, on May 1, 1957 (for a conference of the College or Preachers on nuclear energy, held in conjunction with the 50th anniversary of the laying of the cornerstone of the Washington Cathedral), p. 7, as found in Box 16, Reinhold Niebuhr Papers, Manuscript Division, Library of Congress, Washington, DC.

not want the United States to see itself simply as "righteous" and the Soviet Union as "evil," as he never thought things were so simple given the darkness he saw in human nature generally. Moreover, he emphasized at the time that the Soviet threat was primarily ideological, not military. In subsequent chapters Niebuhr's views of communism will be further developed, but suffice it to say that he viewed communism as dangerous, or, more specifically, "the most dynamic and demonic world politico-religious movement in history."[15] His assessment of the Soviet threat as more ideological and political than military was similar to that of George Kennan, father of the containment policy and author of the famous "X" article in which he first argued that the United States should pursue a policy of containment of the Soviet Union.[16] In his *Memoirs* Kennan later said that he never meant containment "by military means of a military threat, but the political containment of a political threat."[17] Like Kennan, while Niebuhr initially worried that Washington was too slow to respond to the Soviet threat, instead he began to fear that American policy toward the USSR might go too far and become too aggressive. Niebuhr in particular feared that Americans might become too self-righteous, too aggressive, and too full of hubris in their anticommunism. Unfortunately for both Kennan and Niebuhr (and many others), one could argue that at times during the Cold War this is exactly what occurred, the most prominent examples being the McCarthy-era anticommunist witch hunt and the Vietnam War.[18]

As communism made gains in Asia in the late 1940s and 1950s, Niebuhr had much to say. Regarding China, he agreed with U.S. policy under Dean Acheson that the United States had no moral obligation to save the corrupt Chiang Kai-shek regime. He did not see Mao and the Chinese communists as an immediate threat to the United States at the time, but saw them instead as simply nationalists seeking to liberate their country from poverty and imperialism. In a background check (a "loyalty test" in fact) done when he served as a State Department consultant in late 1950 and into 1951, J. Edgar Hoover's FBI was highly suspicious of Niebuhr, finding him to be too tolerant of Chinese communism.[19] That did not, however, stop Niebuhr from

---

[15] RN, *World Crisis*, p. 16.

[16] George F. Kennan (known as "X" here), "The Sources of Soviet Conduct," *Foreign Affairs* XXV (July 1947): 575.

[17] George F. Kennan, *Memoirs: 1925–1950* (Boston: Little, Brown, 1967), p. 358.

[18] A deeper discussion of Niebuhr's approach to communism and the Vietnam War will be joined below.

[19] Fox, *Reinhold Niebuhr*, p. 242.

continuing to be a darling of the Washington, academic, and theological establishments of the day.

When the Korean War broke out in 1950, Niebuhr feared the United States would get bogged down in a land war on the Asian continent that could weaken and distract the nation and that might allow the Soviets gains in Europe, which he viewed as much more important to US interests than Asia. He even proposed trading Taiwan to the Chinese communists in exchange for a cease-fire on the Korean Peninsula (he made this proposal after the United States/UN had approached the Yalu River, in effect occupying most of Korea).[20] In the end, despite the realization of his fears when Chinese troops later intervened, he defended the U.S. defense of South Korea, seeing it as a necessity in the face of North Korean aggression.

The Vietnam War and U.S. Policy

Throughout the early Cold War period, Niebuhr supported, and was supported by, the large anticommunist Washington establishment, his brand of political Realism attracting many admirers. However, by the 1960s, as the United States began to become embroiled in an undeclared war in the jungles of Vietnam, Niebuhr's tone began to shift, and with it his level of support in the Washington establishment also shifted. Niebuhr would once again show the sincerity of his dedication to his own search for truth and the objectivity of his social and political views by giving up his status as one of the Washington establishment's favorite intellectuals to turn his critical pen on the country he so loved.

Niebuhr was a friend and admirer of Hubert Humphrey, a liberal senator from Minnesota who became vice president under Lyndon Johnson in 1964. While Niebuhr was a great supporter of Humphrey for his role in passing the civil rights laws under the Johnson administration, Niebuhr was not a fan of Johnson's, and by association Humphrey's, policies on Vietnam. In a letter written to Humphrey in the runup to the 1968 presidential election, in which Humphrey eventually became the Democratic Party's candidate, Niebuhr spoke truth to power"

---

[20] Fox, *Reinhold Niebuhr*, p. 240.

Dear Mr. Vice President:

For old times' sake, in terms of our friendship, I should address you—
"My Dear Hubert."

The purpose of this letter is to inform you that I have been asked to be
on a [Eugene] McCarthy Committee and also on a [Nelson] Rockefeller
Committee. Both of these committees are exploiting the disaffection which
the Vietnam policy has created in our religious and learned communities. I would favor that disaffection, because this is a futile war, costly and
bloody, and also violates one of the principles of a just war that the means
should be proportionate to the end.

I have said that I would do nothing without giving you an advance notice.
I feel a sense of tragedy about this impasse because as you know, I and many
of your ADA[21] friends have a great admiration for you and wish you well. At
the same time, we must be true to our convictions as Abraham, "We must be
firm in the right as God gives us to see the right". And many of us feel that
the Vietnam war is a tragic disaster. I do not presume to influence your judgment because you have your firmness in the right, so I am only writing you
this letter to reveal to you how deep my convictions are which have dictated
these drastic steps involving a rift with a cherished old friend.[22]

In the end, neither McCarthy nor Rockefeller won the 1968 Republican
nomination, but Richard Nixon, running against the Democrats' Hubert
Humphrey. Niebuhr had never been a fan of the Republicans and even called
himself "a lifelong opponent of the Republican party,"[23] but Rockefeller was
a relatively liberal, progressive Republican candidate for president whom
Niebuhr agreed to support if Rockefeller won the Republican nomination.
Given the friendship Niebuhr had with Humphrey and the disaffection he
had with the Republicans historically, support of a Republican candidate
(even Rockefeller) in this race indicated the vehemence with which Niebuhr
opposed the Vietnam War.[24]

---

[21] The Americans for Democratic Action was founded in 1947 by American progressives, including Niebuhr, Humphrey, Walter Reuther, and Eleanor Roosevelt.

[22] Letter from RN to Vice President Hubert Humphrey, dated July 26, 1968, Box 49, Reinhold
Niebuhr Papers, Manuscript Division, Library of Congress, Washington, DC.

[23] RN, "The West and Asia," p. 5, original manuscript found in Box 17, Reinhold Niebuhr Papers,
Manuscript Division, Library of Congress, Washington, DC. No further information on date or
whether it was published is available in the box/folder, but a hand-written note on page one says,
"The New Leader," in which it may have been published. The discussion of the fall of Dien Bien Phu
suggests the date may have been 1954.

[24] In subsequent letters, Niebuhr expressed some remorse for his strong words to Humphrey and
wished him all the best for the election. Humphrey wrote back to Niebuhr on August 1, saying, "I

Niebuhr once wrote, "The freedom of his [man's] spirit enables him to use the forces and processes of nature creatively; but his failure to observe the limits of his finite existence causes him to defy the restraints of both nature and reason."[25] By Niebuhrian analogy, this phenomenon is yet more pronounced at the level of collective society, the sort of argument Niebuhr used to analyze the United States' involvement in Vietnam. Although early on Niebuhr supported the U.S. policy of trying to help prevent the takeover of South Vietnam,[26] as U.S. involvement in Vietnam escalated, he became increasingly critical of U.S. policy there, leading him to eventually conclude, "For the first time I fear I am ashamed of our beloved nation."[27]

There were several reasons Niebuhr felt the American military presence in Vietnam was wrong,[28] and his reasoning was quite consistent with the classical realist strain of thought. Niebuhr argued early in the Vietnam War era that it was an emergent, radicalized, communist China that the United States feared and sought to contain by U.S. policy in Vietnam.

> Despite the negative attitude of most of our university scholars and experts, an attitude supported by many church leaders and journalists, a shifting proportion of the public, and probably most of the military, support the war effort because they fear an ultimate military conflict with Red China for which our foothold on the peninsula is alleged to be a strategic advantage.[29]

Again, let it be made clear that Niebuhr, arch anticommunist, was not against U.S. efforts to contain the spread of communism and China's influence in Asia.

---

want to express to you my deep appreciation for your thoughtfulness and courtesy. Whatever our differences on Vietnam, we share virtually all the same objectives for our society and even on that issue we are both committed to a political solution as the only rational one. I shall do my earnest best to work for a just and lasting peace in Southeast Asia and retain the hope that we may all soon again work together for a just and compassionate society and peace among nations." Letter from Vice President Hubert Humphrey to RN, dated August 1, 1968, Box 49, Reinhold Niebuhr Papers, Manuscript Division, Library of Congress, Washington, DC.

[25] Kenneth W. Thompson, "The Political Philosophy of Reinhold Niebuhr," in Charles W. Kegley, ed., *Reinhold Niebuhr, His Religious, Social and Political Thought* (New York: Pilgrim Press, 1984), p. 237.

[26] RN, "Vietnam and the Imperial Conflict," *The New Leader* 49/12 (June 6, 1966).

[27] Fox, *Reinhold Niebuhr*, p. 285.

[28] RN, *Faith and Politics*, p. 251.

[29] RN, "The Social Myths of the 'Cold War,'" *Journal of International Affairs* 21 (1967): 40–56, as found in Box 56, Reinhold Niebuhr Papers, Manuscript Division, Library of Congress, Washington, DC.

There is obviously some truth that if we withdraw from Vietnam, other Asian nations, particularly Thailand, Malaysia and perhaps the Philippines, will not be safe against Chinese expansion. Our military presence is obviously necessary in Asia. But it was certainly an error of inadvertence to become involved in South Vietnam by gradually increasing commitments, so that our prestige is involved in the pretense that we are helping a small nation to preserve its independence.[30]

So while he believed a U.S. "military presence [wa]s obviously necessary in Asia," as he said above, he believed U.S. policy in Vietnam was becoming increasingly misguided.

Niebuhr's problems with the growing U.S. involvement in its war in Vietnam were six-fold.[31] First, he did not believe U.S. interests were threatened enough to demand such U.S. action at the costs it would entail. *Second*, he believed U.S. policymakers underestimated the will of the Vietnamese communists to keep Vietnam Vietnamese. He recognized the hopelessness of yet another "foreign imperial force" (from the Vietnamese point of view) entering the nation "to liberate it." The effects of French colonialism were too recent, the feelings of nationalism too intense, he felt, to enable foreign troops to remove by force an indigenous political movement believed by the majority of indigenous peoples to be legitimate anti-imperialist freedom-fighters. Third, Niebuhr believed U.S. policymakers overestimated their own capabilities politically and militarily. They overestimated the political will of the American people to support such a foray and the nation's military ability (within practical political and economic bounds) to root out the Vietcong and their adherents. Fourth, from a moral point of view, Niebuhr believed the U.S. presence in Vietnam was wrong because he believed it was a direct result of America's growing self-righteousness and smug self-importance in world affairs and was based on corrupted motives. He believed that the United States' prideful surety that what it was doing was best for Vietnam was incorrect from the start—that Americans may have thought they were acting in the best interests of the Vietnamese but the majority of the Vietnamese themselves apparently thought otherwise. In 1967, Niebuhr said in a *Christianity & Crisis* editorial, that it was an "error [to] regard the issue

---

[30] RN, "Reinhold Niebuhr Discusses the War in Vietnam," *The New Republic* (January 29, 1966): 16; as found in Box 56, Reinhold Niebuhr Papers, Manuscript Division, Library of Congress, Washington, DC.

[31] RN, *Faith and Politics*, p. 251.

as the containment of communism, when we are in fact dealing with the nationalism of a small nation in Asia."[32] The long-term damage of the war on the people, he felt, was not worth such dubious political gain. Fifth, he felt it extremely arrogant for U.S. policymakers to assume they knew what *was* best for the majority of the Vietnamese people and even more so to carry it out forcefully. Lastly, Niebuhr believed American motives were not purely honorable or without self-interest, but that the patriotic epithets of "making South-East Asia safe for democracy" were rationalizations and justifications for the base advancement of American interests in the region.

Ultimately, as the futility of the American involvement in Vietnam began to reveal itself in the U.S. failure to achieve either its explicit or implicit objectives, Niebuhr felt American rationalizations and justifications were stretched further to cover America's embarrassment at its own folly and ineptitude. They were heightened by fruitless attempts to gain back lost American pride by resorting to increasingly questionable displays of force such as the use of napalm, mass B-52 bombings, and unauthorized[33] operations in other nations. In 1968, Niebuhr wrote,

> Our engagement in Vietnam has consequently forced the Administration to create a series of obvious fictions or myths calculated to obscure the hiatus between our idealism and our hegemonial responsibilities.[34]

In fact, Niebuhr's frustration with American policymakers was already evident in the early 1960s when he stated cynically,

> Perhaps there is not much to choose between communist and anticommunist fanaticism, particularly when the latter, combined with our wealth, has caused us to stumble into the most pointless, costly and bloody war in our history.[35]

---

[32] Mark Hulsether, *Building a Protestant Left: Christianity and Crisis Magazine, 1941–1993* (Knoxville: University of Tennessee Press, 1999), p. 131.

[33] "Unauthorized" here refers to the lack of authorization of U.S. incursions into neighboring countries like Cambodia and Laos (upon which the United States had not declared war or such acts the U.S. government did not always even acknowledge) by either the U.S. Congress or the UN Security Council, for example.

[34] RN, *Faith and Politics*, p. 241.

[35] RN as cited by Walter Lafeber, *America, Russia, and the Cold War: 1945–1971* (New York: John Wiley & Sons, 1972), p. 301

Niebuhr's Realism apparently could not allow him to go along with the American adventure even before it became evident that it would flounder. Niebuhr saw through the moral haze and identified what he saw as a self-righteous justification for the pursuit of narrow national interests beneath. Niebuhr must have been disappointed, yet his own work undoubtedly prepared him for such a development. His realist view of human nature was the antidote to what he saw as misguided U.S. idealism in U.S. Cold War policy.

> The paramount problem for contemporary study of international relations is to supplant the illusions which we have inherited from the French enlightenment and which are most characteristically expressed in the influence of Auguste Comte upon our social thought, with the wisdom of an Edmund Burke (and, one might add, of a Winston Churchill).[36]

Although he considered the American democratic system to be relatively just, its leaders were human beings, home to the same imperfect nature found in human beings in any country or political system in history and therefore subject to folly.

This was part of what Niebuhr called "the irony in American history." Niebuhr's book of the same title

> argued that because of pride, presumed innocence, and lack of restraint, American power was walking the rim of abyss. American idealism, which had been instrumental in developing immense national power, now ironically blinded the U.S. to the dangers of overusing that power.[37]

This must not have surprised Niebuhr, for in his epic *The Nature and Destiny of Man*, he argued that this phenomenon had been the cause of the fall of all the great empires throughout time. Subsequently, U.S. policymakers were, he thought, in danger of overestimating both American virtue and American capability, ultimately threatening to undermine the long-run American interests they sought to protect. Of this, he said, "A wise statecraft attempts to foresee as much of the future as possible but it is also conscious of the limits of man's foreknowledge."[38]

---

[36] RN, "The Moral Issue in International Relations," manuscript submitted to Kenneth Thompson of the Rockefeller Foundation for a conference sponsored by the same, submitted April 2, 1954.

[37] Lafeber, *America, Russia, and the Cold War*, p. 133.

[38] RN, *World Crisis*, p. 38.

Reinhold Niebuhr died before the U.S. role in the Vietnam conflict came to end in 1975 and also before the Cold War ended with the end of the Soviet Union on December 31, 1991. The views he articulated on the Vietnam War, as well as the Cold War more broadly, seem prescient in retrospect. Had he lived to see the 2003 invasion of Iraq by the United States and a cohort of nations supporting the move, I believe Niebuhr would have had many similar observations about that war, with similar themes surrounding the dangers of hubris, overestimation of one's own capabilities and righteousness, and other things. An analysis of that war from a Niebuhrian perspective follows.

7

Niebuhrian Takeaways on the Just War Tradition and the U.S. Invasion of Iraq*

In the next three chapters of this book, I take a new tack, saying in effect, "based on what he did write, what might Reinhold Niebuhr have said about X if he were with us today?" Of course, no one alive today can be sure about what he would have said about the 2003 U.S. invasion of Iraq, the responsibility to protect, or the twenty-first century rise of China (the three major cases I will analyze). At the same time, I believe this is a useful exercise for at least the following reasons. First, it helps us better engage with Niebuhr and his thought as we apply it to contemporary cases, and such engagement with one of the twentieth century's greatest thinkers is one of the goals of this book. Second, it might help us better understand these three cases from an academic perspective as we try to understand how theory and practice meet, and as we attempt to explain how this twentieth-century classical Realist helps us understand the specific cases we are analyzing here. Finally, given his stature and his wisdom, bringing Niebuhr's twentieth-century insights to bear on these contemporary challenges might help policy-makers as they grapple with these challenges going forward. This presentation might bear real-world benefits in terms of enhanced peace and security, as was arguably the case with Niebuhr's impact on foreign and defense policy in his own time.

This chapter analyzes Niebuhr's views of just war and the ways in which he might have applied it to the American decision to invade Iraq in 2003. Here I pose the following questions. What were Niebuhr's views of the just war tradition? How would he have viewed the decision of the George W. Bush administration to invade Iraq in 2003? Would he have viewed it as a just war, or would he have opposed it as he had opposed the Vietnam War?

---

* This section on the Iraq War is a revised and reoriented version of a short piece that appeared on the website of the Council on Faith and International Affairs on January 4, 2008, as Gregory Moore, "Christian Views of War: The Case of Iraq" (http://www.cfia.org/ArticlesAndReports/ArticlesDetail.aspx?id=9214&hId=3672).

Niebuhrian International Relations. Gregory J. Moore, Oxford University Press (2020).
© Oxford University Press.
DOI: 10.1093/oso/9780197500446.001.0001

Love and War

In the international relations literature, Reinhold Niebuhr has perhaps most famously captured the seeming tension between love, forgiveness, and mercy on the one hand, and justice, war, and violence on the other. Of course, Niebuhr was not the first to note this tension, but rather it has its origins in a number of the recorded statements of the biblical Jesus. In Matthew 5:39 Jesus says, "Do not resist the one who is evil. But if anyone slaps you on the right cheek, turn to him the other also."[1] Yet in Luke 22:36, on the night before his crucifixion, Jesus says, "And now let the one who has no sword sell his cloak and buy one." How does one reconcile Jesus' exhortation to turn the other cheek, with his admonition to the disciples to buy swords?[2] This is a question Reinhold Niebuhr grappled with. Those Christians emphasizing the primacy of Matthew 5:39 have belonged to a pacifist tradition in Christian social thought, most famously and perhaps best articulated by John Howard Yoder.[3] Those, like Niebuhr, emphasizing Jesus' words in Luke 22:36, Paul's in Romans 13, and the many Old Testament battles such as those in the book of Joshua as at least potentially normative for the notion of a just use of force domestically and/or in interstate conflicts, however, have belonged to the just war tradition, a tradition articulated by many throughout Western history, including St. Augustine,[4] Michael Walzer,[5] Paul Ramsey,[6] Jean Elshtain,[7] and Niebuhr.[8]

The use of the sword discussed in Luke 22:36 and Romans 13 is quite different contextually from what we normally discuss in international relations, for both of these passages are about the use of force, the sword, in

---

[1] This and following Bible passages are taken from the Holy Bible, English Standard Version (Wheaton, IL: Crossway Publishers, 2001).

[2] Interestingly, in a passage parallel to Luke 22, in Matthew 26:52, after Peter in trying to defend Jesus cuts off a man's ear, Jesus says to Peter, "Put your sword back into its place. For all who take the sword will perish by the sword." This passage is of course viewed as being in line with Jesus' exhortation to turn the other cheek.

[3] See John Howard Yoder, *The Politics of Jesus: Vicit Agnus Noster*, Second Edition (Carlisle, UK: Paternoster and Eerdmans, 1994).

[4] St. Augustine, *City of God* (New York: Image Books, 1958).

[5] Walzer does not articulate a Christian approach to just war, but his work draws heavily on that tradition and has become arguably the most excellent, most systematic, and best-known articulation of the just war tradition today. See Michael Walzer, *Just and Unjust Wars: A Moral Argument with Historical Illustrations*, Third Edition (New York: Basic Books, 2000).

[6] Paul Ramsey, *The Just War: Force and Political Responsibility* (Lanham, MD: Rowman & Littlefield, 2002).

[7] See Jean Bethke Elshtain, *Just War Against Terror* (New York: Basic Books, 2003).

[8] See *Moral Man and Immoral Society* (New York: Scribner's Sons, 1932); *Christian Realism and Political Problems* (New York: Charles Scribner's Sons, 1952), and others.

the domestic political context. Romans 13, for example, is viewed by most Christian thinkers as an elaboration on why and when use of the sword (read here as police power) is legitimate in a society/kingdom/state. The point I am making here is that pacifists generally have made an argument that the biblical Christian understanding of the use of force, whether in the domestic or international context, is off limits across the board for Christians because of Jesus' words in Matthew 5:39 regarding turning the other cheek. In defending their positions, Christian thinkers such as Niebuhr, Ramsey, Elshtain, and others in the just war tradition would include not only passages from Joshua, but Romans 13 as well, in making their claim that Christian views of war and force more generally are not pacifist (read as completely disavowing the use of force) as Yoder would have it.

The Just War Tradition and Niebuhr's Place Therein

Although he did not have a habit of alluding to it explicitly in his writings, I will argue here that Reinhold Niebuhr's approach to international relations is consistent with the just war tradition.[9] Niebuhr argued that pacifism was a reasonable and admirable approach for one to espouse as an individual, but that in the collective life of humankind, he found pacifism problematic, in some cases even irresponsible, where justice can only be maintained by a prudent application of force.

> The pacifists rightly recognize that it may be very noble for an individual to sacrifice his life or interests rather than participate in the claims and counterclaims of the struggle for justice (of which war may always be the *ultima ratio*). They are wrong in making no distinction between an individual act of self-abnegation and a political policy of submission to injustice, whereby lives and interests other than our own are defrauded or destroyed.[10]

---

[9] For more, see Childress's elaboration on this point: James Childress, "Reinhold Niebuhr's Realistic-Pragmatic Approach to War and 'The Nuclear Dilemma,'" in Richard Harries, ed., *Reinhold Niebuhr and the Issues of Our Time* (Grand Rapids, MI: Eerdmans, 1986).

[10] RN, "The Christian Faith and the World Crisis," *Christianity and Crisis* (inaugural issue, February 10, 1941); as found in Harry R. Davis and Robert C. Good (eds.), *Reinhold Niebuhr on Politics* (New York: Charles Scribner's Sons, 1960), p. 151.

Niebuhr's view of pacifism, and its appropriateness at the individual level but not at the foreign policy level, is consistent with his notion that there is a moral dualism as it regards the ethic of individuals on the one hand, and collective life on the other (alluding in the latter to the use of force by police and the military as examples). He charged pacifists with valuing non-violence so highly as to ultimately prefer oppression under tyranny to justified resistance, something he could not countenance.

As the winds of war blew stronger for the United States in February 1941, and Niebuhr saw U.S. neutrality as increasingly untenable, Niebuhr said, "Love must be regarded as the final flower and fruit of justice. When it is substituted for justice it degenerates into sentimentality and may become the accomplice of tyranny."[11] In his discussion of Niebuhr's aversion to political pacifism, Richard Harries imagines an Orwellian moment (alluding to Orwell's *1984*) in which the totalitarian Big Brother makes freedom unobtainable and life unlivable, reminding us all that that we must question that (pacifist) "assumption that war, however terrible, is the worst evil we can conceive of."[12] Niebuhr agreed with Morgenthau and just warriors in general that Neville Chamberlain's policies toward Hitler, his policies of appeasement, were in the end morally irresponsible, though they may have seemed noble and generous-spirited at the time.

Keith Pavlischek argues (I think incorrectly) that Niebuhr's approach was *not* consistent with a just war approach, however.[13] Pavlischek seems to read Niebuhr as saying that using force is evil (necessary though it may be) and that the policymaker who uses force lives in tension with Jesus' exhortation not to use violence. Yet that is not what Neibuhr is saying, as many of his writings make clear, not the least of which is the debate he had with his pacifist brother, Richard, in 1932 over the "grace of doing nothing" versus the necessity to stand up to Japanese brutality in light of Japan's wanton 1931 aggression against China.[14] As his strong stand in defense of China then

---

[11] RN, "The Christian Faith and the World Crisis," *Christianity and Crisis* (inaugural issue, February 10, 1941); in RN, *Love and Justice*, edited by D. B. Robertson (Westminster, UK: John Knox Press, 1957), p. 283.

[12] Richard Harries, "Reinhold Niebuhr's Critique of Pacifism and His Pacifist Critics," in Richard Harries, ed., *Reinhold Niebuhr and the Issues of Our Time* (Grand Rapids, MI: Eerdmans, 1986), p. 118.

[13] Keith Pavlischek, "Reinhold Niebuhr, Christian Realism, and Just War Theory: A Critique," in Eric D. Patterson, *Christianity and Power Politics Today* (New York: Palgrave MacMillan, 2008); also available on the website of the Ethics and Public Policy Center (www.eppc.org/docLib/20080205_palpatterson03.pdf).

[14] H. Richard Niebuhr, "The Grace of Doing Nothing," *Christian Century* (March 23, 1932); and RN, "Must We Do Nothing? A Response to H. Richard Niebuhr's article, 'The Grace of Doing Nothing,'" *Christian Century*, March 30, 1932, as cited by John D. Barbour, "Niebuhr vs. Niebuhr: On

makes clear, Niebuhr agrees with Pavlischek that use of force by a nation is just and good at times and that *not* using force in the face of evil may, in fact, at times be immoral (and unbiblical from a Christian perspective) for the policymaker and/or political authority (as suggested by Paul in Romans 13). Niebuhr, who had himself disavowed pacifism, observed, "it is not possible to disavow war absolutely without disavowing the task of establishing justice."[15] For Niebuhr, justice was something too important to disavow in such a blanket fashion, assuming as he did that such would be the result of a wholesale rejection of the use of force. Niebuhr believed that war was sometimes necessary because of the importance of upholding justice and that in some cases the use of force was not only permissible but also a moral imperative.

As it regards the distinction in the just war tradition between *jus ad bellum* (considerations of justice in going to war) and *jus in bello* (considerations of justice in how war is waged), a bit of elaboration is in order. The principles of *jus ad bellum* include just cause, competent authority (to go to war), right intention (i.e., to restore just peace), last resort, probability of success, and proportionality of projected results (expected good must outweigh expected costs). *Jus in bello* principles include proportionality of the use of force (nothing should be done that generates more harm than good), discrimination (between combatants and noncombatants), avoidance of evil means, and good faith (just treatment of the enemy so as to make later reconciliation possible). Military force could be employed for just reasons but conducted unjustly, or employed for unjust reasons but conducted justly, for these are two separate lines of logic.

Niebuhr spent considerable energy in addressing matters of *jus ad bellum*, while his thoughts on *jus in bello* issues are harder to find in his writings and are a bit equivocal at times. Subsequently, it is probably fair to say that *jus in bello* was an underdeveloped aspect of his work, and critics such as Keith Pavlischek are not incorrect in noting this. Having conceded this point, we would be unfair to Niebuhr to suggest, as Pavlischek does, that Niebuhr holds to a stark "anything goes," "ends justify the means" attitude once the bullets start flying.[16] There certainly *is* a sense in places of measured consequentialism

---

Tragedy in History," *Christian Century* 101/36 (November 21, 1984); and found in Box 56, Reinhold Niebuhr Papers, Manuscript Division, Library of Congress, Washington, DC.

[15] "Christian Faith and Natural Law," in RN, *Love and Justice*, p. 53, as cited in Harries, *Reinhold Niebuhr and the Issues of Our Time*, p. 130.
[16] Pavlischek, "Reinhold Niebuhr, Christian Realism, and Just War Theory," p. 2008.

in his work. For example, in discussing the importance of standing for justice, doing the right thing (in this context, it was a discussion of whether or not to support the use of force against Japan's aggression against China in 1931), Niebuhr said, we "must try in every social situation to maximize the ethical forces and yet not sacrifice the possibility of achieving an ethical goal because we are afraid to use any but purely ethical means."[17] Here I think he means a choice between ethical arguments and brute violence, but one might also read it as meaning a choice between ethical means and unethical means. If one knows his dialectics, his dual morals arguments, one might see where he is going with such arguments. He is highlighting the darkness of war and politics, always noting that we can't shrink from getting involved because we might dirty our hands. In discussing the moral necessity of joining the fight against Hitler prior to Pearl Harbor when American was still neutral, he spoke of the need to do "whatever has to be done to prevent the triumph of this intolerable tyranny," referring to Hitler.[18] This does sound somewhat consequentialist, or at least potentially consequentialist. Yet, with just war expert Michael Walzer, Niebuhr rejected Allied area bombing of Germany in World War II as too "indiscriminate" and not of military necessity. In addition, regarding the U.S. decision to drop the atomic bombs on Japan, he said,

> Critics have rightly pointed out that we reached the level of Nazi morality in justifying the use of the bomb on the ground that it shortened the war. That is exactly what the Nazis said about the destruction of Rotterdam and Warsaw. They claimed that a brief conflict aiming at total destruction was more merciful than a long-drawn-out war. . . . As matters stand now, we have completely lost our moral position, particularly in the Orient.[19]

He was a signatory to a 1946 report that called the nuclear bombing of Japan "morally indefensible" and "irresponsible."[20] He could hardly be accused of

---

[17] RN, "Must We Do Nothing? A Response to H. Richard Niebuhr's article, 'The Grace of Doing Nothing,'" *Christian Century*, March 30, 1932; as cited by John D. Barbour, "Niebuhr vs. Niebuhr: On Tragedy in History," *Christian Century* 101/36 (November 21, 1984); and found in Box 56, Reinhold Niebuhr Papers, Manuscript Division, Library of Congress, Washington, DC.

[18] "To Prevent the Triumph of an Intolerable Tyranny," in *Love and Justice*, p. 275, as quoted in Childress, "Reinhold Niebuhr's Realistic-Pragmatic Approach to War," p. 138.

[19] RN, "The Atomic Bomb," *Christianity and Society* (Fall 1945); in RN, *Love and Justice*, p. 233.

[20] Report of the Commission on the Relation of the Church to the War in Light of the Christian Faith, appointed by the Federal Council of Churches of Christ in America, *Atomic Warfare and the Christian Faith* (March, 1946), as cited in Childress, "Reinhold Niebuhr's Realistic-Pragmatic Approach to War," p. 140. RN to James B. Conant, letter of March 12, 1946; as described and cited

ignoring *jus in bello* considerations across the board. I do concede here, how-ever, that while he was consistent about the moral problems of area bombing and firebombing, Niebuhr waffled on the use of atomic bombs on Japan, as I pointed out in Chapter 2. With his private statement to James Conant that the use of the atomic bombs on Japan was necessary to end the war early, Niebuhr does open himself up somewhat to Pavlischek's charge of "ends justify the means,"[21] and he certainly contradicts himself. Campbell Craig argues persuasively that Niebuhr later came to adopt a just war approach to nuclear warfare, arguing with Bishop Angus Dun that "[t]he notion that the excessive violence of atomic warfare has ended the possibility of a just war does not stand up."[22] Craig characterizes Niebuhr as being in the just war tradition and as accepting the notion that a nuclear war could be just, de-spite the general indiscriminateness of nuclear war. Despite these potential problems of consistency, I believe Niebuhr's work is broadly consistent with the Augustinian, just war tradition, clearly so in the *ad bellum* sense, and generally (though perhaps not always consistently) so in the *in bello* sense.

Niebuhr of course shared Augustine's views of human nature predisposed to sin and self-regard; of the distinction between the ethics of "the city of man" and "the city of God" (this could be applied in Niebuhr's case as Niebuhr's distinction between personal ethics and public/social ethics, respectively); of the use of force as good and necessary in certain circumstances; of the distinctions that must be made as to when the state should resort to force; and so on. Consequently, an application of Niebuhr's thought to the 2003 Iraq War is helpful and serves to bring the fruits of his intellectual rigor to bear on an important issue in the early twenty-first century. Indeed, Niebuhr's name was widely invoked in arguments against the war in the period after the war began.[23] We now turn to the case of the U.S. invasion of Iraq in 2003 in an

---

in Richard Wightman Fox, *Reinhold Niebuhr: A Biography* (San Francisco: Harper & Row, 1985), pp. 224–5.

[21] One might ask, do we believe what the letter to Conant said is the best representation of Niebuhr's thoughts, or the published pieces coming out against the use of the bomb?

[22] RN and Bishop Angus Dun, "God Wills Both Justice and Peace," *Christianity and Crisis* 15 (June 13, 1955), p. 78, as found in Campbell Craig, *Glimmer of a New Leviathan: Total War in the Realism of Niebuhr, Morgenthau, and Waltz* (New York: Columbia University Press, 2003), p. 83.

[23] See Arthur Schlesinger Jr., "Forgetting Reinhold Niebuhr," *The New York Times* (September 18, 2005), Section 7, Page 12; Paul Elie, "A Man for All Reasons," *The Atlantic* (November, 2007), accessed from https://www.theatlantic.com/magazine/archive/2007/11/a-man-for-all-reasons/306337/; David Brooks, "Obama, Gospel and Verse," *The New York Times* (April 26, 2007), accessed from https://www.theatlantic.com/magazine/archive/2002/09/a-man-on-a-gray-horse/302558/; Gregory Moore,

attempt to access the merits of the war in terms of just war and whether or not it accorded with broader Niebuhrian thinking.

The 2003 Iraq War, Niebuhr, and the Just War Tradition

On the night of March 19, 2003 (U.S. time), the United States began its military action against Iraq. President George W. Bush stated that the goals of the operation were to "disarm Iraq, to free its people and to defend the world from grave danger."[24] In his appeal to the American public, this was a case of preemptive war to stop a growing threat.

> The people of the United States and their friends and allies will not live at the mercy of an outlaw regime that threatens the peace with weapons of mass murder. We will meet that threat now with our Army, Air Force, Navy, Coast Guard and Marines so that we do not have to meet it later with armies of firefighters and police and doctors on the streets of our cities.[25]

The president made a number of appeals to just war principles such as just cause, right spirit, discrimination between combatants and noncombatants, good faith, and self-defense.

Yet several elements were missing in the president's *jus ad bellum* calculations from a just war perspective. Here let us consider the *ad bellum* components one by one. In terms of "just cause," it would be difficult to argue that Iraq had done anything to the United States that deserved invasion in response, for there is no evidence that Iraq had any role to play in the 9/11 attacks or any other attacks on the United States. Nor had Iraq attacked a U.S. friend or formal ally, invoking collective security or the like. Also, while the United States made appeals to "right intentions" (normally read as "restoring peace" after an act of invasive violence), Iraq had not attacked the United States and was not disturbing its neighbors at the time. Restoring peace, therefore, could not be a reasonable argument when it was the United

---

"Christian Views of War: The Case of Iraq," Council on Faith and International Affairs (January 4, 2008; http://www.cfia.org/ArticlesAndReports/ArticlesDetail.aspx?id=9214&hId=3672).

[24] David Sanger with John Burns, "Threats and Responses: Bush's Speech at the Start of the War," delivered March 19, 2003, *The New York Times* (March 20, 2003), Section A, page 1.

[25] Bush, "Threats and Responses."

States that actually broke the peace between the United States and Iraq by invading Iraq in March 2003. The application of the just war notion of war as "last resort" is also problematic here because it was clear that many of America's allies and others on the Security Council wanted to see the United States wait until the UN inspection process had run its full course. War was clearly not yet a last resort in March 2003. Even if the United States wanted to make the case that it was enforcing prior UN sanctions, this must give rise to questions about the principle of competent authority (another *ad bellum* consideration), for it would have to be the UN, and not the United States, that would have had to authorize an enforcement of Security Council resolutions not involving matters of self-defense, defense of an ally, cross-border incursions, and so on.

A similar case confronted the United States in April 1965, when President Lyndon Johnson ordered U.S. troops to invade the Dominican Republic to restore order after that country's president had been assassinated in 1961, and the political situation had slowly devolved into civil war. In response to Johnson's foray into the Dominican Republic, Niebuhr opined, "The President thought it so important to prevent the establishment of a new Castroite government in the Caribbean that he did not take time to consult the Organization of American States, which alone could have invested our force with moral authority."[26] Niebuhr clearly believed the OAS's sanction would have given the U.S. action credibility. While, as maintained earlier in this book, Niebuhr did *not* think it wise or necessary for the United States to yield its foreign policy entirely to the UN and to act *only* when the UN approved, clearly in the case of an international intervention such as that in the Dominican Republic or the one in Iraq, *not* having the authority of the OAS or UN, respectively, cast doubt on the legitimacy of the operation in question in Niebuhr's eyes and increased the burden of proof that the operation was consistent with the just war tradition.

Based on the analysis presented here, the 2003 Iraq War falls short of the just war criteria in terms of both *in bello* and *ad bellum* considerations of proportionality (doing more good than harm), for there is good cause to argue that the war has brought greater harm to Iraq's people than would have been the case had Coalition forces not intervened. With the exception of the Kurds in the north, who suffered disproportionately under Saddam and who have

---

[26] RN, "Caribbean Blunder," *Christianity and Crisis* 25 (May 31, 1965): 113–14; as found in Charles C. Brown, *Niebuhr and His Age: Reinhold Niebuhr's Prophetic Role in the Twentieth Century* (Philadelphia: Trinity Press International, 1992), p. 239.

fared disproportionately well (having escaped much of the sectarian vio-lence that followed the U.S. invasion) after the start of the war, the years com-prising the U.S. intervention in Iraq were more violent for average Iraqis than had been the case prior to the invasion, despite the positive good achieved in removing the despotic Saddam Hussein regime. Iraq suffered some 114,725 civilian deaths from the start of the war in 2003 until the end of December 2011, when the United States announced the official end of its role there.[27] Another study, conducted in 2006, estimates that from the start of the in-vasion in March 2003 until the end of the study in July 2006, "about 655,00 Iraqis have died above the number that would be expected in a non-conflict situation."[28] Even without considering the number of Coalition forces lost in the war, it would be difficult to argue that Saddam Hussein would have killed that many people in the same amount of time, or even within several years on either end of the war. In addition to all that has been said heretofore about the inapplicability of the just war tradition's sense of "justice" to this partic-ular war, the leaders of the Coalition forces bear a heavy burden of proof in explaining how unleashing so much death and destruction has lessened the suffering of Iraqis. In the just war tradition, normally *all* of the criteria for *jus ad bellum* considerations are expected to be met before military action is initiated if one wants to claim that a war is "just." A strong argument can be made that this was not the case with this war.

Elshtain vs. Niebuhr

As I continue to build this argument, let us turn to another well-known Christian political philosopher and professed Niebuhr supporter, Jean Bethke Elshtain. Elshtain argues in her book, *Just War Against Terror*, that both the general U.S. war against terror (which included the invasion of Afghanistan and Iraq and many other operations), as well as the U.S. inva-sion of Iraq, were all worthy of the just war moniker.[29] How is it that two great American political philosophers, both very Niebuhrian in their thinking,

---

[27] This estimate comes from "Iraqi Deaths from Violence," 2003–2011," via http://www.iraqbodycount.org/analysis/numbers/2011/ (January 2, 2012; accessed March 12, 2012).

[28] Gilbert Burnham, Riyadh Lafta, Shannon Doocy, and Les Roberts, "Mortality after the 2003 Invasion of Iraq: A Cross-Sectional Cluster Sample Survey," *The Lancet* 368 (October 21, 2006): 1426.

[29] Jean Bethke Elshtain, *Just War Against Terror* (New York: Basic Books, 2003/2004). A useful dis-cussion of the Iraq War was added as an epilogue to the paperback version of this 2003 book, which was issued in 2004, after the war began.

Niebuhr and Elshtain, would come down so differently on the Iraq War? Let me start by saying that I am not alone in opining that Niebuhr would have been against the 2003 Iraq War. Niebuhr experts Alberto Coll, John Patrick Diggins, and Mark Amstutz have all said as much too.[30] In addition, Vibeke Tjalve joins me in noting the interesting divergence between Elshtain, saying Iraq was a just war, and Niebuhr, whom Tjalve says would have been against the war.[31]

In her argument, Elshtain focuses on four *ad bellum* considerations: just cause (or "response to an act of aggression or the threat of such")' open declaration of war by competent authority; right intention (i.e., to restore just peace); and last resort.[32] Elshtain argues that while conceding that Iraq did not attack the United States per se, it was a threat to the United States because of its weapons of mass destruction (WMD) programs, "Saddam's well-documented mass murder of his own people," including "attempted genocide against the Kurds, his destruction of the entire way of life of the marsh Arabs, and his mass murders against the Shiite Muslims in the aftermath of the 1991 Persian Gulf War."[33] She emphasizes not the WMD, however, but the humanitarian dimensions, conceding that while "[t]his was a judgment call," the United States had a just cause in attacking Iraq, primarily because of the threat Saddam Hussein posed to his own people.[34] Open declaration of war by a competent authority can be said to have been met as long as one is arguing that the United States felt threatened or was acting for humanitarian reasons, but if, as some argued, the United States was enforcing UN Security Council (UNSC) resolutions, a concerted effort approved by the UNSC would have made more sense. Elshtain argues that the United States had the right intentions, that it wanted to do the right thing in Iraq, and that it was not swayed by ulterior motives. She also believes that the invasion of Iraq was a last resort, maintaining that the United States waited a long time, that already in 1998 the United States had commenced a bombing campaign over Iraq for

---

[30] See Alberto Coll, "The Relevance of Christian Realism to the Twenty-First Century," in Eric Patterson, ed., *Christianity and Power Politics Today: Christian Realism and Contemporary Political Dilemmas* (New York: Palgrave Macmillan, 2008); John Patrick Diggins, *Why Niebuhr Now?* (Chicago: University of Chicago Press, 2011); Mark Amstutz, "Reinhold Niebuhr's Christian Realism and the Bush Doctrine," in Patterson. *Christianity and Power Politics Today* (2008), pp. 125–33.

[31] Vibeke Schou Tjalve, *Realist Strategies of Republican Peace: Niebuhr, Morgenthau, and the Politics of Patriotic Dissent* (New York: Palgrave Macmillan, 2008), p. 140.

[32] Jean Bethke Elshtain, *Just War Against Terror* (New York: Basic Books, 2003/2004), p. 184. She only considers these four, whereas some people add probability of success and proportionality of projected results (good must outweigh costs).

[33] Elshtain, *Just War Against Terror*, p. 186.

[34] Elshtain, *Just War Against Terror*, p. 188.

failing to keep its commitments to UNSC resolutions, but stopped when the UN promised to ramp up the inspection regime to call Saddam to account for his human rights abuses and weapons programs infractions. With the invasion of Iraq, the United States declared it had waited long enough.

Elshtain cites Niebuhr in her book in support of her general argument that the War on Terror is consistent with the just war tradition, and I think she is right in this broad sense. However, she does not cite Niebuhr in the section of her book (the epilogue) on the Iraq War. Frankly, I don't think Niebuhr would have sided with her in this discussion. As I said earlier, Iraq did not have anything to do with the 9/11 attacks, so this was not a question of responding to an attack. Nor am I persuaded that there was an imminent threat of an Iraqi attack on the United States that warranted all the destruction and bloodshed caused by the invasion and subsequent insurgencies. If this was about a humanitarian impulse to help the Kurds or the marsh Arabs or the Shiites, why did the United States wait so long to act? Most of *that* death and destruction had taken place several years previously. I do not believe *ad bellum* criteria were met, and Elshtain's argument does not persuade me otherwise. Nor do I think it would have persuaded Niebuhr. Moreover, Elshtain argues that the *in bello* case for the war was easily made. Whereas there can be no doubt that U.S. and coalition forces were professional and well trained and did all they could to minimize civilian casualties, there were some problems with the *in bello* criteria as well as the ad bellum criteria. I would argue (and I think my argument is consistent with Niebuhrian thinking) that while indeed the strong U.S. response to 9/11 was warranted and consistent with just war traditions, it is much more difficult to make that case for the invasion of Iraq.

The 2003 Iraq War as Preemptive or Preventive War?

If the standard criteria for a just war do not pass muster in this case, could one argue, as the Bush administration did, that the invasion of Iraq was a matter of preemptive or preventive war? If so, could a case be made that this was a just preemption or a just preventive war? As Michael Walzer, Alan Dershowitz, and others have argued, preemption *can* be consistent with the just war tradition, while preventive war is a bit more controversial.[35] In fact,

---

[35] See Walzer, *Just and Unjust Wars*; and Alan M. Dershowitz, *Preemption: A Knife that Cuts Both Ways* (New York: W. W. Norton, 2006). For elaboration, see below.

Jean Elshtain made the case that this was a preemptive war. Does that make sense in this case?

In fact, the U.S. attack on Iraq in 2003 could *not* be considered a "preemption" as long as a preemption is defined as it traditionally has been: "like a reflex action, a throwing up of one's arms at the very last minute" to parry a blow or land one's own before the attacking blow strikes its target.[36] The 1967 Israeli strike against Egyptian forces massing on its border just prior to invading Israel is the classic example of preemption.[37] Yet in the Iraq case, there had been no reliable and convincing intelligence suggesting that Iraq was preparing to attack the United States or even (as alleged at the time) that Iraq was preparing to share what WMD technology or materials it had with persons, organizations, or states that were prepared to attack the United States or its citizens. Elshtain's argument that the attack on Iraq was preemptive is also problematic for another reason. Deemphasizing WMD in favor of the argument that the United States should invade Iraq on humanitarian grounds as she does makes a preemptive attack less logical. One might make a preemptive argument if one learns the enemy has his finger on the button and has given the order to fire or launch an attack, and then one attacks—this is the logic of preemption. It is difficult to make a preemptive argument in this case, which logically would mean a humanitarian attack was imminent and that the U.S. move was to head it off, stopping it before it happened—it just does not much make sense. I am not aware of any reports that an attack that would cause a humanitarian crisis was imminent when the United States attacked Iraq. Nor did the United States make such an argument. No impending blow to the United States or any civilians or others we know of was on its way. Thus, the U.S. strike against Iraq could not legitimately be considered a preemptive one.

Nor was U.S. action against Iraq in 2003 consistent with a justifiable act of preventive war. If preventive war is considered justified in terms of "an attack that responds to a distant danger," or is that which is "fought to maintain the balance" of power to prevent "a relation of dominance and inferiority,"[38] as preventive war is usually characterized, the attack on Iraq fits no better. In fact, for Walzer, preventive war is never justified.[39] While Dershowitz concludes that preventive war is ultimately a right of democracies and that a

---

[36] Walzer, *Just and Unjust Wars*, p. 75.
[37] Walzer, *Just and Unjust Wars*, pp. 82–5.
[38] Walzer, *Just and Unjust Wars*, pp. 75, 76.
[39] Walzer, *Just and Unjust Wars*, p. 80.

preemptive strike on Iran would be justified under certain circumstances by Israel or the United States if Iran develops nuclear capabilities, he rejects it as a reason justifying the U.S. attack on Iraq in 2003.[40] Even Kenneth Pollack, arguing prior to the war that an attack on Iraq was needed and would be a "just war," had to admit that the United States did not have a "smoking gun" but had only "very strong circumstantial evidence" that Iraq was working on nuclear weapons in 2002–2003, that the United States did not really have a *casus belli*.[41] In fact, Pollack argued that because the United States lacked a proper *casus belli*, it might consider a "covert action campaign" in Iraq to provoke an Iraqi attack on U.S. forces in the region so as to establish a *casus belli*, a highly problematic argument, to say the least. Although one could easily make a case that Iraq under Saddam Hussein posed a potential threat to the United States given the despotic nature of the regime and its open hostility toward the United States, there was no evidence in 2003 (nor has there been after the U.S. intervention) that Saddam had either the capabilities or the intentions of attacking the United States any time in the near future, or that he was working with Al Qaeda and thereby was responsible at least in part for 9/11.[42]

Nor was there any evidence that Saddam was an imminent danger to his neighbors or intent on changing the balance of power in the region. Finally, even if such things in themselves represent justification for preventive war (and again, for many, they do not), they could not be applied in this case, as I have argued above.

The Just War Verdict: War on Terror Yes, War on Iraq No

While recognizing the legitimacy of a U.S. response to the terrorism of 911 and its War on Terror, and even the ultimate justice in the destruction of Saddam's despotic and corrupt regime, there just does not seem to be a convincing case one could make that the U.S. invasion of Iraq was just in the traditional sense of just war, preventive war, or preemptive war in March 2003.

---

[40] Dershowitz, *Preemption,* pp. 210, 239, 343, and 174–89.

[41] See Kenneth M. Pollack, *The Threatening Storm: The Case for Invading Iraq* (New York: Random House, 2002), pp. 365–71.

[42] Mark Mazzetti, "C.I.A. Said to Find No Hussein Link to Terror Chief," *The New York Times* (September 9, 2006), A1; "A Senate Committee Finds That, Contrary to What President Bush Has Said, Saddam Hussein Repulsed Overtures from al-Qaida" (*St. Petersburg (FL) Times,* September 9, 2006), A1.

Others have reached the same conclusion, arguing that the line of thought expressed here is consistent with Niebuhr's own approach to war initiation and conduct.[43] For example, Alberto Coll, a well-known Niebuhr expert, argues that the Iraq War "fell far short of meeting the 'last resort' requirement of just war theory," that the weapons inspectors could have been given more time,[44] and that "the Christian Realists would have cautioned us about the use of 'just war' theory to support the unmeasured militaristic policies of the Bush administration in the Middle East."[45] In summing up what he concludes Niebuhr's view of the Iraq War would have been were he alive, Coll put it this way.

> For Niebuhr the September 11 attacks certainly would have justified a response against its perpetrators—the Al Qaeda terrorist network—and that response could have included military attacks designed to destroy the network and prevent it from reconstituting itself. It is dubious that September 11 would have justified a full-scale war against a secular regime that had not been involved in the attacks."[46]

As I noted above, John Patrick Diggins, too, argued that Niebuhr could not reasonably be invoked, as many did at the time, in support of the Iraq War.[47] Likewise, Mark Amstutz has argued that although there were some similarities in George W. Bush's and Niebuhr's worldviews in their appreciation for the importance of power and the need for power to be united with morality in international relations, for politics based on a Christian/dualistic view of human nature, and the priority of freedom and democracy, Niebuhr's and Bush's approaches had important points of divergence as well. Amstutz is correct to argue that Niebuhr would have disagreed with the "excessive social engineering" that the Iraq War came to represent, the "excessive optimism"

---

[43] Again, in addition to the sources below, see Arthur Schlesinger Jr. "Forgetting Reinhold Niebuhr," *The New York Times* (September 18, 2005), Section 7, Page 12; Paul Elie, "A Man for All Reasons," *The Atlantic* (November 2007), accessed from https://www.theatlantic.com/magazine/archive/2007/11/a-man-for-all-reasons/306337/; David Brooks, "Obama, Gospel and Verse," *The New York Times* (April 26, 2007), A25; and Gregory J. Moore, "Christian Views of War: The Case of Iraq," Council on Faith and International Affairs (January 4, 2008), accessed from http://rfiaonline.org/extras/articles/310-the-case-of-iraq, invoking Niebuhr against the war.

[44] Coll, "The Relevance of Christian Realism to the Twenty-First Century," in Patterson (2008), p. 32.

[45] Coll, "The Relevance of Christian Realism to the Twenty-First Century," in Patterson (2008), p. 27.

[46] Coll, The Relevance of Christian Realism to the Twenty-First Century," in Patterson (2008), p. 28.

[47] John Patrick Diggins, *Why Niebuhr Now?* (Chicago: University of Chicago Press, 2011), p. 5.

of Bush toward history and the potential for bringing about political change, the "excessive moralism" (and moral universalism) of Bush policy, and Bush's "excessive self-confidence" about his foreign policy.[48]

Lessons from Vietnam

It is argued here that the assumptions inherent in the decision to take the United States to war in Iraq in March 2003 fail to live up to the standards of the just war tradition, and were Reinhold Niebuhr alive at the time, he would undoubtedly have been "a voice crying in the wilderness." He would certainly have opposed the war in Iraq, just as he opposed the war in Vietnam. Indeed, many of the same reasons he offered for opposing the Vietnam War could also be invoked in the case of the Iraq War.

Here, referring back to arguments I made in Chapter 6, I directly compare the six reasons Niebuhr opposed the war in Vietnam[49] with what I conclude would be the reasons he would have opposed the war with Iraq. First, as with Vietnam, I believe he would have concluded that U.S. interests were not threatened by Iraq in such a way as to justify a war that would last more than eight years and cost thousands of American and Iraqi lives. There was no evidence that Iraq had been involved in the 9/11 attacks on the United States, nor was it clear that Saddam was preparing an attack on the United States or any of America's allies or interests in the region.

Second, as was the case with Vietnam, I think he would have concluded that U.S. policymakers overestimated the amount of support they would receive from antiregime forces in Iraq, and underestimated the level of anti-American opposition they would face. They clearly underestimated both the level of regional foreign penetration in support of anti-American operations and the complexity of cobbling together a new government in an ethnically and religiously diverse state such as Iraq (noting divisions between Shia, Sunni, and Kurdish factions in particular), neither of which was a major factor in Vietnam.

Third, as in Vietnam, Niebuhr believed that U.S. policymakers overestimated their own political and military capabilities. It has been

[48] Mark Amstutz, "Reinhold Niebuhr's Christian Realism and the Bush Doctrine," in Patterson (2008), 125–33.

[49] One might consult Niebuhr's arguments against the Vietnam War in RN, *Faith and Politics* (New York: George Braziller, 1968), p. 251.

easier in the case of Iraq than in Vietnam to maintain popular support for the U.S. military presence over the years, perhaps because of a lower level of U.S. casualties in Iraq and/or the more comprehensive U.S. victory over Saddam Hussein's forces and consequent sense of more complete control over the political situation after the invasion. Although the invasion of Iraq was arguably easier and came at a lower cost (in terms of U.S. troops lost) than the U.S. military estimated, the insurgency that followed and the infiltration of foreign fighters/jihadis into Iraq were issues the U.S. government was not well prepared for. Nor was it well prepared for the state-building role it had to undertake following the quick success of its invasion in overthrowing Saddam Hussein. The successful incursion of the militant group ISIS (Islamic State of Iraq and Syria) into Iraq in 2014 illustrates well the remaining ethnic and religious tensions and unresolved problems in Iraq. Planting a democracy in a Muslim nation by force was not as easy as many in Washington believed.

Fourth, as with Vietnam, I believe Niebuhr would have viewed the U.S. presence in Iraq as wrong because he would have viewed the reasoning behind it as having tainted motives as a direct result of American self-righteousness and self-importance in world affairs after the end of the Cold War and beyond the terrorist attacks of September 11, 2001. As with Vietnam, I believe he would have attacked the American surety that what it was doing was best for Iraq, for in a poll of Iraqis in March and April of 2005 conducted by USA TODAY/CNN/Gallup, when asked, "Taking everything into account, do you think the coalition invasion of Iraq has done more harm than good or more good than harm?" 46 percent said "more harm than good," while 33 percent said "more good than harm." In the same poll, when respondents were asked, "Do you think now of Coalition forces mostly as occupiers or mostly as liberators?" 71 percent said occupiers, 19 percent said liberators, and 8 percent said both.[50] In a December 2005 poll, less than half of Iraqis polled (46 percent) said the country was better off then than it was before the war, and half said it was wrong for U.S.-led forces to have invaded Iraq (this was up from 3 percent in 2004). The poll also said that the number of Iraqis opposing coalition forces in Iraq was then two-thirds, up 14 percent from February 2004.[51] While the American chapter in Iraq ended officially

[50] USAToday/CNN/Gallup, "Key Findings: Nationwide Survey of 3,500 Iraqis," *USA Today* (May 20, 2005; http://www.usatoday.com/news/world/iraq/2004-04-28-gallup-iraq-findings.htm).

[51] Gary Langer and Jon Cohen, "Poll: Broad Optimism in Iraq, But Also Deep Divisions among Groups," *ABC News*, December 12, 2005 (http://abcnews.go.com/International/PollVault/story?id=1389228). The optimism alluded to in the title of the article stems from increasing optimism

in December 2011 and it is true that Iraq became a free, democratic nation, there appears to be a large gap between the way in which the U.S. government portrayed the war and the way in which the Iraqis have viewed it.[52] Niebuhr would have been bothered by this disconnect.

Fifth, while most Iraqis were glad to see Saddam Hussein go, as in the case of Vietnam Niebuhr would have judged it as being arrogant for U.S. policymakers to assume they knew what was best for the majority of the Iraqi people. Specifically, he would have objected to the United States carrying out a policy that would violently and profoundly remake Iraq without the people's real participation until after the invasion and the first Iraqi elections on January 30, 2005.

Lastly, as in Vietnam, Niebuhr would have viewed American motives in Iraq as not being purely honorable or without self-interest. In the Vietnam case, the United States argued that it was protecting South Vietnam from a communist takeover, "making South-East Asia safe for democracy" and preventing the domino theory from being realized—in other words, preventing the spread of communism in Southeast Asia. In the case of Iraq, the argument was primarily that of liberating Iraqis from despotism, "making the Middle East safe for democracy" and working "to keep the world's most dangerous weapons out of the hands of the world's most dangerous people," as George Bush put it. While in both cases Niebuhr might have accepted the argument that these were real concerns in Washington, his Realism would have led him to (what for him would be) the inescapable likelihood that these interests were not in themselves worthy of leading Washington to risk American lives for them. Rather, Niebuhr would likely have suspected that at best they were only a small part of Washington's interest calculations, and more likely were rationalizations and justifications for the more fundamental motivation of the advancement of American interests in the region.

---

about prospects for their lives personally as electricity and water are increasingly available and more Iraqis had returned to work. They were much more pessimistic about the affairs of their country in . general, however.

[52] The data here were originally presented in a paper I presented to faculty and students during a Faculty Fellows Forum at Eckerd College, St. Petersburg, Florida, on February 15, 2006 (Gregory J. Moore, "The Christian Love Ethic, Christian Views of War, and the War in Iraq").

The Irony of America's Iraq Policy

Were Niebuhr alive in 2003, he might have repeated what he penned in 1952. This quotation from his *The Irony of American History* is so apropos as to be worth quoting in full, for it might just as well have been written in 2003.

> We . . . as all "God-fearing" men of all ages, are never safe against the temptation of claiming God too simply as the sanctifier of whatever we most fervently desire. . . . Strangely enough, none of the insights derived from this faith are finally contradictory to our purpose and duty of preserving our civilization. They are, in fact, prerequisites for saving it. For if we should perish, the ruthlessness of the foe would be only the secondary cause of the disaster. The primary cause would be that the strength of a giant nation was directed by eyes too blind to see all the hazards of the struggle; and the blindness would be induced not by some accident of nature or history but by hatred and vainglory.[53]

These words were directed to an earlier generation of American leaders during the Cold War years. Though that was a struggle of a different nature than the one the United States found itself in during the years following September 11, 2001, the advice given is fitting in an uncanny way. The strongest nation in the world had been brought to its knees by a motley band of terrorists working out of caves and camps in Afghanistan. In its quest for security, the strongest nation in the world had, with its Iraq invasion, set in motion a series of events that would lead to the marked rise of Iranian influence in Iraq and Syria, the rise of Russian influence across the Middle East, the rise of ISIS (or the Islamic State of Iraq and Syria) in the region, and could arguably be linked to a financial crisis that crippled America in 2008, all of which undermined U.S. security, again arguably, more than the threat posed to America by Saddam Hussein. As Solomon said to a still earlier generation, "What has been is what will be, and what has been done is what will be done, and there is nothing new under the sun."[54] All of this only serves to remind us again of Niebuhr's continuing relevance.

---

[53] RN, *The Irony of American History* (New York: Charles Scribner's Sons, 1952), pp. 146 and 173–74.

[54] The Holy Bible, Ecclesiastes 1:9 (English Standard Version).

8

Niebuhrian Takeaways on Humanitarian Intervention and the Responsibility to Protect

In her powerful, Pulitzer Prize-winning book, *A Problem from Hell—America and the Age of Genocide*, Samantha Power documents the painful legacy of the twentieth century in terms of genocide, a word first coined by Raphael Lemkin, a Polish Jew who fled the Nazi onslaught against European Jews, to reside in the United States where, failing to win support to help the Jews in Europe until it was too late, he successfully carried forward a campaign to build a regime within the new United Nations that would protect vulnerable people groups from the ultimate crime, genocide.[1] The twentieth century may best be remembered as a century of world wars and Cold War, but more common were the many internecine wars, many of which included genocide: notably, the Turkish massacre of the Armenians in 1915 (some 1 million dead); the Nazi German "Final Solution" against the Jews (some 6 million Jews dead, plus thousands of others); the "killing fields" of Cambodia with the Pol Pot Khmer Rouge regime between 1975 and 1979 (some 2 million Cambodians dead); the streets of Rwanda in 1994 (some 800,000 killed). And the century did not end before another series of genocides in the Balkans between 1992 and 1999 left some 200,000 Bosnians and 11,300 Kosovar Albanians dead, among others.[2] Man's inhumanity to man had taken a nasty, modern, and profoundly brutal turn, creating the necessity for a new term to describe it—*genocide*, or the killing of (or attempt to kill) an entire race or ethnic group.

With the passing of the very bloody twentieth century and the dawn of the twenty-first came a new movement, spawned by a small group of activists

---

[1] Samantha Power, *A Problem from Hell—America and the Age of Genocide* (New York: Basic Books, 2013 [2002]), p. xix.
[2] Power, *A Problem from Hell*, pp. xix–xx, 472.

Niebuhrian International Relations. Gregory J. Moore, Oxford University Press (2020).
© Oxford University Press.
DOI: 10.1093/oso/9780197500446.001.0001

and several national governments, the most important of which perhaps was the Canadian government, to create a new concept, norm, or principle that would enshrine in international law—or at least in the international consciousness and practice—the principle of what came to be called the responsibility to protect, or R2P for short. R2P embodies the recognition that states have a responsibility to protect their own citizens and that the international community has a collective responsibility to act to protect vulnerable individuals when states fail to do so. The Canadian government initiated the International Commission on Intervention and State Sovereignty in 2000, and with the strong support of UN Secretary General Kofi Annan it was voted on and approved first by the world's leaders at the 2005 World Summit on UN reform and then by the UN Security Council in 2006. As James Pattison put it,

[A]t the 2005 UN World Summit (the High-Level Plenary meeting of the 60th session of the General Assembly, with over 160 heads of state and government in attendance), states agreed that there exists a universal responsibility to protect populations. In doing so, they indicated their preparedness to undertake action "should peaceful means be inadequate" and when "national authorities are manifestly failing to protect their populations from genocide, war crimes, ethnic cleansing and crimes against humanity."[3]

As problems in Darfur, Libya, Syria, and elsewhere in the new century quickly illustrated, the acceptance of R2P did not immediately usher in a new, peaceful age in international relations. As Alex Bellamy has argued,

We should . . . recognize that the R2P endorsed by world leaders in 2005 and by the UN Security Council in 2006 did not include criteria for the use of force . . . but did point towards a heavy agenda of institutional reform and behavioural change geared towards preventing and mitigating genocide and mass atrocities.[4]

---

[3] James Pattison, *Humanitarian Intervention and the Responsibility to Protect: Who Should Intervene?* (New York: Oxford University Press, Kindle Edition, 2010), p. 3. In this quotation, Pattison quotes and cites the following: United Nations, *2005 World Summit Outcome*, A/RES/60/1 (http://www.un.org/summit2005/documents.html; 2005).

[4] Alex J. Bellamy, *Responsibility to Protect* (Cambridge, UK: Polity Press, 2009), pp. 3–4.

The normalization of R2P as an internationally accepted principle has been a significant event in international relations. For while

> decisions about intervention will continue to be made in an ad hoc fashion by political leaders balancing national interests, legal considerations, world opinion, perceived costs and humanitarian impulses . . . [w]here R2P can make a real difference is in reducing the frequency with which world leaders are confronted with the apparent choice between doing nothing and sending in the Marines.[5]

The acceptance of R2P internationally has been a major step forward in building a community of mutual accountability among nations and an important step toward ending genocide. If Reinhold Niebuhr had been alive to see these developments, I believe he would have been an enthusiastic supporter of the principle of R2P, even while being cautious about the interventionist potentialities it entailed and understanding the limits on foreign policy altruism posed by the foibles of human nature, group dynamics, politics, and international anarchy.

Niebuhr's Observations on Humanitarian International Relations and Early R2P-esque Cases

As I have argued earlier, particularly in Chapter 5 on the United Nations and the potential for national transcendence, while Reinhold Niebuhr was a Realist through and through, he did believe that individuals and nations had a moral responsibility to act to help others in need. He also believed that wealthy and powerful nations like the United States in particular had a responsibility to those in need abroad. A "head in the sand" policy was not an option for the United States or any responsible power, in Niebuhr's view. As Niebuhr said, "the [biblical] commandment 'Thou shalt love they neighbor as thyself' brings us under religious and moral compulsions to eliminate the violations of brotherhood in the field of race relations"[6]; here he was alluding to race relations in the broader sense, that is, not just within the United

---

[5] Bellamy, *Responsibility to Protect*, pp. 3–4.
[6] RN, "Christian Faith and Political Controversy," *Christianity and Crisis* (July 21, 1952); as found in RN, *Love and Justice*, edited by D. B. Robertson (Westminster, UK: John Knox Press, 1957), p. 60.

States. While "eliminating the violations of brotherhood in the field of race relations" might be said to be only one dimension of what we know as R2P, and one of the loftier aspects thereof, Niebuhr's endorsement of that notion is indicative of his sensitivities to the moral dimension of domestic and international politics.

Niebuhr's work contains many quotes that allude to his recognition of what is now called the responsibility to protect, but the following is of particular interest in its general appeal to an ethic of care for others facing danger.

> When a great fire has broken out in a small town, responsible citizens who are in a position to do something about it do not draw their shutters, lock their doors, and crawl under their beds. To do so would be to forget forever moral authority in their community. The Christian ethic requires these citizens to go out on the street and do whatever may be necessary to help their fellows bring the fire under control.[7]

Niebuhr made this comment in response to a pre-Pearl Harbor 1941 debate in the United States about a U.S. policy to remain neutral in the face of Nazi and Japanese aggression. He found the policy of neutrality morally irresponsible, akin to an individual going to sleep rather than helping while one's neighbor's house burned down. In many places in his work, Niebuhr spoke of a community of nations, or the notion that international relations is about a community of nations. So, I conclude that this domestic analogy is an apt description of Niebuhr's understanding of nations' mutual responsibilities. He thought that individual nations in a community of nations had some measure of mutual responsibility when it came to calamities transpiring within the bounds of their neighbor's territory, whether the neighboring government itself was responsible or whether the calamity was what insurance companies used to call "an act of God." But what were those responsibilities, and how did they relate to another important concept in Niebuhr's writing, state sovereignty?

To underline my point about Niebuhr's commitment to mutual responsibility in a community of nations and the dilemmas of sovereignty they sometimes engendered, it will be useful to consider some examples of wars and crimes against humanity that occurred during his lifetime, with an eye to searching out his responses at the time so as to ascertain what he might

---

[7] RN, "Repeal the Neutrality Act!" *Christianity and Crisis* (October 20, 1941); as found in RN, *Love and Justice*, p. 19.

have said about later humanitarian crises and international responsibility. Although R2P is a more recent concept, and even humanitarian intervention as we understand it today was not a major trend in international relations discussions/literature in his time, Niebuhr was a prolific writer and commentator on current affairs in his day, so he did leave us much to consider in this respect.

Below are several examples of such events and Niebuhr's commentary on each of them. Not all are classic examples of what we would understand as R2P today. Some fall more appropriately in the category of collective security. All, however, touch on the notion of moral responsibilities across borders, and they are therefore useful to our discussion.

Japanese Invasions of China, 1931, 1937

In 1931 Japan invaded China's Manchurian provinces. Niebuhr expressed strong opposition to Japan's policy and argued that the United States had a responsibility to oppose Tokyo. In considering a proper U.S. response to this invasion, Niebuhr's brother, H. Richard Niebuhr, penned "The Grace of Doing Nothing," arguing that it was better that the United States did not get involved.[8] Reinhold vigorously responded the following week in the same publication.

> It would be better to come to terms with the forces of nature in history, and try to use ethically directed coercion in order that violence may be avoided. . . . In practical, specific and contemporary terms this means that we must try to dissuade Japan from her military venture, but must use coercion to frustrate her designs if necessary, must reduce coercion to a minimum and prevent it from issuing in violence, must engage in constant self-analysis in order to reduce the moral conceit of Japan's critics and judges to a minimum, and must try in every social situation to maximize the ethical forces and yet not sacrifice the possibility of achieving an ethical goal because we are afraid to use any but purely ethical means.[9]

---

[8] H. Richard Niebuhr, "The Grace of Doing Nothing," *The Christian Century* (March 23, 1932): 378–80.

[9] RN, "Must We Do Nothing? A Response to H. Richard Niebuhr's article, 'The Grace of Doing Nothing,'" *Christian Century* (March 30, 1932): 415–17; as cited by John D. Barbour, "Niebuhr vs. Niebuhr: On Tragedy in History," *Christian Century* 101/36 (November 21, 1984): 1096–99; and found in Box 56, Reinhold Niebuhr Papers, Manuscript Division, Library of Congress, Washington, DC.

Niebuhr's message was that the United States could not stand by and allow Japan to have its way in Asia. It must stand up to Japan, taking coercive measures if necessary. This was a bit of a dilemma in light of Niebuhr's pacifism of the time, to say the least, but the Christian Realist in him was already beginning to surface in his impatience with the United States and other nations which were doing nothing in the face of evil. As he said in *Moral Man and Immoral Society*, published in December 1932, not long after Japan's takeover of Manchuria in 1931, "the dream of perpetual peace[10] and brotherhood for human society is one which will never be fully realized . . . " for society is "in a perpetual state of war."[11] The position he took through this statement might be read as follows: if physical force, "violence," could be avoided, this was best. However, if this failed, one must not be "afraid to use any but purely ethical means," meaning violence.

When Japan expanded its invasion of China in 1937 to much of the rest of the country, Niebuhr was not silent. In one 1937 piece for *Christian Century* about the war in China, he offered some of his best opinions about the responsibility to protect and intervene on behalf of China in the face of Japanese brutality and imperialism and an overwhelming apathy and/or public sense of isolationism in the United States at the time.

> The argument that we have no "moral responsibility" to aid one side against the other so long as we do not have the support of some international group is a curious bit of casuistry. . . . But it is very confusing to identify such a question with right and wrong and insist that our isolated position absolves us of moral responsibility. We happen to live in an internationally anarchic world. There is at present no international policeman upon whom we may call. Whether in such a situation it is either wise or good to shut ourselves in our castle and wash our hands of responsibility is a question which cannot be decided abstractly. Both the expediency and morality of our policy would depend on how great the risks are of aggravating the conflict or the hope of mitigating it.[12]

Niebuhr went on to argue that in the case of coming to the assistance of China against Japan in 1937, the risks were *not* too great for the United States

---

[10] Note here the allusion to Kant.

[11] Chapter 1 of RN, *Moral Man and Immoral Society* (New York: Scribners, 1932).

[12] RN, "America and the War in China," *Christian Century* (September 29, 1937): 1195–6, as found in Box 56, Reinhold Niebuhr Papers, Manuscript Division, Library of Congress, Washington, DC.

to avoid acting. Here it would be difficult to argue that it was an abiding national interest in defending China that drove U.S. policy, though certainly China's defeat would not have been in America's interest. It seems clear to me that for the United States, perhaps the most important reason for its decision to intervene against Japan prior to Pearl Harbor was a sense that Japan's actions in China were brazen and highly offensive to American sensibilities. Hence, this issue is relevant to our discussion of R2P. Another point worth making here, is that in lieu of actions from the League of Nations (which did little in this case) and prior to the United Nations, Niebuhr was arguing that individual nations had a responsibility to act to protect nations like China in such circumstances, even when there was no sanction offered by an international organization like the League or the UN, particularly when (always the Realist) it is clear that 1. moral responsibility, 2. national interests, and 3. a realistic hope for success converge. The expedience or prudence in Niebuhr's call here is a part of his realism, and I will return to this matter later.

Italian Invasion of Abyssinia/Ethiopia, 1935

Following Japan's invasion of Manchuria, things got worse for those, like Niebuhr, who believed in the importance of a foreign policy that fostered international community, peace, and brotherhood, and in the viability of international organizations such as the League of Nations. For soon after the Japanese invasion of Manchuria came the Italian invasion of Abyssinia (or Ethiopia) in 1935. Again, as in the case of Japan's invasions of China, the League of Nations failed to do anything meaningful to hold Italy accountable. The League struggled to put together sanctions on Italy, but in the end it only managed to impose very small, relatively painless penalties. Niebuhr spoke out against what he saw as the capitulation of the international community to such naked aggression. "One must support sanctions in the hope that they will not lead to war. But if they should, one can hardly withdraw from the political consequences of such a policy."[13] Niebuhr then criticized British Foreign Secretary Samuel Hoare for resigning over his refusal to implement sanctions against Mussolini, and the subsequent failure of Britain to meaningfully oppose Italy in this respect. He believed Britain should have

---

[13] RN, "Why Sanctions Are Good," *Radical Religion* (Fall, 1935); as found in RN, *Love and Justice*, edited by D. B. Robertson (Westminster, UK: John Knox Press, 1957), p. 167.

adopted a more robust policy toward Italy and argued that the United States should have at least supported the (mild) League of Nations sanctions against Italy but did not even do this. Niebuhr feared a world war was imminent and hoped that by holding Italian imperialists accountable for their acts against an innocent nation, the international community might deter further imperialism and avoid greater conflicts. This was, after all, the ultimate raison d'etre of the League of Nations upon its establishment at the end of World War I. As Niebuhr put it, "The best we can do for the moment is to prevent the outbreak of a world war, in the hope that its postponement may increase the possibility of its prevention."[14] His fears were well grounded, of course, as we all know in hindsight, for the failure of the League of Nations to stand up to Japan or Italy in 1931 and 1935, respectively, was followed by Nazi Germany's military occupation of the Ruhr Valley in 1936 (which occurred against the Versailles provisions), Japan's expansion of its invasion of China in 1937 (meaning Japan invaded southern and central China in addition to its holdings in Manchuria), Nazi Germany's general launching of World War II in Europe in the following two years, and the further expansion of Japan's imperialism, and ultimately war, in the Asia-Pacific as well as Pearl Harbor and further Japanese exploits thereafter.

The Holocaust, 1933–1945, and World War II, 1939–1945

When Adolf Hitler took power in Germany in 1933, Niebuhr, a fluent German speaker with family and friends still in Germany, began to be greatly concerned about what he saw happening in the country. He understood the danger Hitler posed and foresaw the horrors of the Holocaust before many in the United States did. In fact, he called for U.S. action as early as August 1933, just months after the Nazis took power in Germany, when he registered his concern about the plight of the Jews in Germany under the new Hitler regime. Already in 1933 he was arguing that America's Christian churches had "a clear obligation laid on them to offer every possible resistance to the inhumanities of the present German regime" toward the Jewish people.[15] What was happening to the Jews in Europe was "for him one of the key arguments for intervention," Richard Fox argues, adding, "By the early thirties he [RN]

---

[14] RN, "Why Sanctions Are Good," as found in RN, *Love and Justice*, p. 168.
[15] RN, "The Germans Must Be Told!" *The Christian Century* (August 9, 1933), as found in Box 15, Reinhold Niebuhr Papers, Manuscript Division, Library of Congress, Washington, DC.

had made the ethical leap to coercion, and grasped that Hitler was bent on the cultural annihilation of the Jews. From that time on he was a firm, though sometimes qualified, backer of the Zionist cause."[16] Niebuhr's remarks about the *Anschluss*, Nazi Germany's forceful takeover of Austria in 1938, are telling of his views on totalitarian Nazism, his understanding of the responsibility of others to stand up for oppressed peoples elsewhere, and his specific concern for the plight of the Jews in the face of the Nazi onslaught.

> With the entrance of the Nazis into Vienna their anti-Semitic fury has reached new proportions. Here was a city in which Jewish intelligence played a significant role in the cultural achievements of the nation, particularly in medicine and music. The Nazis swooped down upon the city and wreaked indescribable terror. The Jews have been spared no indignity. . . . The tragic events since the taking of Austria allow us to see the racial fanaticism inherent in the Nazi creed in boldest outline. This is really the final destruction of every concept of universal values upon which Western civilization has been built.[17]

For Niebuhr, the Holocaust alone was reason enough for the United States to enter the war against Nazi Germany, let alone to support Britain, America's closest ally, and defend Western civilization from Nazi barbarism. This was true even without the German invasion of Poland and France, and the bombardment of Great Britain. Yet, to Niebuhr's grave disappointment, America stood by in neutral abandonment.

Prior to the U.S. entry into the twentieth century's second great war in Europe, with the isolationist mood that characterized American popular sentiment of the time the U.S. Congress passed several Neutrality Acts between 1935 and 1939, designed to keep the United States out of the war in Europe. The final act passed in 1939 reaffirmed U.S. neutrality, but President Roosevelt got added to the language a clause allowing a robust arms trade with U.S. allies Britain and France, ending the arms embargo the United States had upheld until then. While Niebuhr supported the end of the arms embargo, he lamented that the United States was still standing aside and not supporting its allies, even after the allies had bravely declared war on

---

[16] Richard W. Fox, *Reinhold Niebuhr: A Biography* (New York: Pantheon, 1985), pp. 209 and 209–10, respectively.
[17] RN, "Anti-Semitism," *Radical Religion* 3 (Summer 1938), as found in John Patrick Diggins, *Why Niebuhr Now* (Chicago: University of Chicago Press, 2011), p. 3.

Germany in 1939 following Germany's invasion of Poland. His words are significant and merit quoting at length here.

> We demand the immediate repeal of the Neutrality Act because it is one of the most immoral laws that was ever spread upon a federal statute book. Its immorality was accentuated by the misguided idealism that was evoked in its support. The essence of immorality is the evasion or denial of moral responsibility. When a man refuses to recognize his obligations as a member of a community, when he isolates himself from the affairs of his community, when he acts as a completely unrelated individual, he is an immoral man. Morality consists in the recognition of the interdependence of personal life. The moral man is the man who acts responsibly in relations to his fellows, who knows the duties that communal life requires, and who is willing to accept the consequences that these duties impose. As with men, so with nations.[18]

As Niebuhr clearly stated, such moral responsibility to come to the aid of those in need was not a personal responsibility only, but rather was required of nations as well.

Alluding to notions of what we would now call globalization, Niebuhr continued, noting that modern technology and logistics united the world in a way that made it increasingly difficult for peoples to eschew their interconnectivity.

> Two or three hundred years ago . . . [t]he oceans were then so vast that there was some reason for thinking of the Americas as a separate world from Europe. But the mechanical revolution of the last one hundred years has destroyed the distinction between the Old World and the New. . . . We belong to a common community and we have acquired immense communal responsibilities as a result of that fact. To deny these responsibilities is unchristian and unethical. This is exactly what the Neutrality Act did.[19]

Niebuhr then turned his guns on American isolationism as he continued to emphasize "interdependence" in a time when the term had not yet been

---

[18] RN, "Repeal the Neutrality Act!" *Christianity and Crisis* (October 20, 1941), as found in RN, *Love and Justice*, pp. 17–8.

[19] RN, "Repeal the Neutrality Act!" *Christianity and Crisis* (October 20, 1941), as found in RN, *Love and Justice*, p. 18.

made famous in international relations parlance by Keohane and Nye,[20] who later made the term *complex interdependence* famous.[21] As Niebuhr said,

> Do-nothingness for the sake of peace is not moral. It is pure escapism in a world where nations can escape no longer from the ethical consequences of their interdependence. . . . When a great fire has broken out in a small town, responsible citizens who are in a position to do something about it do not draw their shutters, lock their doors, and crawl under their beds. To do so would be to forget forever moral authority in their community. The Christian ethic requires these citizens to go out on the street and do whatever may be necessary to help their fellows bring the fire under control.[22]

For Niebuhr the concept of interdependence was linked to the Christian notion of "Everyone to whom much was given, of him much will be required."[23] To him, pitching in to help was a moral issue (a biblical mandate), a practical issue (helping friends/allies), and a social responsibility (interdependence in an international community). Niebuhr was always disappointed that it was not until the Japanese bombing of Pearl Harbor, only on December 7, 1941, that his beloved nation finally declared war on Nazi Germany (and Japan and Italy). Although he agreed, he felt it was better late than never.

Support for the New State of Israel, 1940s

Niebuhr was a passionate supporter of Israel and the Zionist cause, given all that the Jewish people suffered in Europe during the Holocaust. As discussed earlier, he believed the Holocaust was "one of the key arguments for intervention" in the war by the United States, and he expressed grave disappointment (and even physical illness) because of the United States' slow awakening to the importance of intervening on behalf of the Jews and others in the face of Hitler's onslaught.[24] Hitler's attempt to exterminate the Jewish people

---

[20] Robert O. Keohane and Joseph S. Nye, *Power and Interdependence: World Politics in Transition* (Boston: Little, Brown, 1977).

[21] As a reviewer pointed out to me, the term *interdependence* was first made famous by Nobel Prize-winning author Norman Angell in his 1910 book, *The Great Illusion: A Study of the Relation of Military Power to National Advantage* (English edition in 1910; Amazon Digital Services, 2012).

[22] RN, "Repeal the Neutrality Act!" *Christianity and Crisis* (October 20, 1941); as found in RN, *Love and Justice*, p. 19.

[23] Luke 12:48b, the Holy Bible, English Standard Version.

[24] Fox, *Reinhold Niebuhr*, pp. 209–10.

made it clear to Niebuhr that the Jewish people needed a homeland of their own; therefore, not surprisingly, he became an ardent champion of Zionism during and after the war.[25] He became an activist after the war to press for the rights of Jewish refugees to settle in the British mandate of Palestine, but the British government was doing little to address the problem. To press the case for establishing a Jewish homeland, as early as 1942 Niebuhr wrote an article titled "Jews after the War" for *The Nation* in which he made the case that American and British power should be used to establish a Jewish state in Palestine after the war.[26]

Richard Fox recounts an interesting episode of Niebuhr's proactivity on behalf of the Jewish people in the shadow of genocide.[27] The British and American governments had formed an Anglo-American Committee of Inquiry on the question of the status of Europe's Jews after the Holocaust, and when they convened a meeting in Washington, Niebuhr arrived with a statement prepared on behalf of the Christian Council on Palestine. Though not invited to the meeting, after waiting for hours, Niebuhr was given a chance to speak at the end of the meeting. He argued for a Palestinian state with a Jewish majority, a speech which a Zionist lawyer called "the finest presentation of the Zionist case that I have ever heard," and he observed that Niebuhr's "closing of the case made all the difference in the world and may fundamentally affect the decision."[28] A few months later, the committee *did* recommend to the British government that it admit 100,000 refugees to Palestine to begin to address the Jewish refugee problem. Off course, eventually, in 1948, the State of Israel was established. Reinhold Niebuhr, a German American and a Christian, was one of the strongest supporters of the new Jewish homeland.

U.S. Intervention in the Dominican Republic, 1965

Niebuhr also had words about U.S. intervention in (or some would call it an invasion of) the Dominican Republic in 1965 and (for our purposes here) about the importance of international organizational sanction to convey additional legitimacy on such interventions. From Niebuhr's perspective, this

---

[25] Fox, *Reinhold Niebuhr*, pp. 209–10.
[26] RN, "Jews after the War," *The Nation* (February 21 and 28, 1942), as found in Box 17, Reinhold Niebuhr Papers, Manuscript Division, Library of Congress, Washington, DC. See also RN, Letter to the Editor, *Christian Century* (May 27, 1936), as cited in Fox, *Reinhold Niebuhr*, p. 210.
[27] Fox, *Reinhold Niebuhr*, p. 226.
[28] Fox, *Reinhold Niebuhr*, p. 226.

was a case of how *not* to conduct an intervention in the face of an international crisis. When in 1961 the pro-U.S. Dominican President Rafael Trujillo was assassinated, unrest followed. The United States helped broker a deal that included an election, which took place in 1963. However, a candidate with leftist sympathies won, prompting a counterintervention by anticommunist military units, which charged the new government with pro-Castro leanings. This led to the outbreak of a civil war. In April 1965, U.S. President Lyndon Johnson ordered U.S. troops to invade the Dominican Republic to restore order. In response, Niebuhr opined, "The President thought it so important to prevent the establishment of a new Castroite government in the Caribbean that he did not take time to consult the Organization of American States, which alone could have invested our force with moral authority."[29] In fact, within a week of the U.S. intervention, Organization of American States peace delegates were in the capitol, and a day later they established what was called "the Inter-American Peace," which brought in more than 1700 OAS member soldiers to maintain the peace while elections were organized and then held. Niebuhr's statement made it clear that while he thought unilateral U.S. intervention in the Dominican Republic was unwarranted because of the United States' ulterior motives, he believed the authority, the sanction of international organizations like the OAS, could help play an important role in conferring legitimacy upon international interventions such as this one and in the end bring about better outcomes, in both moral and political terms.

Conclusions: Niebuhr and R2P

Reinhold Niebuhr passed away in 1971. What might he have said about human rights disasters in Cambodia (1975–1979), Rwanda (1994), or the Balkans (1991–1999)? What counsel would he have given Presidents Obama and Trump on the Syrian crisis in recent years? While it's not easy to say what his counsel would have been on specific cases, as each case had its particularities, we can draw some general conclusions based on Niebuhr's writings on moral responsibility in foreign policy and on cases he did discuss in his day.

---

[29] RN, "Caribbean Blunder," *Christianity and Crisis,* 25 (May 31, 1965): 113–4, as found in Charles C. Brown, *Niebuhr and His Age: Reinhold Niebuhr's Prophetic Role in the Twentieth Century* (Philadelphia: Trinity Press International, 1992), p. 239.

Niebuhr would remind us that "the children of light" who are in positions of political responsibility must do what is necessary to uphold justice, and that this responsibility was not relegated simply to the domestic political sphere. Yet while remaining wary of the wiles and ways of "the children of darkness," "the children of light" must not allow themselves to succumb to the hubris and folly of "the children of darkness" and of means–ends calculations that might make them no better than "the children of darkness" in the end. For Niebuhr, "the children of darkness" can account for the policies of both those who perpetrate genocide and other crimes against humanity, but also those who stand idly by, unwilling to help the victims. Several nations, including France, Canada, and some U.S. states, have the "duty to rescue" laws that make it a crime *not* to come to the aid of someone in distress. In fact, in the United States, all states have some form of Good Samaritan Law, which protects from liability those who come to the aid of those in peril. As is the case in those nations or U.S. states with such "duty to rescue" laws, those who stand by and do nothing to help victims of crimes when they are witnesses to such crimes and have the power to act, are in effect aiding and abetting the crime and are in effect accomplices to the criminals involved. So too for nations, Niebuhr would argue.

Here I think Niebuhr's Realism clashes somewhat with his idealism, leading to yet another example of the proverbial Niebuhrian dialectic. For while Niebuhr knew what nations *should* do (i.e., help their suffering brothers and sisters out), he was not surprised, given his perspective on human nature and the politics of collective society and international relations, when in many cases they failed to do so. "[I]deally we ought to resist injustice done to others as much as we resist it when done to ourselves. But we do not. The force of self-interest alone finally makes the will strong enough to meet its obligations to others.[30] In her study of "America and the Age of Genocide" (the subtitle of her book), Samantha Power draws a conclusion that Niebuhr would have understood.

> The real reason the United States did not do what it could and should have done to stop genocide was not a lack of knowledge or influence but a lack of will. Simply put, American leaders did not act because they did not want to. They believed that genocide was wrong, but they were not prepared

[30] RN, Letter to the Editor, *Christian Century* (May 27, 1936), as cited in Fox, *Reinhold Niebuhr*, p. 210.

to invest the military, financial, diplomatic, or domestic political capital needed to stop it.[31]

Niebuhr would not have been surprised at Power's findings, for he always emphasized both the foibles of human nature and the limitations of human concern for others. Yet Niebuhr concluded, "Man is not totally depraved. We should not believe" he says, that man "acts only from motives of self-interest." He continued, "Man has a dim sense of awareness of his obligations to his fellows and a weak desire to fulfill those obligations. But the desire is not strong enough to produce action until self-interest and social interest reach some kind of coincidence."[32] Niebuhr is correct here, for we have seen this phenomenon in the world's slow response to Japan's and Italy's adventurism in the 1930s, to the horrors of the Holocaust, the Cambodian killing fields, the Balkans and Rwanda in the 1990s, and on and on. Herein is a word of wisdom from Niebuhr for today's policymakers and activists. When there is a fire that needs U.S./international help in suppressing and Washington and/ or the international community is slow and/or reluctant to respond, showing policymakers not only their moral responsibility, but the realities of their (or their nation's) self-interests in acting (or the political, economic, and/or strategic costs of *not* acting), is fundamental to spurring on action toward such desired ends.

In 1937, in the face of the Americans' overwhelming preference for isolationism, after Japan's brazen invasion and brutalization of China (following its initial invasion of northeastern China in 1931), Niebuhr penned the following.

The argument that we have no "moral responsibility" to aid one side against the other so long as we do not have the support of some international group is a curious bit of casuistry. . . . But it is very confusing to identify such a question with right and wrong and insist that our isolated position absolves us of moral responsibility.[33]

---

[31] Power, *A Problem from Hell*, p. 508.

[32] RN, "History (God) has Overtaken Us," *Christianity and Society* (Winter 1941), as found in RN, *Love and Justice*, pp. 293–4.

[33] RN, "America and the War in China," *Christian Century* (September 29, 1937), pp. 1195–6, as found in Box 56, Reinhold Niebuhr Papers, Manuscript Division, Library of Congress, Washington, DC.

Moral responsibility was moral responsibility in Niebuhr's view. In other words, the duty to act was there, whether or not the rest of the international community was on board. Yet Niebuhr recognized the importance of interests in foreign policymaking, that "moral responsibility" alone was not always a powerful enough motivation to gain support for a policy.

> We happen to live in an internationally anarchic world. There is at present no international policeman upon whom we may call. Whether in such a situation it is either wise or good to shut ourselves in our castle and wash our hands of responsibility is a question which cannot be decided abstractly. Both the expediency and morality of our policy would depend on how great the risks are of aggravating the conflict or the hope of mitigating it.[34]

In the end, while the moral case for intervention might be compelling in a given case, Niebuhr (always the Realist) understood that effective policy would not be undertaken until or unless a national interest could be invoked and a realistic path to implementing the policy could be demonstrated.

Similarly, Niebuhr's Realism would necessitate a concomitant warning as regarding potential interventions in the name of R2P. Given his view of politics and the self-interested realities of human nature in individuals and national political leaders as they make policy, Niebuhr would see the dark potential of the possibility of exploitation of R2P for political gain. Just as the Russians and Chinese and others have argued about (against) Western "humanitarian interventions," some observers see humanitarian intervention as simply a cover for great power politics, for using lofty rhetoric to advance baser political and strategic interests. Niebuhr would have taken this seriously. I believe he would have supported the creation and maintenance of the norm of UN Security Council sanction for more robust interventions in the name of R2P. While cognizant of the value of having the sanction of international organizations to provide additional legitimacy, as was evident in his statements about the role of the OAS in the Dominican intervention, I don't read Niebuhr as supporting the notion that the United States (or other concerned nations/actors) could act *only* when the UN or other international organizations gave sanction. Moral responsibility or political necessity *could* move a nation or group of nations to act with or without such sanction.

---

[34] RN, "America and the War in China," *Christian Century* (September 29, 1937): 1195–6, as found in Box 56, Reinhold Niebuhr Papers, Manuscript Division, Library of Congress, Washington, DC.

Yet I think Niebuhr's Realism would have led him to be fairly conservative with regard to advocating non-UN Security Council-sanctioned interventions. Just as he recognized the wisdom of the UN Security Council (UNSC) veto, which was designed to prevent great power conflict by requiring great power consensus on the most important matters of peace and security, so too humanitarian interventions can have important implications for relations between great powers today. Moreover, the sanction of the UNSC resolution provides many guarantees against the possibility that such an intervention could draw the great powers into conflict. I think this is evident in Niebuhr's criticism of the United States for not seeking OAS endorsement before intervening in the Dominican Republic in 1965.

In the end, Niebuhr would commiserate with those of us, like Samantha Power, who are saddened by the world's cold willingness to ignore genocide and other atrocities and to stand by and do nothing in so many such cases. Yet with the increasing international acceptance of the principle of R2P and the growing international recognition that "[w]e—even here—hold the power, and bear the responsibility," to quote Abraham Lincoln[35] (one of Niebuhr's personal heroes), Niebuhr would find hope as he reminds us of the following.

> The insistence of the Christian faith that the love of Christ is the final norm of human existence must express itself socially in unwillingness to stop short of the whole human community in expressing our sense of moral responsibility for the life and welfare of others.[36]

Although the term *R2P* would not be coined for many years after his death, Niebuhr understood what we now know as the responsibility to protect, whether in one's own neighborhood or on the global stage, to be a moral imperative for individuals *and* nations, even while understanding the difficulty of mobilizing such good will and social action socially and politically.

---

[35] This quotation from Abraham Lincoln was found as deployed in Samantha Power's *A Problem from Hell*, standing alone on the page preceding the Table of Contents.

[36] RN, *The Children of Light and the Children of Darkness* (New York: Charles Scribner's Sons, 1944), pp. 188–90; as found in Harry R. Davis and Robert C. Good, eds., *Reinhold Niebuhr on Politics* (New York: Charles Scribner's Sons, 1960), p. 342.

9

Niebuhrian Takeaways for the West Regarding the Twenty-first Century Rise of China

The rise of China is the most important international relations event of the twenty-first century. China presently has the largest population in the world, the third largest land mass in the world (after Russia and Canada), the second largest economy in the world (after the United States, though in purchasing power parity (PPP) terms it is already the largest), the second largest military expenditures in the world (after the United States), and the largest number of active duty military personnel in the world, to cite a few important indicators of comparison. It is, very obviously, extremely important how the United States in particular, as the most powerful nation in the world, will handle the emergence of China as a true peer competitor in the coming decades. International relations (IR) theories, IR theorists, China specialists, security studies experts, diplomats, and pundits have had much to say on this topic, and were he alive, surely Reinhold Niebuhr would be an important voice among them, weighing in on this vital subject as well. What would he have said about China's rise? Given his intellectual gravitas and the influence he wielded in the twentieth century, what words of wisdom might his work offer us as we consider one of the most intractable international challenges of the twenty-first century, the rise of China? Despite the challenges of sifting through all of Niebuhr's disparate (and largely obscure, hard to find, and/or out of print) writings on public policy issues, this study seeks to answer these questions.

This chapter starts with a discussion of what Niebuhr *did* say about China in his lifetime, followed by a discussion of what factors would be most important in considering how one should view China's rise today from a Niebuhrian perspective, concluding with advice for policymakers drawn from Niebuhr's writings applying to the issue of China's rise in the twenty-first century. In sum, although Niebuhr was a defensive Realist like Henry

Niebuhrian International Relations. Gregory J. Moore, Oxford University Press (2020).
© Oxford University Press.
DOI: 10.1093/oso/9780197500446.001.0001

Kissinger, Niebuhr would be quite hawkish on China today, parting ways to some degree with the legacy of the Kissingerian Realist approach to China, the pragmatic yet strategic engagement that made Kissinger famous as the architect of Nixon's rapprochement with China in 1971–1972. While Niebuhr probably would have supported Kissinger's approach to China in 1971, I argue that Niebuhr would emphasize the potential danger China's rise poses to its neighbors and the United States today, but that this would *not* be because it was based primarily on the sorts of factors that structural and offensive Realist John Mearsheimer has identified as salient, that is, latent material power and material power structures. Rather, Niebuhr's stress on human nature and the importance of ideology and regime type would lead him to argue that today's China is a potentially dangerous power.

What Niebuhr Did Say about China in His Lifetime

The various stages of Reinhold Niebuhr's intellectual development had important implications for his views on international affairs. He was a liberal Protestant in his youth, turned leftist/Marxist in his early professional life, after which he settled on Christian Realism, the worldview he held at the high point of his career until the end of his life.[1] During the leftist stage of his intellectual development, he held highly sympathetic, even favorable, views of Soviet communism, though he always opposed the excesses of Stalinism. By the time Mao and the Chinese Communist Party had taken power in China in 1949, Niebuhr had moved to a hawkish view of Soviet communism. He was much more sympathetic toward Chinese and Vietnamese communism, both during his leftist and Christian Realist stages, for he viewed both as more nationalist than communist per se, more a reaction to global imperialism than an indication of identification with the world communist movement ideologically. Next I present an overview of some of Niebuhr's views of China and events in China, based on his own writings.

Niebuhr was an advocate of U.S. support for the Republic of China as it stood up to Japan from 1931, when Japan invaded northeastern China, through 1937 when Japan expanded its invasion to the rest of China, up until

---

[1] For more, see Richard Wightman Fox, *Reinhold Niebuhr: A Biography* (San Francisco: Harper & Row, 1985); Ronald Stone, *Reinhold Niebuhr: Prophet to Politicians* (Abingdon, MD: Abingdon Press, 1972); and above.

the end of World War II when Japan was ultimately defeated. In the aftermath of Japan's invasion of China in 1931, Niebuhr said that "we must try to dissuade Japan from her military venture, but must use coercion to frustrate her designs if necessary."[2] Niebuhr not only supported U.S. intervention against Japan, but also was among the early American voices calling for U.S. action against Nazi Germany, as early as 1933 raising the alarm about "the German Nazi effort to extirpate the Jews in Germany."[3]

After World War II, as the United States continued to support Chiang Kai-shek's Nationalist government, it became increasingly clear that Chiang was losing the civil war in China. In 1949, Niebuhr made the following observation:

> The Chinese government is slowly disintegrating; and we face the cheerless prospect of a triumphant communism in China. There are those who think this . . . has taken place because we did not come to the aid of [Nationalist] China early enough or with sufficient generosity. But even those who criticize our policy must admit that the [Nationalist] Chinese government is corrupt and that it has steadily lost moral prestige in recent years.[4]

As he emphasizes, Niebuhr did not agree with those in the United States who believed China was "lost" to the communists because the United States did not invest enough to save the Nationalists there. He concluded that Chiang lost because Chiang's own regime was corrupt and inept. He explains, "In China . . . communism conquered the nation precisely because the Nationalist government lacked the moral and political virtue necessary to claim the allegiance of the vast mass of the Chinese people."[5] Yet the debate in America was about who should be blamed for the "loss" of China. As Niebuhr observed,

---

[2] RN, "Must We Do Nothing? A Critique of H. Richard Niebuhr's Article, 'The Grace of Doing Nothing,' in Last Week's *Christian Century,*" *Christian Century* (March 30, 1932): 415–7, as found in Box 15, Reinhold Niebuhr Papers, Manuscript Division, Library of Congress, Washington, DC.

[3] RN, "The Germans Must Be Told!" *The Christian Century* (August 9, 1933), as found in Box 15, Reinhold Niebuhr Papers, Manuscript Division, Library of Congress, Washington, DC.

[4] RN, "The Dilemma in China," *Messenger* 14 (January 4, 1949): 4, as found in Charles C. Brown, *Niebuhr and His Age: Reinhold Niebuhr's Prophetic Role in the Twentieth Century* (Philadelphia: Trinity Press International, 1992), p. 148.

[5] RN, "Should We Be Consistent?" *Christianity and Crisis* 10 (February 6, 1950): 1; Davis Harry R. and Robert C. Good (eds.), *Reinhold Niebuhr on Politics* (New York: Charles Scribner's Sons, 1960), p. 309.

In Asia we are in the toils of a fiction that the communists triumphed in China because we gave inadequate support to the Nationalists. This fiction binds us to the Chinese Nationalists and makes us adamant in the refusal to admit Communist China to the United Nations.[6]

As early as 1957, Niebuhr argued for admitting the People's Republic of China (PRC) to the UN, though he also favored continued military support of Taiwan.[7] Although the U.S. government continued to support the Nationalists and refused to recognize the PRC during Niebuhr's lifetime, with the Kissinger/Nixon entente with China beginning in 1971, the United States eventually worked to admit the PRC into the UN in September 1971, just months after Niebuhr's passing.

Niebuhr's primary reason for advocating American nonsupport for Chiang Kai-shek was Chiang's own ineptitude and his Nationalist regime's corruption. But there was yet another important reason. Niebuhr pointed out that a "communist China is not as immediate a strategic threat as imagined by some. The Communism of Asia is primarily an expression of nationalism of subject peoples and impoverished nations."[8] While famously arguing (in agreement with George Kennan) for containment of Soviet communism in Europe, he did not argue for a similar sort of "boots on the ground" containment of communism in Asia, including China. In a *Christianity and Society* piece, he added,

The line against communism in Europe must be rigorously held. But no line can be held in China. Communist victory is a reality. Furthermore, it offers no foreseeable strategic threat as in Europe. What is more to the point, however, is that communism in the whole of Asia is created by two great forces, the hopes and fears of the abjectly poor and the resentment of "colored" peoples who are in revolt either against their colonial status or against the moral arrogance of the white man.[9]

---

[6] RN, "British Experience and American Power," *Christianity and Crisis* 16 (May 14, 1956): 57; Davis and Good, p. 303.

[7] RN, "China and the United Nations," original manuscript sent to *The New Leader* for publication on March 26, 1957; as found in Box 15, Reinhold Niebuhr Papers, Manuscript Division, Library of Congress, Washington, DC.

[8] RN, "Streaks of Dawn in the Night," *Christian Century* (December 12, 1949): 162–4; and Fox, *Reinhold Niebuhr,* p. 240.

[9] RN, "Communism in China," *Christianity and Society* 15 (Winter 1949–1950): 6; also found in Charles C. Brown, *Niebuhr and His Age: Reinhold Niebuhr's Prophetic Role in the Twentieth Century* (Philadelphia: Trinity Press International, 1992), p. 148.

Whereas the Soviet Union had imposed communism in Eastern Europe and maintained it by force, Niebuhr viewed the spread of communism to China (and Vietnam) as being of a different order, as he makes clear here. In his view, communism was attractive to Asian peoples because of its focus on poverty alleviation and anticolonialism, issues, issues that they cared about deeply.

Westerners sometimes forget this point, or miss it altogether. Communism in Asia was anticolonial and anti-imperialistic, and it had a clear message about both the reality and origins of imperialism. It was a narrative that made sense to Vietnamese, Chinese, and others in the wake of their shared harsh experiences of imperialism and colonialism. Western liberalism for these peoples was associated with the very imperialist nations from which they sought to win their liberation. Niebuhr expressed his feelings about the potential of democracy taking root in the developing world as follows.

The essential problem which democracy faces in Asia and Africa can be briefly stated: Democracy is at once a more tainted and a more impossible ideal than we have realized. It has been tainted for the Asian and African nations because the democratic nations are also the technically most pow-erful nations, whose initial impact on the continents was imperialistic. Democracy seems an impossible ideal because it appears to lack the essen-tial conditions for attaining justice and stability, within the framework of a free society. Asians and Africans also usually lack the religiocultural foun-dation for individual freedom;[10] their religions either lose the individual in the social whole, the family, or the tribe (as in Confucianism and in the more primitive religions of Africa), or are mystical religions which seek for the annulment of individuality. But even if these peoples should manage to gain an appreciation of the value of the individual, more like our own, they must still prove that individual liberty, so much prized by the West, can be made compatible with *both* [emphasis in the original] justice and stability. Freedom is not an absolute value.[11]

Westerners see democracy as a universal value and freedom as an absolute value, attained by democracy. The Chinese and Asians more generally, as

---

[10] Today we know that democracy *has* come to Japan, Taiwan, South Korea, India, African states and others, so Niebuhr's statement here seems out of step with today's political reality.

[11] RN, "A Qualified Faith," *New Republic* 134 (February 13, 1956): 14–5; Davis and Good, pp. 310–11.

Niebuhr notes, tend to believe that while democracy is attractive, it "appears to lack the essential conditions for attaining justice and stability, within the framework of a free society." It therefore seems out of reach, an unaffordable luxury. The Chinese Communist Party has gone to great lengths to make sure that this narrative is widely believed, I might add—in other words, fostering the notion among its people that democracy is in fact out of reach, not for them (at least in the near term). This is just as true today as it ever was in the era when the Chinese Communist Party (CCP) ruled China. Because of China's national or social conditions (*guoqing*, 国情) and the success of China's Patriotic Education Campaign, coupled with comprehensive state control of media sources and content, most Chinese accept this as truth, despite the reality of a vibrant democracy in Taiwan and the democratic inclinations of some thinkers in China, such as Yu Keping.[12]

As it regards China, democracy seems as far away today as it did in Niebuhr's day. The vast majority of Mainland Chinese citizens simply cannot imagine freedom, as Westerners frame it, as being compatible with the economic success and stability they expect for their society. Here I am speaking generally about Chinese raised under the socialization of the CCP. Obviously, I think, there is no reason Chinese people cannot participate in and enjoy the fruits of democracy save that in Mainland China people have been taught that true (i.e., Liberal) democracy is incompatible with Chinese society. They have been led to believe that democracy is not possible in China and, in fact, that it is actually undesirable, considering the West's many social ills (drug abuse, crime, sexual unorthodoxy, family breakdown, racism, social tensions, etc.). These talking points are presented to the people as what the government would label the liabilities of political liberalism. Despite the truths in some of these critiques of Western liberalism, most Mainland Chinese have actually never understood democracy nor the fact that democracy is the most important guarantor of prosperity, justice, stability, and the rule of law, if done right. Moreover, in my experience,[13] few Chinese have understood the dangers that a lack of democracy poses to justice, stability, and the rule of law in their own society in the long run. Vested political interests in China (i.e., the CCP) have worked hard to make sure the Chinese people do not understand this, lest they find democracy attractive and press for it.

---

[12] Keping Yu, *Democracy Is a Good Thing: Essays on Politics, Society and Culture in Contemporary China* (Washington, DC: Brookings Institution, 2011).

[13] I would note that, in addition to being a political scientist and an IR specialist, I am a Sinologist and have lived and worked in China for over 14 years at the time of writing.

Turning to a discussion of international relations and global communism, we find that Niebuhr's responses to the Korean and Vietnamese wars
were indicative of his views of the different challenges communism posed to
U.S. security in Europe and in Asia. He argued emphatically that the United
States should *not* get involved in a land war on the Asian continent. While
in the Korean case the Soviet Union had, as in Eastern Europe, installed a
pro-Soviet, communist government, he believed anti-imperialist nationalism appealed to Koreans just as it did to Chinese and Vietnamese. More
importantly, he feared Chinese intervention if the United States got involved.
His fears were realized, of course, for after the United States crossed the 38th
parallel and approached China's borders, the Chinese finally decided to enter
the war, and the United States found itself fighting not only North Korea but
China has well. Niebuhr saw Asian communism (North Korea's, China's,
Vietnam's) as primarily nationalistic, and not truly doctrinaire communism,
so he differentiated it from the Soviet threat. He believed the United States
had to take a stand against communism in Europe, even if it meant a land war,
but that the United States should avoid a land war against communist powers
in Asia. He said that the "free world can live if we lose Asia, but we cannot
live in security if Russia should come into possession of the economic and
technical resources of Europe."[14] At one point, he even proposed abandoning
Taiwan to the Chinese communists in exchange for a cease-fire in Korea.
This proposal led some to question his judgment and even his patriotism.[15]

In like manner, Niebuhr was famous for his opposition to the U.S. war in
Vietnam, where China was also involved in the early years of the conflict,
prior to the Sino-Soviet split, when Vietnam leaned to one side (the Soviet
side) and China was subsequently pushed out of the picture by Hanoi. Joining
the other classical Realists of the day (e.g., Kennan, Morgenthau, Thompson),
he vehemently opposed the U.S. war in Vietnam, maintaining that the United
States had slipped into hubris and had been blinded by its own sense of self-
importance. He argued with the other Realists that U.S. interests would be
better served if it would stay out of the war.[16] While he endeared himself to
antiwar intellectuals of the day, Niebuhr fell out of favor in Washington as a
result.

[14] RN, Letter to the Editor, "Our Position in Asia," *The New York Times*, December 23, 1950, and
found in Fox, *Reinhold Niebuhr*, p. 241.

[15] For more, see Fox, *Reinhold Niebuhr*, pp. 241–2.

[16] See Fox, *Reinhold Niebuhr*, p. 241. RN, Letter to the Editor, "MacArthur Statements Contrasted,"
The New York Times, December 6, 1950; RN, Letter to the Editor, "Our Position in Asia," *The New York
Times*, December 23, 1950.

The USSR and Today's China Compared

It is clear that at the time of writing China is the only world power with the potential to be a true peer competitor to the United States in the coming decades. While there are many incompatibilities when we compare today's China with the Soviet Union (and these will be addressed), it is still instructive to look back at the period when the Soviet Union rose, following World War II, to become a nondemocratic peer competitor to the United States, and to compare the USSR then to the People's Republic of China today. As mentioned earlier, during the Marxist phase of his intellectual development (the 1920s and early 1930s), Niebuhr was sympathetic to Soviet communism. As the excesses and violence of Stalinism became more and more apparent in the 1930s, however, he became increasingly critical of Stalin and Soviet communism. As he moved out of an explicit Marxist orientation into his Christian Realist phase, Niebuhr began to see Soviet communism in an increasingly ominous light. In particular, he noted that what made the Soviet Union particularly dangerous in his view was the universalism of its aspirations, its universalistic "creed." Communism was an ideology that was in fact an all-encompassing social, economic, and political program, a belief system that demanded the absolute obedience and devotion of its adherents and/or subjects. It was "evangelical" in nature, meant to reach every far-flung corner of this earth, with a gospel of social, economic, and political liberation and equality.

Despite its rosy platitudes about egalitarianism and its bid to create a "workers' paradise," Niebuhr very bluntly called international communism "the most dynamic and demonic world politico-religious movement in history."[17] He used the words "dynamic and demonic" because he saw communism as suppressing freedom and human initiative, removing political accountability between government and people, and allowing a single party or even a single ruler to rule with absolute power, which he saw as extremely dangerous given his views of human nature (to be elaborated upon further later in this chapter). In reference to the religious allusions of the statement above, in Niebuhr's view, "Communism, in its pure form, is a secularized religious apocalyptic creed."[18] Considering the Chinese context in the 1960s,

[17] RN, "Our Moral and Spiritual Resources for International Cooperation," *Social Action* 22 (February 1956): 5–12; in Good and Davis, p. 240; and in *"World Crisis and American Responsibility; Nine Essays,"* Ernest W. Lefever, ed. (New York: Association Press, 1958).

[18] RN, "The Communist Party and Russia," *Christianity and Society* 9 (Spring, 1944): 8; and in Good and Davis, p. 261.

calling communism religious is not much of a stretch, given the at times literal worship of Mao that occurred in China. Mao's picture typically was hung in almost every home and office; Mao's "Little Red Book" was studied, memorized, and recited; a supernatural veneration was accorded Mao. While few venerate Mao in such a way today, it is still not uncommon to see a decorative photo of Mao hanging from the rear-view mirror of a taxi for good luck, much as a Catholic will display the St. Christopher image as protection for the traveler. Niebuhr adds to his description of religiocommunism: "Hell knows no fury like the fanaticism of the prophets of a secular religion who have become the priest-kings of an utopian state."[19] He explained: "the communist movement has managed to compound power lusts with utopian dreams in such a way as to give its totalitarian practices a dynamism and a plausibility which no one could have foreseen in this age which prides itself on its enlightenment."[20]

While nationalism itself could be seen as antithetical to this universal creed (and was regarded as such by many communist leaders), Niebuhr observed that many communist parties tapped into nationalism for the advancement of the greater leftist cause. This was true of leftist Russians, Koreans, Chinese, Vietnamese, and others historically. Niebuhr had an appreciation for the appeal of nationalism to Asian peoples and for the utility of leftist creeds to nationalist political movements in Asia. He argued that this was the best way to understand communist successes in nations such as China and Vietnam, that it was not so much communist ideology in and of itself, but the nationalism it came to be yoked to under leaders such as Kim, Mao, and Ho that provided the strong motivation for leaders and peoples to embrace communism in the 1950s, 1960s, and 1970s during communism's heyday. He notes that Marx himself would have opposed, and would have been surprised by, Stalin's use of (Russian) nationalism to stoke the fires of continuing revolution (and repression) in the USSR, for again, communism is a universalistic, not particularistic/nationalistic, belief system.[21] Like Stalin, Ho, Mao, and others found it quite amenable to nationalism, revolutionary movement formation, and regime maintenance, however. Niebuhr understood this well, perhaps better than many American policymakers as it regarded both the

---

[19] RN, "Hazards and Resources," *Virginia Quarterly Review* 25 (Spring 1949): 204; and Davis and Good, p. 262.

[20] RN, "Our Moral and Spiritual Resources for International Cooperation," *Social Action* 22 (February 1956): 5–12; and in Davis and Good, p. 240.

[21] RN, *The Structure of Nations and Empires* (New York: Scribner's, 1959/1977), p. 241.

"communist takeover" of China and, later, the successes of the communists in Vietnam.

Today's China does *not* have a pure, universal communist creed, but instead has what the Chinese call "socialism with Chinese characteristics" and many other allusions to Chinese exceptionalism. This is quite the opposite of Soviet Marxist universalism and its sense of being the international avant-garde. There has been talk among academics, pundits, and policymakers of a "Beijing consensus," defined as a state-dominated market economy paired with a harsh, illiberal, authoritarian political system.[22] However, Chinese government spokespersons say there is no "Beijing consensus"; they argue instead that China's political and economic system is unique to China and is not readily transferrable to other countries. While it may be true that China's economic successes in the past 35 years may be an encouragement to dictators elsewhere and may in some ways justify some of their repression as they experiment with some of China's political and economic methods, there is no evidence that Beijing is in fact actively promoting such a model outside of China.[23]

Consequently, China can in no way be compared to the Soviet Union in terms of the danger that it will spread its "creed" to other nations and actively overthrow other nations. The China of the 1960s, with Mao's radical foreign policy,[24] was comparable to Soviet "leftist evangelism" as Mao sought to export the Maoist revolution around the world, but that policy was abandoned in the 1970s and has not been resurrected. Robert Kagan has made the case that China and Russia may be indirectly undermining democracy by being models of "antidemocracy"—that their relative success (especially prior to the drop in oil prices and the world's sanctions against Russia over its adventures in Ukraine, when Russia was riding high) might be seen as "proof" to autocrats that some degree of market economics could be combined with statist economic policy and authoritarian politics with good

[22] See Joshua Cooper Ramo, *The Beijing Consensus* (London: Foreign Policy Centre, 2004); Stephen Halperin, *The Beijing Consensus: How China's Authoritarian Model Will Dominate the Twenty-First Century* (New York: Basic Books, 2010); and Scott Kennedy, "The Myth of the Beijing Consensus," *Journal of Contemporary China* 19/65 (June 2010): 461–77.

[23] I will note, however, that for the first time since Mao a Chinese leader has suggested that China's model could be suitable for, and an inspiration to, other nations. For more, see Xi Jinping's speech at the 19th Party Congress of the CCP in October 2017.

[24] For more information on this phase of Chinese foreign policy, see Peter Van Ness, *Revolution and Foreign Policy: Peking's Support for Wars of National Liberation* (Berkeley: University of California Press, 1970).

effect.[25] This is certainly problematic, but it does not compare to the threat the Soviet Union posed as a bulwark against freedom and democracy.

It is also true that China cannot be compared to the Soviet Union in terms of the geopolitical threat it poses to the United States and the Western powers today. The Soviet Union had occupied Eastern Europe and North Korea, it was orchestrating revolution in Vietnam, Africa, Latin America, and elsewhere, against the interests of the Western powers, and it could be argued against the interests of the peoples in those targeted nations. China has no such expansionist policy today. It *does* have designs on Taiwan, but that is a unique historical case. Taiwan was an island once ruled by China, but it separated from the Mainland because of the outcome of the wars with Japan, the Chinese Civil War, and then the Cold War. China might be said to have expansionist tendencies in terms of its maritime policy in the East and South China Seas, but even at its most aggressive, China's policies in recent years would not compare to those of the Soviet Union during the heyday of the Cold War.

I do not think Niebuhr would today compare China to the former Soviet Union in terms of either ideological or military expansionist threat potential. That does not mean he would be dovish toward China. On the contrary, I believe he would be quite hawkish regarding today's China. Let me now explain why.

Four Reasons Niebuhr Would Be Hawkish Toward Today's China

Following is a discussion of four factors that complicate China's ability to rise peacefully. In other words, I believe that, based on Niebuhr's perspective, it would be highly unlikely for China to rise peacefully, and there are our key reasons I believe Niebuhr would be hawkish about China today: (1) the regime type and structure of China's political system; (2) the master narrative of the PRC under the Chinese Communist Party today; (3) the inescapable role of human nature, and (4) the opportunities China's growth in material capabilities (i.e., and related defense spending) presents Chinese leaders.

[25] Robert Kagan, *The World America Made* (New York: Alfred A. Knopf, 2012).

1. The Regime Type and Structure
of China's Political System

Were Niebuhr around today to comment on the 21st-century rise of China, I believe the first factor he would identify as making China a potentially difficult power to deal with, from the perspective of the Western democracies, would be China's regime type and the consequent power structure of its political system. In his writings during the World War II and Cold War eras, one of the things Niebuhr identified about both the Soviet and Nazi German regimes that made them particularly dangerous, was their authoritarian/totalitarian regime types.[26] They did not allow democratic elections or regular political participation,[27] they were ruthlessly authoritarian (totalitarian), they were inherently insecure regimes that crushed dissent, they murdered opponents, they allowed little or no media freedom, they ruthlessly brainwashed their citizens with mind-numbing propaganda, and they generally ruled with an iron fist. I would like to point out here that talking about politics or regime type is not anathema to classical Realists, as Jonathan Kirshner has pointed out, but rather, "politics matters."[28]

While today's China cannot be compared either to the USSR of the Stalin era or to Nazi Germany, the CCP's rule from at least the late 1950s to the mid-1970s was no less draconian, brutal, or even totalitarian. Yet importantly, in today's China the CCP holds the tools of state repression in a deeply authoritarian system that is still largely unaccountable to the people, which means that many of the political problems of Stalinist Russia and Nazi Germany remain in today's China as well. The CCP does not allow democratic elections or regular political participation. It is an inherently insecure regime that crushes dissent, freely imprisons opponents,[29] allows little or no true media freedom, systematically brainwashes its citizens with mind-numbing propaganda, generally rules with an iron fist, and is ruthlessly authoritarian.

---

[26] Nazi Germany can be considered totalitarian for most of Hitler's tenure, while the USSR was in and out of totalitarianism, but certainly totalitarian during Stalin's rule, as Hannah Arendt has famously argued. Hannah Arendt, *The Origins of Totalitarianism* (New York: Schocken Books, 1951).

[27] In the German case, of course, the Nazis came to power by democratic election in 1933, but within months of their being elected, they dismantled the democracy they had taken over and did not allow democratic participation or accountability again while they ruled.

[28] Jonathan Kirshner, "The Tragedy of Offensive Realism: Classical Realism and the Rise of China," *European Journal of International Relations* 18/1 (2010): 65.

[29] Chris Buckley, "China Is Detaining Muslims in Vast Numbers. The Goal: 'Transformation,'" *The New York Times*, (September 8, 2018; https://www.nytimes.com/2018/09/08/world/asia/china-uighur-muslim-detention-camp.html).

Niebuhr explains in a very general sense why communist parties such as China's are so draconian and incapable of tolerating dissent. He starts his explanation by noting that all governing authorities strive for national unity as a core element of national strength. "The nation is a corporate unity, held together much more by force and emotion than by mind. Since there can be no ethical action without self-criticism," ethical conduct for governments is less likely than ethical conduct for individuals because "self-criticism is a kind of inner disunity, which the feeble mind of a nation finds difficulty in distinguishing from dangerous forms of inner conflict."[30] True to a degree of any nation, hence the moral dualism[31] Niebuhr famously identified, the problem is particularly acute in the Chinese communist regime in that the lack of democratic legitimacy means it will always be insecure politically as long as it disallows democratic freedoms. It can never be sure that it has the people's support, so it must clamp down on dissent, whether in print, in educational circles,[32] on the web, or in public displays. In the last few years, it has become apparent that China's regime has become more draconian and more, not less, authoritarian in its patterns of rule.[33]

Niebuhr often discussed the problems of the Soviet and Nazi German regimes and their implications for the democratic powers. In discussing the fact that both the USSR and the United States called their systems democratic (as does China, we might note), Niebuhr noted that the Soviets would not allow a real debate about what democracy was.

> [T]he Russians are having no part in the debate. They seal off every organ of communication that would make an exchange of interpretations possible. . . . It is precisely because Russian communism legitimatizes a corrupt

---

[30] RN, *Moral Man and Immoral Society* (New York: Scribner's, 1932), p. 88.

[31] I speak here of Niebuhr's expectations of the potential for moral behavior from individuals (higher) as opposed to groups/nations (lower), as indicated by the title of his 1932 book, *Moral Man and Immoral Society*, which he later stated should have been titled *Immoral Man and Less Moral Society*.

[32] Tom Phillips, "China Universities Must Become Communist Party 'Strongholds,' Says Xi Jinping," *The Guardian* (December 9, 2016; https://www.theguardian.com/world/2016/dec/09/china-universities-must-become-communist-party-strongholds-says-xi-jinping).

[33] See Elizabeth Economy, "China's Imperial President: Xi Jinping Tightens His Grip," *Foreign Affairs* (November/December, 2014): 80–91; David Shambaugh, "The Coming Chinese Crack-up," *The Wall Street Journal* (March 6, 2015), accessed from https://www.wsj.com/articles/the-coming-chinese-crack-up-1425659198; Kerry Brown, *CEO, China: The Rise of Xi Jinping* (New York: I. B. Tauris, 2016); Elizabeth Economy, *The Third Revolution: Xi Jinping and the New Chinese State* (New York: Oxford University Press, 2018); and Nicholas Lardy, *The State Strikes Back: The End of the Economic Reform in China?* (Washington, DC: Peterson Institute for International Economics, 2019).

politics by utopian illusions that it is so dangerous to the world and so blinding to its devotees.[34]

Just as was the case in Soviet Russia, the Chinese leadership does not allow debates about democracy or any discussions about anything that would challenge the dominant narratives of the Party. Its censorship system and patriotic education are probably the most advanced the world has ever seen. The Chinese people are increasingly cut off from the rest of the world by the great firewall and the highly sophisticated system of censorship built by the CCP to manage narratives about topics it deems important to state security and regime stability. In this respect, what Niebuhr said about the USSR is true about today's People's Republic of China as well.

Niebuhr also discussed the party machinery and dictatorship that Lenin set up in the USSR. Although Lenin was "more subtle than Stalin," Niebuhr nonetheless saw problems, for

> without real freedom, either within the party or in the community, there was nothing to prevent a shrewd manipulator, Stalin, from bringing all the organs of power into his own hands, from liquidating even the generation of newer oligarchs—many of whom owed their positions to his favor and had helped him to eliminate his foes. It is this absolute monopoly of power which proved to be so vicious and which is not defined by Khrushchev's [the Soviet premier during 1953–1964] euphemism, "the cult of personality."[35]

The centralized power structure, the coverup of information that might expose dirty deeds, and the near-absolute lack of accountability of the regime/party/leader to the people (or even to the party leadership) made the Soviet Union particularly dangerous in Niebuhr's eyes. There are in fact many parallels to today's Chinese political system, and were Niebuhr still with us today, he would surely not miss them.

Reading Niebuhr's description of Stalin's takeover of the Soviet party and state apparatus, though not suggesting absolute equivalency in quality or degree, one cannot help but think of China today: President Xi Jinping

---

[34] RN, "The Quaker Way," *Christianity and Society*, (Winter 1949–1950), as found in Davis and Good, p. 296; and RN, *Love and Justice*, edited by D. B. Robertson (Westminster, UK: John Knox Press, 1957), pp. 297–8.

[35] RN, "Is This the Collapse of a Tyranny?" *Christianity and Society* 21 (Summer 1956): 4–6; and Good and Davis, 263.

has consolidated an enormous amount of power since he assumed the presidency in 2012. He came to power following a major high-level scandal and the dramatic arrest/purge of his primary competitor for rule, Bo Xilai (and his all-powerful lieutenant, spy-master Zhou Yongkang).[36] During this period of uncertainty, Xi himself[37] disappeared for a short time, and there was a delayed outcome at the Beidaihe leadership retreat prior to the18th Party Congress in 2012 where the new leadership was supposed to be selected. Xi was ultimately christened that year as the new leader of China. China has three major power positions: first and foremost is the office of the CCP general secretary; second is the chairmanship of the Central Military Commission, and third is the presidency, representing power over the party, the military, and the state apparatus, respectively. Mr. Xi holds all three posts, and under his rule China has seen a tightening of state control over propaganda, security, the Internet, religion, and many other facets of life in China, as many have observed.[38] Perhaps more importantly, with the 19th Party Congress held in 2017, we learned that the Chinese constitution would be altered so that Xi Jinping's name and thought would be enshrined there and the top leaders would no longer face term limits. This was a significant change considering that these term limits were one of the most important reforms of the post-Mao era. All of this has paved the way for President Xi to rule indefinitely, with most experts believing he will rule past the previously normal two terms and on into a third term, with possibly more to come.[39]

While Niebuhr would likely concede that China today does not have the messianic impulse or ideology of the old USSR, nor does it appear to have the expansionist tendencies of the Soviet Union during the Cold War, the

[36] Zhou at the time might be compared to J. Edgar Hoover at the height of his power in U.S. politics. For more on the fall of Bo Xilai, see John Garnaut, *The Rise and Fall of the House of Bo* (New York: Penguin, 2012).

[37] Tania Branigan, "Xi Jinping, China's Expected Future Leader, Has Not Been Seen for 10 days," *The Guardian* (September 11, 2012; https://www.theguardian.com/world/2012/sep/11/xi-jinping-china-not-seen).

[38] For example, see Elizabeth C. Economy, "China's Imperial President: Xi Jinping Tightens His Grip," *Foreign Affairs* (December 1, 2014; http://www.foreignaffairs.com/articles/142201/elizabeth-c-economy/chinas-imperial-president); David Shambaugh, "The Coming Chinese Crack-up," *The Wall Street Journal* (March 6, 2015; https://www.wsj.com/articles/the-coming-chinese-crack-up-1425659198); Elizabeth Economy, *The Third Revolution: Xi Jinping and the New Chinese State* (New York: Oxford University Press, 2018), etc.

[39] David Dollar, "Xi's Power Grab Gives a Short-term Boost with Long-term Ramifications," *Order from Chaos*, Brookings Institution (February 27, 2018; https://www.brookings.edu/blog/order-from-chaos/2018/02/27/xis-power-grab-gives-a-short-term-boost-with-long-term-ramifications); Susan Shirk, "China in Xi's 'New Era': The Return to Personalistic Rule," *Journal of Democracy* 29/2 (April 2018; https://www.journalofdemocracy.org/article/china-xi's-"new-era"-return-personalistic-rule), pp. 22–36.

highly centralized and undemocratic nature of the Chinese Communist regime described here would be a source of grave concern to him. He would remember too well the lessons of the patterns of the undemocratic regimes of the past century, regimes like Hitler's Germany, Stalin's USSR, and the military clique that ruled Japan during World War II. Niebuhr argued against idealists who said the Cold War was simply a misunderstanding between peoples:

> The Russian people are, in fact, wonderful people. But this sentence makes it appear that the primary difficulty lies in misunderstandings between the peoples, which is not a fact.... [On the call for more exchanges between the USSR and the USA, Niebuhr said . . .] [t]he Russian dictatorship cannot afford these interchanges. It keeps up a constant barrage of propaganda that makes the noncommunist world appear to be perishing in a mire of misery, and therefore it cannot afford to let the Russian people discover the truth.[40]

In the same way, I think Niebuhr would agree that the Chinese are a wonderful people with a fantastic culture and a positive and profound civilizational influence on the world. Yet, like "the Russian [Soviet] dictatorship," the Chinese dictatorship "keeps up a constant barrage of propaganda" portraying the United States and other Western powers as corrupt, hypocritical, and imperialistic, making democracy look like something undesirable, irrational, debauched, unstable, something the Chinese people should not want[41] (and could not afford, even if admitting it did have merits). Like the former Soviet regime, the Chinese Communist Party "cannot afford to let the [Chinese] people discover the truth." With its general lack of democratic accountability, which Democratic Peace theorists suggest make foreign policy adventurism more likely, the CCP has considerable ability to shape the behavior of China's citizens at home and abroad in ways that ensure domestic support for most any foreign policy they advocate, and can manifest themselves in hypernationalist, antiforeign, anti-Liberal ways at home and abroad, as events in Australia surrounding protesting Hong Kong students there in

---

[40] RN, "The Quaker Way," *Christianity and Society* (Winter 1949–1950); and *Love and Justice*, p. 297.

[41] Bethany Allen-Ebrahimian, "How China Won the War against Western Media," *Foreign Policy* (March 4, 2016). https://foreignpolicy.com/2016/03/04/china-won-war-western-media-censorship-propaganda-communist-party).

2019,[42] and U.S. data about Chinese students in the United States[43] make evident. All of this will have important implications for China's people and for China's relations with the world for many years to come.

2. The Master Narrative of the PRC Today

The second factor that would have led to Niebuhr's being hawkish toward China today is the nature of China's current master narrative—in other words, the CCP's self-proclaimed raison d'etre, its mission, its self-styled narrative about its place in history. I draw here from Peter Gries[44] and Zheng Wang[45] primarily, as I believe they have best captured the dynamic I have observed in Chinese political life and Chinese foreign policy.

Peter Gries, writing about Chinese nationalism, paints a picture of a very insecure, authoritarian regime that has increasingly come to rely on nationalism as a way to shore up support for itself. The regime has come to draw heavily upon what Gries calls "the victimization narrative," which is based on the *true* story of China's victimhood from 1839 until 1949, what is often called China's "hundred years of humiliation." The year 1839 marks the onset of the Opium Wars with Great Britain, in which China was forced into a series of unequal treaties that led to the ceding of Hong Kong to Britain and the opening up of special treaty ports to foreign traders operating under the principle of extraterritoriality. These ports were on Chinese territory but were not subject to Chinese law, so foreign operators where in effect above the law in these territories and beyond the reach and/or accountability of Chinese law and authority. This period of victimhood continued in 1860 when foreign armies invaded Peking, China's capital, and ransacked the Yuanming Yuan imperial gardens (and again in 1900 when foreign armies again invaded Beijing to punish Chinese authorities for the Boxer Rebellion, which killed

---

[42] See Andreas Fulda, "Beijing Is Weaponizing Nationalism Against Hong Kongers: Hong Kong's Unique Identity Threatens Xi Jinping's Rhetoric of Greatness" *Foreign Policy* (July 29, 2019; https://foreignpolicy.com/2019/07/29/beijing-is-weaponizing-nationalism-against-hong-kongers).

[43] Marie Royce presents data showing that 84 percent of Chinese students in the United States rely solely on Chinese websites for news about the United States and continue to use state-managed WeChat for their main form of communication. U.S. Assistant Secretary of State for Educational and Cultural Affairs Marie Royce, "The U.S. Welcomes Chinese Students," EducationUSA Forum, Washington, DC (July 30, 2019).

[44] Peter Hays Gries, *China's New Nationalism: Pride, Politics, and Diplomacy* (Berkeley: University of California Press, 2004).

[45] Zheng Wang, *Never Forget National Humiliation: Historical Memory in Chinese Politics and Foreign Relations* (New York: Columbia University Press, 2012).

foreign citizens and harmed foreign interests in China). The story of victimhood continued with 1894–1895 when Japan imposed war and then defeat upon China, taking as booty the island of Taiwan. This was a great humiliation given that China had always been at the apex of power in Asia as lord of the tributary system, and Japan the lesser power that paid tribute to China and its emperors. Now it was Japan that had taught China a lesson in military and economic modernization. China's victimhood deepened with the end of World War I and the ceding of former German holdings in China to Japan instead of being returned to Chinese sovereignty. China's struggles at the hands of foreign powers continued in 1931 when Japan invaded northeast China and set up a puppet state called Manchukuo. Then in 1937 Japan launched a full-scale invasion of the rest of China, including the horrible rape and murder fest in the Chinese capital of Nanking.[46] China's humiliation was complete. It was, in the master narrative, only in 1949 that China's people "stood up," as Mao put it, throwing off the yoke of foreign imperialism and Chinese rulers under the influence of foreign powers (the latter is how Mao viewed Chiang Kai-shek and the Nationalist regime).

The story recounted here is a *true* story, a *real* history the Chinese people endured.[47] Although the term *narrative* is used, it is not intended that this be read as only a story or just someone's interpretation. These things happened. The Chinese people suffered immensely. China's dignity was squashed for a long period of time. And now it has been restored in many respects. These are very real sentiments shared by the vast majority of the Chinese people.

Chinese scholar Zheng Wang captures something few outside of China and perhaps most Chinese themselves have not well understood. Wang argues that the Chinese Communist Party has gone through several iterations of narratives about its raison d'etre, its own telling of its historical importance and mission. He contends that the first stage was revolution and the liberation of Mainland China from subjugation by foreign and bourgeois "running dogs of the imperialists." The second stage came with the passing of Chairman Mao and the rise of Deng Xiaoping's pragmatism in the Four Modernizations. Put simply, economic modernization was the CCP's raison d'etre during this second stage, which lasted until only very recently

---

[46] See Iris Chang, *The Rape of Nanking: The Forgotten Holocaust of WW II* (New York: Basic Books, 1997).

[47] I think this is an accurate history, and I sympathize greatly with the suffering of the Chinese people during this time. My only difference of opinion with this narrative might be that I'd mark the end of the foreign encroachment at 1945 and the defeat of the Japanese, not 1949, as I don't see Chiang Kai-Shek as a puppet of foreign imperialists.

in Wang's telling. In very recent years, and especially evident now with Xi's rise, a new narrative is being written for the CCP. I don't think it necessarily means the Party's legitimacy is no longer linked to economic performance, but as the nation has reached new heights of economic modernization, the Party leaders have sought a new narrative to supplement and perhaps replace the economic narrative. Wang argues that this has been especially important as leaders have considered the possibility of economic slowdown, or even economic meltdown given the vicissitudes of the global and Chinese economies in periods such as those represented by the economic crises of 1997, 2008, and 2015.

The new (third) narrative, the new raison d'etre, of the Chinese Communist Party is what Wang calls "never forget national humiliation,"[48] or put another way, the party's role is that of the "most throughgoing patriot," as he puts it, the last and best bulwark against foreign encroachment and greater national humiliation at the hands of foreign forces. This is to say, nationalism is the new driving force, but more specifically the Party is the only salvation, the only protection for the Chinese people and of Chinese territory from the humiliation produced by foreign attacks and foreign-imposed indignities such as those suffered by the Chinese during the hundred years of national humiliation. The Patriotic Education Movement has become the primary socialization tool of the party–state to inculcate in its people's minds, hearts, and memories the humiliations of China's past, fostering a belief (a knowledge) that the CCP is the force that defeated the Japanese and other threatening foreign forces and that drove out the Kuomintang (KMT)/Nationalists who failed to stand up for China's dignity but in fact compromised too often with foreign powers (Japan and the United States in particular). In fact, it was only Mao Zedong and the CCP who finally and completely cast aside the shackles of China's subjugation to such powers and allowed the Chinese people to stand up, as Mao said on October 1, 1949, at the south balcony of the Forbidden City, a memory indelibly etched in the minds of every Chinese citizen. China had stood up.

The truth is not quite so simple, however. The KMT *did* fight the Japanese, and more often and harder than the CCP, who for the most part (with a few important exceptions) rode out the war against Japan in the wilds of Yan'an, rebuilding for the fight against the KMT that came with the end of the war against Japan. It was largely the Americans, and to a lesser extent the KMT,

---

[48] *Wuwang guochi* or 勿忘国耻 in Chinese.

who carried the battle against Japan in the end, but this is not part of the master narrative and is not well known by most people in China. In fact, the CCP did *not* defeat Japan. The United States did, with a supporting role from Chiang Kai-shek and the KMT, whose forces held thousands of Japanese troops at bay on the Mainland, which helped facilitate the American island-hopping strategy that eventually, along with Washington's fire-bombing and atomic bombing strategies, brought Japan to its knees in 1945.

The implications of this "never forget national humiliation" narrative are important, as Wang argues effectively. For example, because of this narrative the CCP cannot afford to compromise on issues like Taiwan or the Diaoyu Islands, the latter being disputed territories claimed by both Japan and China. The South China Sea issue takes on greater meaning and urgency as well, having also been cast as a "core interest" of China's in the statements of at least some Chinese officials.[49] This is another example of China's ancient territories that have been (and are being) encroached upon by foreign powers. And talk about the true autonomy of Xinjiang or Tibet is out of the question. Moreover, backing up those foreign powers is the United States, who in the Maoist days prior to 1971 and again in recent years was seen as a primary "evil" in its efforts to block China's return to great power status, to reclaim its rightful position among the nations, according to this master narrative. Wang's "never forget national humiliation" narrative portrays Japan and the United States in particular as the forces that have brought the greatest humiliation upon China and are the greatest forces blocking China's regaining of Taiwan, the Diaoyu Islands, and other maritime features that Beijing maintains have been China's "since time immemorial." This state of affairs, in Wang's telling, makes for a very prickly China, a China that will not (cannot!) compromise on such territorial issues now that this narrative has come to the fore.

Wang's thesis is, in effect, that the dynamics of domestic politics, in this case the Party's master narrative, has shaped or even determined its foreign policy choices. Consequently, these territorial disputes and cases involving in particular Japan and the United States, have become extremely sensitive and are very provocative to the Chinese, making China much more sensitive about such issues than would have been the case without the master narrative presented here. This master narrative is propagated in state-run

---

[49] See Gregory J. Moore, "Bismarck or Wilhelm? China's Peaceful Rise and the South China Sea," *Asian Perspective* 42 (2018): 265–83.

education and in state-run media, and is basically inculcated in the Chinese people from cradle to grave. Censorship, net nannies, and the "*wumaodang*" (or fifty cent party)[50] shape public opinion on such issues that are important to Party leaders to ensure that the master narrative is upheld and is not challenged. Recent protests against Mainland Chinese policies in Hong Kong have also elicited a strong resort to nationalism according to some observers.[51] Nationalism, then, has become a driving force, an institutionalized part of China's political and foreign policy process.

Niebuhr had a lot to say about nationalism in his day, and his words are helpful as we consider China today. Niebuhr noted how, in the Soviet Russian case, what made the USSR particularly formidable was the "meretricious compound of Russian nationalism with communist dreams of world dominion; and the creation of a tyrannical oligarchy devoid of either internal or external checks upon its power."[52] In China's case, while today's China does not have the religio-fanatic component of communism Niebuhr mentions, it does have the nationalist component, and perhaps because of the lack of Marxist-Leninist zeal and the messianic message it brings, nationalism is relied upon in today's China *even more so* than was the case in Russia under Soviet communism.

This kind of nationalism at the hands of an authoritarian party–state also means that democratic reforms and the fruits of the "democratic peace" are also unlikely to be seen in the Chinese case in the near term. Niebuhr had interesting observations about this issue as well. In 1952, in discussing why democracy had not found fertile ground in the nonindustrial nations, speaking specifically of "the great traditional cultures of the Orient," Niebuhr observed that "[t]hey combined very refined cultures with very low forms of social integration, the village and the family remaining the only communities of significant loyalty."[53] For a non-Asian scholar, Niebuhr offers a profound understanding of Eastern/Chinese culture, social structure, and politics here. He discusses the historical lack of individualism under Confucianism (noting that individuals were always subordinate to the family, the group, the

---

[50] This term refers to a group of people who monitor the Internet for the state, shaping opinion and guiding the conversation where possible in social media spaces. They are supposedly being paid *wumao* (50 cents, rmb) for each post, or act.

[51] Andreas Fulda, "Beijing Is Weaponizing Nationalism Against Hong Kongers: Hong Kong's Unique Identity Threatens Xi Jinping's Rhetoric of Greatness," *Foreign Policy*, (July 29, 2019; https://foreignpolicy.com/2019/07/29/beijing-is-weaponizing-nationalism-against-hong-kongers).

[52] RN, "Hazards and Resources," *Virginia Quarterly Review* 25 (Spring 1949): 204; and Davis and Good, p. 262.

[53] RN, *The Irony of American History* (New York: Scribner's, 1952), p. 115.

village, etc.), and explains how and why Confucianism was able to offer little resistance to communism (which completely undermined it), when it came.

> Its [Confucianism's] lack of historical dynamism makes it an easy prey to communism, particularly among the youth; and the lack of individual independence and the strong emphasis upon prudential rather than heroic virtue, predisposes even opponents of communism to bow to its power. . . . Resentment against feudal injustice easily prompts the youth of decaying feudal societies to espouse the cause of a new collectivist culture, which promises justice. They do not understand the tyrannical consequences of this new form of totalitarianism. But even if they did understand, they cannot be expected to feel the loss of liberty with the same sense of grievous deprivation as in the West.[54]

Niebuhr was correct, and this same penchant toward prudentialism makes it difficult for anyone in China to be an instigator of political change today.

> A democratic society requires some capacity of the individual both to defy social authority on occasion when its standards violate his conscience and to relate himself to larger and larger communities than the primary family group.[55]

Few foreigners understand these truths, and in fact it is rather amazing that a Western, non-Asianist like Niebuhr was able to detect these nuances in Chinese culture and politics and so accurately pinpoint the key issues at stake. A democratic transition in China does not seem likely in the near future, nor would it be easy if it became possible. Westerners and Chinese liberals must face this reality. At the same time, Americans and other Liberals must not lose hope in the universal value of democracy, pluralism, human rights, rule of law, and freedom. They are indeed as important for the Chinese as they are for anyone else. In due time, this fact will be realized in China, from the cities to the villages, from the halls of academe to the noodle shops on the side streets.

Until that time comes, however, the CCP will continue to run the show in China, as far as we can see. While China has come a long way politically and,

---

[54] RN, *The Irony of American History*, pp. 125 and 126.
[55] RN, *The Irony of American History*, pp. 125–6.

in particular, economically in recent years, the challenges presented by CCP rule will remain. Niebuhr's observations have shed light on some of the most profound elements of the challenge these realities will likely present to the United States and the other democracies.

3. The Role of Human Nature

Third, and perhaps most fundamental for Niebuhr, is the role of the inescapable realities of human nature. While, as Waltz[56] and others have pointed out, human nature is a constant, the point here is that the realities of human nature would make Niebuhr skeptical about Chinese claims that it will rise peacefully or Chinese assertions that Chinese society is more "harmonious" in nature and its people more peaceful than others. Human nature would, therefore, provide another reason Niebuhr would be hawkish toward China as its growth and power continues to reach new heights, for he would not see it as highly likely that China would be able to rise peacefully. He would reject exceptionalist arguments that suggest China is fundamentally different from other powers. His would not be a critique of the Chinese people or culture, but simply, as Mearsheimer has said, a tragic part of international political reality (though for different reasons than Mearsheimer has argued).[57] Niebuhr very famously argued that human nature is a key variable in coming to an accurate understanding of human (and interstate) behavior in any social, cultural, or political context. One observer said of human nature that it was "the basis of his [Niebuhr's] whole thought."[58] Another has said, "Niebuhr explicitly assumes that an understanding of political phenomena, whether international or domestic, is inseparable from a clear picture of human nature."[59] Given that the Chinese state is run by humans, Niebuhr's views of human nature as applied to China must be part of his discussion of China and its rise, just as was the case with his views of Soviet or American politics and foreign policy. Mostly simply, as China's material capabilities grow year on

---

[56] Kenneth Waltz, *Theory of International Politics* (Reading, MA: Addison-Wesley, 1979).

[57] John J. Mearsheimer, *The Tragedy of Great Power Politics* (New York: W.W. Norton, 2001). Mearsheimer, of course, would argue that it was the structural realities of great power politics and great power competition that would make a peaceful rise difficult, whereas Niebuhr would argue that it was the realities of sinful, greedy, power-seeking human nature.

[58] William John Wolf, "RN's Doctrine of Man," in Charles W. Kegley, ed., *Reinhold Niebuhr, His Religious, Social and Political Thought* (New York: Pilgrim Press, 1984), p. 306.

[59] Kenneth W Thompson, "The Political Philosophy of RN," in Charles W. Kegley, ed., *Reinhold Niebuhr, His Religious, Social and Political Thought* (New York: Pilgrim Press, 1984), p. 235.

year and its defense spending continues to grow as well, his view of human nature would not allow him to be sanguine about the Chinese leadership's claims that China will not misuse its power or pose a threat to other nations, or about Chinese assertions that China is not like other states but will rise peacefully and harmoniously.

Niebuhr's traditional biblical, Christian view of human nature maintains that humans are born with a penchant for sin, for selfishness, that cooperation and altruism must be taught because they do not come naturally to humans. In other words, self-interested behavior and disregard for others are far more common in human interrelations than brotherly love. This view of human nature forms the core of his Christian Realism and the Realism of the early classical Realists, including Niebuhr and Hans Morgenthau. Niebuhr's insistence on the universalism of this understanding of human nature forms the basis of his arguments that Russian, Vietnamese, American, and any other nation's policies are all subject to myopia, self-interest, hubris, and national blindness about the inadequacies of the national self, coupled with overoptimism about one's own nation's virtue.[60]

Seemingly flying in the face of this are official Chinese statements that amount to what may be called "Chinese exceptionalism.[61] Chinese government spokespersons, official Chinese White Papers on foreign policy, and official websites all describe China's approach to foreign policy as unique, different, and, well, exceptional. China will not, these narratives argue, rise like a warlike power as did Napoleonic France, Wilhelmine Germany, Nazi Germany, or Athens in Thucydides' day, alluding to Graham Allison's piece, "The Thucydides Trap."[62] In fact, Allison is wrong, the official narrative goes. China will avoid the Thucydides Trap and will in fact rise peacefully, avoiding the temptations of great power aggrandizement. China will instead create what government spokespersons have deemed "a new type of great

---

[60] For more, see RN, *The Nature and Destiny of Man*, Volumes I and II (New York: Scribner's, 1941 & 1943); and elsewhere in this volume.

[61] For more on this issue, see Qin Yaqing (2011) "A Chinese School of International Relations Theory: Possibility and Inevitability," in William A. Callahan and Elena Barabantseva, eds., *China Orders the World? Soft Power, Norms and Foreign Policy* (Washington, DC: Woodrow Wilson Center Press, 2011), pp. 37–53; Yan Xuetong (2011), *Ancient Chinese Thought, Modern Chinese Power* (Princeton, NJ: Princeton University Press); Shaun Breslin (2011), "The 'China Model' and the Global Crisis: From Friedrich List to a Chinese Mode of Governance?" *International Affairs* 87(6): 1323–43; and William A. Callahan (2012), "Sino-Speak: Chinese Exceptionalism and Politics of History," *The Journal of Asian Studies* 71(1): 33–55.

[62] Graham Allison, "The Thucydides Trap: Are the US and China Headed for War?" *The Atlantic* (September 24, 2015; http://www.theatlantic.com/international/archive/2015/09/united-states-china-war-thucydides-trap/406756).

power relations," or great power relations built not on "the great game" or great power competition à la the common expectations of Realism, but on Chinese Confucian and Daoist norms of harmony-centrism.[63]

Niebuhr would find this perspective nonsensical and flying in the face of empirical, historical facts. He viewed war as an inescapable part of human history, for all nations, without exception. He would agree with CCP narratives that Chinese people are wonderful people and that China has suffered much at the hands of imperialist foreign powers; he might even be persuaded that Chinese leaders do not have imperialistic designs on the Asia Pacific. Yet, as all good Realists would point out, benign intentions do not necessarily mean benign outcomes in the world Realists describe. Niebuhr would point out that human nature seeks security, that the will-to-power is the most elementary way to get security, and that while seeking power to enhance one's own security, projected to the national level one nation's security seeking appears threatening to others' sense of security and a security dilemma emerges, using a later Realist term. Niebuhr saw this vicious cycle of security-seeking as inescapable in international relations.

Another problem Niebuhr pointed out regarding human nature is that of moral dualism, which he most famously described in *Moral Man and Immoral Society* (1932). Niebuhr maintained that moral behavior between individuals was possible, though not likely; here again he was alluding to the Christian view of fallen man and self-interested human nature. With individuals he thought that it might be possible to construct a situation in which individuals came to trust each other and work together (particularly when they embraced the gospel of Jesus Christ, from his perspective), getting God's help and the moral instruction of the Holy Scriptures. He saw things differently with groups (and nations), however. Niebuhr said that

society . . . merely cumulates the egoism of the individual and transmutes their individual altruism into collective-egoism so that the egoism of the group has double force. For this reason no group acts from purely unselfish motives or even mutual intent and politics is therefore bound to be a contest of power.[64]

---

[63] See, for example, Yan Xuetong, *Ancient Chinese Thought, Modern Chinese Power.*
[64] RN, "Human Nature and Social Change," *Christian Century* 50 (1933): 363.

Hence, Niebuhr saw that interpersonal ethics and international ethics had to be viewed in distinct terms. He was not optimistic that high ethics would or could guide foreign policymaking in international relations. He argued that unity was the glue that held groups together. Yet for ethics to guide decision making, a high degree of introspection and humility must guide policy debates. Questioning the morality of decisions was bound to challenge unity in his view, and leaders feeling challenged would ultimately interpret it as a lack of support, even betrayal, challenging and/or weakening the unity that is essential in wartime and in making all weighty foreign policy decisions. Hence, because of the need for unity in groups and nations, the introspection and humility needed for ethical decision making was not likely to surface in important national security decision-making fora. Consequently, as Niebuhr observed with sorrow, self-interest (not morals) and national narcissism (not international cooperation) leading to likely conflict were the inevitable pattern of international relations, hope though he might that it was not so.

For these reasons, from a Niebuhrian perspective, Chinese government statements that China will not pursue hegemonic foreign policy patterns, that it will not throw its weight around militarily, that it will rise peacefully, that it is different from other rising powers, cannot be taken seriously. Niebuhr would not bet that China can escape the "Thucydides Trap" that Graham Allison has described.[65] Human nature is, for Niebuhr, universal, and Chinese policymakers are human after all. Therefore, from a Niebuhrian perspective, they will be under the same pressures to expand their country's power and seek greater security for their people as any group of national leaders would be, and this will likely lead to conflict with China's neighbors and, likely, the United States as well. In fact, given all that has been said about the first two complicating factors, it may be even more difficult for China to rise peacefully than some other great powers, despite best intentions.

---

[65] See Graham Allison, "The Thucydides Trap: Are the US and China Headed for War?" *The Atlantic* (September 24, 2015; http://www.theatlantic.com/international/archive/2015/09/united-states-china-war-thucydides-trap/406756); Gregory J. Moore, "Avoiding the Thucydides Trap in Sino-American Relations: And 7 Reasons Why That Might be Difficult," *Asian Security* 13/2 (2017): 98–115.

4. The Opportunities China's Growth in Material Capabilities Presents Chinese Leaders

Lastly, as with any good Realist, Niebuhr would take seriously the reality of military capabilities, and in particularly the growing military capabilities of a rising power like China. Therefore, a brief overview of China's growing defense spending and a comparison of that with trends in U.S. defense spending seems apropos.[66]

Given the growth in China's economy in recent decades, it comes as no surprise to anyone that China's defense spending has also increased year on year for some time and continues with no signs of abatement. At the same time, U.S. defense spending saw a general decline over the same period (until a recent increase under Trump), closing the gap in defense spending between the two powers, as the following statistics indicate.

Based on data from the International Institute of Strategic Studies' annual *Military Balance* report (based on numbers for 2012–2018—see Table 9.1),[67] it is clear that Chinese defense spending is on the rise, and that China has been rapidly closing the gap on U.S. spending as measured in U.S. dollars. From a 2012 starting point up until the most recent budget period in 2018, Washington's defense spending has declined 3.7 percent and China's was up 64.3 percent. The gap between them is indeed closing. This picture appears to have changed a bit with the presidency of Donald Trump, as he raised U.S. defense spending to a budgeted $643.3 billion for 2019, significantly reversing the trend of declining U.S. defense spending. Even with the Trump bump, however, the picture doesn't change given China's increased spending patterns, year-on-year, as the data below shows.

I agree with analysts like Michael Beckley that the United States is not a declining power and is not in danger of being eclipsed by China anytime soon,[68] for defense spending does not in itself measure quality or effectiveness of fighting forces on the

---

[66] This section draws in part from data presented in Moore, "Avoiding the Thucydides Trap in Sino-American Relations.

[67] International Institute of Strategic Studies, *The Military Balance 2013, The Military Balance 2014, The Military Balance 2015, The Military Balance 2016, The Military Balance 2017, The Military Balance 2018, The Military Balance 2019* (London: Taylor & Francis, 2013, 2014, 2015, 2016, 2017, 2018, 2019).

[68] Michael Beckley, "China's Century? Why America's Edge Will Endure," *International Security* 36, No. 3 (Winter 2011/12): 41–78.

Table 9.1 China–U.S. Defense Spending Compared

2013 data (based on 2012 numbers, in billions of U.S. dollars):
  U.S. = 645.7; China = 102.4; so China is 15.8% of U.S.
2014 data (based on 2013 numbers, in billions of U.S. dollars):
  U.S. = 600.4; China = 112.2; so China is 18.7% of U.S.
2015 data (based on 2014 numbers, in billions of U.S. dollars):
  U.S. = 581.0; China = 129.4; so China is 22.2% of U.S.
2016 data (based on 2015 numbers, in billions of U.S. dollars):
  U.S. = 597.5; China = 145.8; so China is 24.4% of U.S.
2017 data (based on 2016 numbers, in billions of U.S. dollars):
  U.S. = 604.5; China = 145.0; so China is 24.0% of U.S.
2018 data (based on 2017 numbers, in billions of U.S. dollars):
  U.S. = 602.8; China = 150.5; so China is 25.0% of U.S.
2019 data (based on 2018 numbers, in billions of U.S. dollars):
  U.S. = 643.3; China = 168.2; so China is 26.1% of U.S.
**Conclusions: Over 2012–2018, U.S. defense spending is down 3.7%;
China's is up 64.3%.**

Source: Author calculations based on International Institute of Strategic Studies (IISS) numbers. International Institute of Strategic Studies, *The Military Balance 2013, The Military Balance 2014, The Military Balance 2015, The Military Balance 2016, The Military Balance 2017, The Military Balance 2018, The Military Balance 2019* (London: Taylor & Francis, 2013, 2014, 2015, 2016, 2017, 2018, 2019); as cited in part by Gregory J. Moore, "Avoiding the Thucydides Trap in Sino-American Relations: And 7 Reasons Why That Might Be Difficult," *Asian Security* 13/2 (2017): 98–115.

battlefield, nor technological or other superiorities.[69] Though defense spending alone is *not* a sufficient measure of a nation's power or capabilities, or its rise or fall, it certainly *is* an important indicator. Given that neither China's military reach nor its responsibilities nor its commitments are as broad as those of the United States, its ability to concentrate its forces on defense of the homeland and its near (South and East) seas is a significant factor, indicating that it *does not* need defense spending parity with the United States to achieve power parity with the United States in East Asia.

These trends and figures in Chinese and American defense spending are facts and are not in and of themselves threats to Sino-American relations,

---

[69] On this point, see Stephen Biddle, *Military Power: Explaining Victory and Defeat in Modern Battle* (Princeton, NJ: Princeton University Press, 2006). On the disadvantages in battlefield effectiveness faced by armies (such as the PLA) built to protect authoritarian regimes from domestic unrest, see also Caitlin Talmadge, *The Dictator's Army: Battlefield Effectiveness in Authoritarian Regimes* (Ithaca, NY: Cornell University Press, 2015).

nor are they reasons for increases in tension. However, they reveal the reality of a rising China that is increasingly seen as a military as well as an economic power, a China that is rising in the midst of the increasingly tense Sino-American security milieu discussed in this study. If the UK or America's other NATO partners were increasing their military spending 10 or 12 percent per year, the United States would likely not only *not* be worried but might be gratified (though perhaps a little confused as to the rationale for the increases). When an authoritarian power like China raises its defense spending in such a fashion, however, in the context of all the mutual strategic distrust with which China and the United States are confronted, with China's penchant to steal intellectual property and engage in corporate cyber espionage, with its recent assertive/aggressive policies in the East and South China Seas, and its recent cozying up to an increasingly aggressive and authoritarian Russia, the United States has reason for concern according to a Niebuhrian analysis of the situation.[70]

Niebuhr would have decried the Obama era declines in U.S. defense spending and saluted Donald Trump's increases given trends in China's defense spending, China's relations with authoritarian Russia, and China's foreign policy toward greater assertiveness, and because of the nature of the Chinese communist regime, as has been elaborated upon above, among other things. I don't think Niebuhr would advocate a full Reaganesque military buildup for the United States because the Chinese regime does not (at least now) pose the sort of double-edged threat (ideological and military) that the Soviet Union posed during the Cold War. Niebuhr would, however, advocate a significant increase in U.S. defense spending and an upgrade of U.S. defense capabilities to deal with the potential of confrontation with China in coming years, just as Donald Trump has in fact done. As was the case during the Cold War in dealing with the Soviet Union, Niebuhr would likely argue that, while engaging in proactive and peaceful diplomacy and

---

[70] See Ryan Hass and Zach Balin, *US-China Relations in the Age of Artificial Intelligence* (Washington, DC: Brookings Institution; Thursday, January 10, 2019); Larry Diamond and Orville Schell, co-chairs, *Chinese Influence and American Interests: Promoting Constructive Vigilance*, a Report of the Working Group on Chinese Influence Activities in the United States (Stanford, CA: Hoover Institutions Press, 2018); Alex Joske, *Picking Flowers, Making Honey: The Chinese Military's Collaboration with Foreign Universities*, Australian Strategic Policy Institute Policy Brief 10 (Canberra: Australian Strategic Policy Institute, October 2018); Alexander Korolev, "The Strategic Alignment between Russia and China: Myths and Reality," *The Asan Forum* (May 4, 2015); Marcin Kaczmarski, "The Sino-Russian Relationship: Fellow Travelers in the West-dominated World," *China Quarterly* 236 (December 2018): 1197–1205; Bill Hayton, *The South China Sea: The Struggle for Power in Asia* (New Haven, CT: Yale University Press, 2014).

seeking not to provoke a rising China, the United States has the moral and strategic responsibility to be ready to hold China accountable, to continue to model responsible democratic politics at home and responsible foreign policy in the international milieu. Unless or until China undertakes democratic reforms and moves in a more liberal, politically accountable direction, it appears that the United States will have to remain ready to defend its interests, ideals and allies in the Asia-Pacific region. It is likely that this may well bring it into direct conflict with a very powerful Chinese Communist regime, and that state it commands, in coming years.

Niebuhrian Insights on the Need for Sobriety, Humility, and Guards against Hubris

With China's rise, I believe there might be another aspect of Niebuhr's thought that might be important regarding the role of the Western powers. Niebuhr often wrote on the need for humility among the Western powers, especially among the Anglo-Saxon powers. He feared that hubris among the established democracies might be just as great a danger as the despotism of the authoritarian powers, though the danger he alluded to would be manifested in different ways. He saw all humans as "sinful," fallible, and subject to hubris, bar none. This was the Christian notion of "original sin" in his thought.

> The idea that we have a right to rule because of our superior virtue is of a higher order than the amoral idea that we have a right to rule because of our power. It recognizes the moral element in history. It is nevertheless a dangerous idea because it obscures the immoral elements in all historical processes.[71]

In his day, Niebuhr argued that the United States had no reason to be smug as it considered the virtues of its political system or the challenges of China's or Russia's. He pointed out that the United States was, in fact, quite fortunate in its geographical position, its historical trajectory, and its demographic realities. China, on the other hand, has the worst of all fortunes in terms of its

---

[71] RN, "Anglo-Saxon Destiny and Responsibility," *Christianity and Crisis*, October 4, 1943; and in *Love and Justice*, p. 186.

geography, its borders with many nations, and its proximity to many potentially adversarial nations.

> We know that we [the United States] have the position we hold in the world today partly by reason of factors and forces in the complex pattern of history that we did not create and from which we do not deserve to benefit. If we apprehend this religiously, the sense of destiny ceases to be a vehicle of pride and becomes the occasion for a new sense of responsibility.[72]

He argued for a renewed sense of Anglo-Saxon compassion toward and responsibility to the poorer, less developed nations of the world, which (still) should include not only Russia, but China.

> Without a religious sense of humility and responsibility the Anglo-Saxon world will fail to come to terms with the two great non-Christian nations, Russia and China. It will fail to understand to what degree what is good in the [then] new Russian order represents values of equal justice that we should have, but did not, achieve, and to what extent the evils of tyranny in Russia are simply a false answer to our own unsolved problem of social justice. It will fail to understand to what degree the white man's pride is the chief obstacle in building a world community that brings Asia fully into the world community.[73]

His argument included a profound self-reflection and introspection about the American response to the evils of the Nazi German regime that is helpful today as well, particularly as the Western democracies consider the challenges presented by communist China.

> Any theory that assumes that we can solve the world's problem merely by fathoming the depth of evil in the German soul and seeking to suppress it betrays us into the evils into which self-righteousness is always betrayed. It does not understand that the evil against which we contend is only a different, and probably a more extravagant, form of the evil that is in our soul also.[74]

---

[72] RN, "Anglo-Saxon Destiny and Responsibility," *Christianity and Crisis*, October 4, 1943; and in *Love and Justice*, p. 187.

[73] RN, "Anglo-Saxon Destiny and Responsibility," *Christianity and Crisis*, October 4, 1943; and in *Love and Justice*, p. 187.

[74] RN, "The German Problem," *Christianity and Crisis*, January 10, 1944; and in *Love and Justice*, p. 226.

Niebuhr's words are wise, and the leaders of the Western democracies would be wise to heed them, lest they stumble as they consider China and other authoritarian nations today.

In like manner, Niebuhr warned of a messianic impulse in American history that first came in the form of a broader French Anglo-American messianism. With the decline of France and Britain's power after World War II and the end of the colonial era, what remained was the notion that the United States was the final representative and guarantor of that liberal enlightenment project that must stand against tyranny. It was the decline of France and Britain as liberal standard bearers, in Niebuhr's opinion, that left "America as the prime bearer of this hope and dream. From the earliest days of its history to the present moment, there is a deep layer of Messianic consciousness in the mind of America [sic]."[75] Americans came to view their country as "the darling of divine providence,"[76] which, in line with their understanding of "manifest destiny," Americans were blessed and put in a specific place at a specific time in history to play a role preordained for them by God. Their power, prosperity, and greatness were seen not simply as things to be enjoyed or taken for granted. "But the legitimization of power is generally subordinate in the American dream to the fact that the concept that a divine favor upon the nation implies a commitment 'to lead in the regeneration of mankind.'"[77] Niebuhr noted that this is something Americans shared with the communists of the Cold War era. I would note again that this sense of exceptionalism is something that the Chinese also see as true of themselves and their own great nation. However, "in the Liberal versions of the dream of managing history, the problem of power is never fully elaborated."[78] This lack of understanding of the role of power (both for good and for evil) was one of the things that provoked Niebuhr's ire most about Western liberalism and for which his Christian Realism had a ready solution.[79] Important to this discussion is the Americans' commonly held notion that "American government is regarded as the final and universally valid form of political organization. But, on the whole, it is expected to gain its ends by moral attraction and imitation,"[80] by what we know of today as "soft power."

---

[75] RN, *The Irony of American History*, pp. 68–9.
[76] RN, *The Irony of American History*, p. 70.
[77] RN, *The Irony of American History*, pp. 71–2.
[78] RN, *The Irony of American History*, p. 73.
[79] For more on this, see earlier sections of this book.
[80] Niebuhr, *The Irony of American History*, p. 74.

While Americans have, in Niebuhr's view (and rightly in my own) recognized how important the role of power and advantageous geography has been in the success of their own liberal project, the Chinese leadership, on the contrary, has never fully understood, in my view, the attraction and "pull" of the nonmaterial (soft power and ideational) elements of the liberal American project. Nor do they today, I would argue. With their largely material-reductionist view of power, hierarchy, and status,[81] they cannot bring themselves to terms with the success of liberal, Western/American ideas and/or the universal truisms across time, space, and culture to which they appeal. The Chinese leadership simply seems to conclude that America is like the Pied Piper, in the lead in the eyes of most, because it is presently (and temporarily, in their view) "*lao da*" (老大) or number one in the social hierarchy,[82] and that when a new "*lao da*," a new number one, steps up onto the stage, the world will rush after that new preeminent power just as the world now follows and admires the United States.[83] There may be here a profound lack of understanding and appreciation of the importance of ideas, of soft power, of the content of statements and representations of leadership of the present "*lao da*" on China's side. This is disturbing because if the argument presented here is correct, China's leaders (and its people, and perhaps the world's people) are in for a rude awakening, for China may overplay its hand, just as Niebuhr's analysis warns us it is (and most other nations in its position would be) likely to do. While it may be true in China that he who pays the piper calls the tune (and the one paying is primarily the party-state in China), it does not appear that such is universally true in time, space, and culture. America's hegemony has not come simply because it is "*lao da*," the strongest power. This is part of it, to be sure, but more importantly, there is indeed "pull" from, attraction to, and resonance with these liberal, democratic, anti-authoritarian ideals for which Americans stand, at least when Americans are not fighting unpopular wars in Vietnam and Iraq, among other things.

---

[81] Singaporean elder statesman, Lee Kuan Yew, in an interview with Joshua Cooper Ramo, said the same thing. See Joshua Cooper Ramo, *The Beijing Consensus* (London: Foreign Policy Centre, 2004), p. 69.

[82] *Lao da* literally means "old big" in Chinese, or it can be translated as "eldest," but it is used most commonly to describe the oldest child in a family or simply to mean number one in a social hierarchy, of which a hierarchy of nations could be one use.

[83] Michael Pillsbury develops this line of thought in *The Hundred Year Marathon: China's Secret Strategy to Replace America as the Global Superpower* (New York: Henry Holt, 2015).

Conclusions

Though much has changed in the world since his passing in 1971, Reinhold Niebuhr's wisdom is still worthy of our consideration. This is true in particular as it concerns the rise of China and the double dangers of embracing either a Mearsheimerian fatalism about the likelihood that China and the United States will fall into the "Thucydides Trap" on the one hand, or a sense of idealist or naïve complacency, that there is no danger of Sino-American conflict on the other hand.

There are several things we might take away from Niebuhr's writings as we consider China's rise. First, I think Niebuhr would warn the United States and the Western democracies against being too smug, of being too sure of their own righteousness as they consider the political problems in China and their management of their policies toward China. Niebuhr had a good understanding of the origins of Asian (and Chinese) nationalism and the historical and cultural reasons democracy did not find fertile ground there historically,[84] and so he would urge humility and caution as Westerners seek to foster greater openness and political accountability in China. In the same way, he would urge Western leaders to consider the truths inherent in China's "victimization narrative," to try to understand why the Chinese are so sensitive to foreign encroachment. These are real memories, real emotions, real histories, even if they are stoked for political purposes by an insecure party–state. He would say China and the dreams of China's citizens should be respected and that room should be made at the table for a rising China.

Yet Niebuhr would not shy away from calling a spade a spade, from recognizing and even calling out the authoritarian excesses of China's party–state, of recognizing the dangers it poses not only to its own people but to its neighbors as well. He might criticize the Obama Administration and European leaders in recent years for pandering to China's economic power while saying little about its human rights problems and the dangers, to its own people and to the world, of its authoritarian ways. While recognizing the legitimate hopes and dreams of the Chinese people and the successes of the CCP's reforms, he would highlight the dark side of the party's authoritarian power structure, reminding Westerners that Beijing's disdain for political openness and true political accountability

---

[84] Though, of course, it has in Japan, Taiwan, and South Korea (the latter two in the 1980s, after Niebuhr's passing).

is not a benign force internationally, particularly in tandem with Russian authoritarianism. Illiberal Chinese trade practices, intellectual property rights violations, illiberal media practices, and state-led hacking activities have already had a deleterious effect on global affairs,[85] and Niebuhr would say we cannot be naïve about it as China's global influence continues to grow.

Niebuhr would advocate a strong foreign policy stance for the United States and its allies against Chinese adventurism if it should grow. He' would think it likely but would not encourage the democracies to do anything to provoke it. He would remind us that "[m]ilitary force is always the *ultima ratio* in the contest between nations,"[86] that a strong defense is a powerful deterrent. Niebuhr would support the existing U.S. policy of preventing China from attaining Western stealth technology, supercomputers, and other sensitive defense-related technologies, a policy that has its origins in the sanctions following the events of June 4, 1989 (known in the West as the Tiananmen Square massacre). He would advocate the continued maintenance of close U.S. security cooperation with Japan, South Korea, the Philippines, and Australia, among others in the region, as a hedge against any Mainland Chinese adventurism.

Niebuhr lived through the Holocaust and Cold War eras and had much to say about dealing with authoritarian and totalitarian regimes that could be of benefit today. In 1947, he argued that we should not equate the Soviets and the Nazis and thereby assume that Moscow was bent on world conquest as Hitler had been.[87] In the same way, though also a large power ruled by a communist party, China cannot and should not be equated with the Soviet Union. This is not to say that Niebuhr would not recognize important parallels, however. Martin Halliwell notes that "when Karl Barth commented in the mid-1950s that communists were not as bad as the Nazis because they

---

[85] Larry Diamond and Orville Schell, co-chairs, *Chinese Influence and American Interests: Promoting Constructive Vigilance*, a Report of the Working Group on Chinese Influence Activities in the United States (Stanford, CA: Hoover Institutions Press, 2018); Alex Joske, *Picking Flowers, Making Honey: The Chinese Military's Collaboration with Foreign Universities*, Australian Strategic Policy Institute Policy Brief 10 (Canberra: Australian Strategic Policy Institute, October 2018)

[86] RN, "A Qualified Faith," *New Republic* 134 (February 13, 1956): 15; and in Davis and Good, p. 312.

[87] Martin Halliwell, *The Constant Dialogue: Reinhold Niebuhr and American Intellectual Culture* (Lanham, MD: Rowman and Littlefield, 2005), p. 197, citing RN, "Our Chances for Peace," *Christianity in Crisis* (February 17, 1947): 1.

didn't exterminate Jews, Niebuhr retorted that both were barbaric regimes deriving from 'the same monopoly of irresponsible power.' "[88] For despite the important differences between the USSR and today's PRC, as I've noted again and again in this study, much of what he said to his contemporaries during the Cold War era has a parallel in America's situation today as it considers relations with China. He would call for a strong American defense and heightened vigilance about an increasingly powerful China ruled by leaders with great power, facing great temptations, with little domestic political accountability. He would urge Americans and their allies not to be naïve. I think he would worry about wishful thinking as it regards China, speaking specifically about Western hopes/beliefs that China will become a liberal democracy any time soon, or that China's rise is benign, and/or that China's regime is unlike other regimes because of stated preferences for harmony and Confucian forms of pacifism.

Again, I find four primary reasons Niebuhr would have been rather hawkish toward today's China. First is the regime type and structure of China's political system, which points to a party–state that is and will be perpetually insecure because of its lack of democratic legitimacy, and that has a formidable ability to shape public opinion, wield immense amounts of financial resources because of its increasingly centralized economic system, and to do what it wants with little political accountability. Second is the master narrative of the PRC today and the reliance of the CCP on fostering a form of nationalism that results in a noteworthy international prickliness. Third is the role of human nature, particularly in the context of the CCP's authoritarian political system and the relatively unrestrained power it affords its top leaders. Fourth is the growth in China's material power capabilities and the opportunities (and temptations) this will present Chinese leaders. Niebuhr simply would not find the peaceful rise narrative of the Chinese leadership very persuasive for these four reasons.

Niebuhr would not, however, locate this conclusion, as other Realists like Mearsheimer do, solely in the simple, raw rise of Chinese material power/capabilities. Niebuhr believed that material matters and that power matters—very much so. However, from an IR theory perspective, Niebuhr's perspective is somewhat unique among today's Realists. Reflecting his classical, human nature Realist bent, Niebuhr's perspective on China's rise draws

---

[88] Halliwell, *The Constant Dialogue*, p. 197, citing RN, "Why Is Barth Silent on Hungary?" *Christian Century* (January 23, 1957): 109.

much from factors that today's Realists tend *not* to major in—politics, regime type, human nature, even ideas, alluding to ideology in his day and factors such as the government's "never forget national humiliation" narrative in the contemporary Chinese context.[89]

Niebuhr's contribution to IR theory has been an important one. Realists have long recognized this contribution, but it may be the case that future IR theorists and policy practitioners may be able to draw from new wellsprings of useful insights in Niebuhr's work, no matter what their theoretical or political inclinations. There is no more important phenomenon in IR in the present era than the rise of China, and so if Reinhold Niebuhr would have anything useful to contribute to our discussions of contemporary IR theory or relations between states, it should be here. In fact, Niebuhr *does* have much to add to our discussions, as this chapter has tried to make plain. Niebuhr's arguments are worth remembering as he spoke truth to power in his day, even as we consider the challenges we face in our own.

---

[89] Zheng Wang, *Never Forget National Humiliation: Historical Memory in Chinese Politics and Foreign Relations* (New York: Columbia University Press, 2012).

10

Locating Reinhold Niebuhr
in Contemporary IR Theory

Where might we locate Reinhold Niebuhr in contemporary IR theory? As we
will see, there is much more to Niebuhr's thought, and his impact on international relations ([IR] and IR theory) was deeper and more profound, than
has been commonly acknowledged. Not surprisingly, then, IR's own political
Realism, likewise claimed by liberal internationalists and neoconservatives,
though perhaps in different variations, is the IR approach with which
Niebuhr is traditionally and rightly associated. Niebuhr has been a seminal
figure in the Realist movement. But there are deep strains of existentialism
in his work as well, whereas existentialism is usually associated with postmodernist and post-structuralist approaches. One might also find roots of
today's democratic peace theory or traces of what Daniel Deudney has called
republican security theory in Niebuhr's work. So, too, one might see themes
in Niebuhr's work that would later be taken up in the English School and
among constructivists. In this chapter, I reconsider Reinhold Niebuhr's work
in IR in relation to IR theory—I hope in the process more adequately and systematically locating his work in IR theory—considering both his influences
and the influences he has had therein and thereupon.

Niebuhr and the Realisms

Let us first consider Reinhold Niebuhr the Realist. While political Realism
is the IR approach that best represents Niebuhr's work on IR, there are really two kinds of "realism" at work in Niebuhr's writing, IR Realism being
the second.[1] First and more fundamentally, while both kinds of realism in
Niebuhr's work have been rightly called Christian Realism, Niebuhr's realism

[1] Again, I denote IR's form as Realism (with a capital R), and the general sense of something being
realistic as realism (with a small r).

Niebuhrian International Relations. Gregory J. Moore, Oxford University Press (2020).
Oxford University Press.
DOI: 10.1093/oso/9780197500446.001.0001

is in the more general sense what Robin Lovin calls a pragmatic "theolog-ical realism." Here Lovin is using the term *realism* in a different sense than IR and foreign policy people use it, meaning making real the truths found in the scriptures to a world filled with unbelievers as well as believers and, in the process, "illuminat[ing] the specific difference it makes to affirm that God is the center of meaning in a morally coherent universe."[2] Yet in doing so the point was not to make explicit theological or scriptural arguments so much as to simply apply Christian understandings of truth to real-world problems in various fields of application, Niebuhr's interest, of course, being social problems, politics, and IR. The result is that listeners from other faith commitments or of no faith commitment at all can benefit from the dis-course. This helps explain the wide appeal of his work.

Second, despite these genealogical differences, Niebuhr's approach to IR can also rightly be called Christian Realism, or Niebuhrian Realism, a subset of IR's human nature-driven classical Realism. His general realism fits hand in glove with the classical IR Realism that was born after World War I. Although classical Realism was made famous by E. H. Carr and Hans Morgenthau in IR circles, both Carr and Morgenthau owe an important debt of gratitude to Niebuhr in their own understanding of the problems of ide-alism and utopianism.[3] Again, Niebuhr had been a Marxist and then a liberal Protestant before turning from both in frustration owing to what he saw as their naïve idealism because of their failure to appreciate the implications of human nature, among other things. His critique of idealism then became fundamental to his whole approach to social phenomena. Consequently, the realism he developed in his own work fit naturally with and subsequently morphed into the IR Realism that became his hallmark approach to inter-national relations. These critiques of idealism and utopianism are of course themes that Carr, Morgenthau, and other Realists later developed in their own work as well and with which, along with Niebuhr, came to form the core of the classical Realist tradition of IR.

Moving to Niebuhr's place in conventional IR theory, many have ac-knowledged his importance to the establishment of contemporary polit-ical Realism. Michael J. Smith has said that "E. H. Carr was only the first of

[2] Robin Lovin, *Reinhold Niebuhr and Christian Realism* (Cambridge, UK: Cambridge University Press, 1995), p. 33.

[3] Edward Hallet Carr, *Twenty Years' Crisis, 1919–1939: An Introduction to International Relations* (New York: Palgrave Macmillan, 2001[1939]); Hans Morgenthau, *Politics among Nations*, 3rd ed. (New York: Alfred A. Knopf, 1960).

the Anglo-American realists to adopt some aspect of Reinhold Niebuhr's thought: its range, depth, and complexity make Niebuhr without question the most profound thinker of the modern realist school."[4] Of course because most IR theorists consider Carr to be one of the founders of the modern IR approach that we know as Realism, this in itself establishes Niebuhr's importance in the heritage of IR theory. There is of course much more to say about Niebuhr's role in early Realism. Campbell Craig says that Niebuhr's 1932 classic, *Moral Man and Immoral Society*, "constitutes the birth of modern American Realism."[5] George F. Kennan said of Reinhold Niebuhr and his relation to the early Realists: "he is the father of all of us."[6] At a colloquium in Niebuhr's honor in 1961, one of Realism's most influential thinkers, Hans Morgenthau, said of Niebuhr, "I have always considered Reinhold Niebuhr the greatest living political philosopher of America, perhaps the only creative political philosopher since Calhoun."[7] Niebuhr's Realism is a formative part of that which we tend to call classical Realism's human nature tradition. An argument for a prominent place in that tradition is easily made for Niebuhr, for he was a founding member of it and was both well known and well respected by modern Realism's early thinkers, including E. H. Carr, Hans Morgenthau, George Kennan, Kenneth Thompson, and (later) Henry Kissinger.[8] Niebuhr also shared much theoretically with two other early British IR thinkers, Herbert Butterfield and Martin Wight. Butterfield of Cambridge University was the founder of the British Committee on the Theory of International Relations, and as Kenneth Thompson notes, "much of the thrust of the British Committee and of Butterfield's scholarly writings overlapped with Niebuhr's interests," though the two did not see eye to eye, being of different disciplines and political sensibilities (Butterfield was a historian, Niebuhr a theologian/ethicist).[9] Wight, a member of the same

---

[4] Michael J. Smith, *Realist Thought from Weber to Kissinger* (Baton Rouge: Louisiana State University Press, 1986), p. 99.

[5] Campbell Craig, *Glimmer of a New Leviathan: Total War in the Realism of Niebuhr, Morgenthau, and Waltz* (New York: Columbia University Press, 2003).

[6] This is what Kenneth W. Thompson recounts George Kennan saying of Niebuhr. Kenneth W. Thompson, "Niebuhr and the Foreign Policy Realists," in Daniel F. Rice, ed., *Reinhold Niebuhr Revisited: Engagements with an American Original* (Grand Rapids, MI: Eerdmans, 2009), p. 139.

[7] Hans Morgenthau, "Niebuhr's Political Thought," in Harold R. Landon, ed., *Reinhold Niebuhr: A Prophetic Voice in Our Time* (Greenwich, CT: Seabury Press, 1962), p. 109.

[8] For more, see Charles W. Kegley, ed., *Reinhold Niebuhr, His Religious, Social and Political Thought* (New York: Pilgrim Press, 1984); and Daniel F. Rice, *Reinhold Niebuhr and His Circle of Influence* (Cambridge, UK: Cambridge University Press, 2012).

[9] Thompson, "Niebuhr and the Foreign Policy Realists," in Rice, ed., *Reinhold Niebuhr Revisited*, p. 143.

committee, also shared many interests and philosophical proclivities with Niebuhr and was influenced by him.[10] Wight's more typically British historical approach to IR led him down roads that spawned both the English School (Hedley Bull, perhaps the English School's most important progenitor, drew heavily from Wight[11]) and constructivism (Wendt's three cultures of anarchy flow directly from Wight, and Wendt intentionally references Wight in this respect[12]).

In the late 1970s, Realism began to morph into a structural variant, thus beginning the hegemony of Kenneth Waltz's structural Realism (or Neo-Realism) among Realists and in IR theory circles.[13] I believe it is clear that Niebuhr would not have followed Waltz down this road and would have found many reasons to disagree with Waltz's structural Realism. This would be primarily because Waltz explicitly disavowed much of what Niebuhr felt was so important in IR: chiefly, the roles of human nature, ideology, regime type, racism, and politics. For Waltz those things were all inside the black box of state, thus unobservable, and were best left out of the analytical equation so as to achieve the parsimony Waltz valued so highly. The same would have been true of a Niebuhrian view of John Mearsheimer's later offensive Realist version of structural Realism, which of course built on the foundation Waltz laid. Niebuhr would have been more comfortable with the Waltzian, defensive version of structural Realism than Mearsheimer's offensive Realism because Mearsheimer's structural determinism is even more pronounced, giving even less role for the agency of states and their leaders than that of Waltz. For example, Mearsheimer has famously argued that China's rise will likely end in conflict with the United States, so the United States should contain China and seek to limit its material power gains.[14] Yet, Niebuhr might argue, surely an overt U.S. attempt to contain China might bring about the very war(s) Mearsheimer hopes to avoid, for all the reasons presented above about the difference between Soviet Russia and today's China. Leadership,

[10] See Guilherme Marques Pedro, *Reinhold Niebuhr and International Relations Theory: Realism Beyond Thomas Hobbes* (Basingstoke, UK: Routledge, 2017), p. 36, Kindle Location 1019.

[11] Hedley Bull, *The Anarchical Society: A Study of Order in World Politics* (New York: Columbia University Press, 1977).

[12] Alexander Wendt, *Social Theory of International Politics* (New York: Cambridge University Press, 1999).

[13] Kenneth Waltz, *Theory of International Politics* (New York: Addison-Wesley, 1979)

[14] See, John J. Mearsheimer, *The Tragedy of Great Power Politics* (New York: W. W. Norton, 2001/ 2014); and John J. Mearsheimer, "The Gathering Storm: China's Challenge to US Power in Asia," *The Chinese Journal of International Politics* 3 (2010): 381–96.

politics, individuals (and their foibles), and of course the role of human nature, were matters too important to be black-boxed for Niebuhr.

I think Niebuhr would have appreciated the Neo-Classical turn in Realism taken by Neo-Classical Realists like Randall Schweller.[15] Because the Neo-Classical Realists were willing to bring politics back in and to consider variables other than structure and the distribution of capabilities.[16] While understanding the importance of the balance of power in international politics and yet not losing the explanatory power of power, Niebuhr would also have appreciated the Neo-Classical Realists' understanding of the limits of balance of power, as Randall Schweller has so ably pointed out.[17] For Niebuhr, one could have no systematic understanding of IR without the role of domestic politics and the impact it has on foreign policymaking, whichever level of analysis one's study operated at. He would likely have concluded, however, that Neo-Classical Realists still underestimate the role of human nature (at the first level of analysis) and the lingering problems presented by human folly and raw "evil" in human conduct.

What of Jeffrey Legro and Andrew Moravscik's argument that Realism had become too much a "big tent" and was in danger of losing its way when they asked, "Is anybody still a Realist?"[18] Niebuhr would have understood their argument and might have agreed with elements therein, in particular that there is a core truth that sets Realism apart from other approaches and that Realism is limited in how far it can go in terms of accommodating other approaches. However, I don't think he would have agreed with the way in which they reduced Realism to three simple core assumptions, namely, (1) "the nature of the actors: rational, unitary political units in anarchy"; (2) "the nature of state preferences: fixed and uniformly conflictual goals"; and (3) "international structure: the primacy of material capabilities."[19] Regarding the first, in his discussion of human nature, Niebuhr deconstructed the Greek and modern Liberal understandings of rational human nature and behavior and so would not have embraced any notion that humans or states were rational actors per se. He believed that human greed, pride, and will-to-power sometimes

[15] For example, see Randall Schweller, *Unanswered Threats: Political Constraints on the Balance of Power* (Princeton, NJ: Princeton University Press, 2008).

[16] See Gideon Rose, "Neoclassical Realism and Theories of Foreign Policy," *World Politics* 51/1 (1998): 144–72.

[17] Randall Schweller, *Unanswered Threats: Political Constraints on the Balance of Power* (Princeton, NJ: Princeton University Press, 2008).

[18] Jeffrey W. Legro and Andrew Moravscik, "Is Anybody Still a Realist?" *International Security* 24/2 (Fall 1999): 5–55.

[19] Legro and Moravscik, "Is Anybody Still a Realist?," pp. 12–8.

drove humans (and states) to do things that were not "rational" or in their interest from any "objective" perspective. He would agree with a Realist assumption that individuals and states do what is in their *perceived* interest, but I don't think he'd agree that their behavior is necessarily rational by any objective standard. With regard to the second assumption, he would not have a problem with a general notion that state preferences are fixed and generally conflictual, as long as this left a lot of room for agency, politics, and local particularities defined broadly. This seems to be how Legro and Moravscik define it in fact. He would have more trouble with the third, however, the importance the authors give to structure. He is not a material determinist in the Waltzian or Mearsheimerian structural sense. In general, his analytics are probably less material driven than even those of most classical Realists, and he is definitely not a structuralist. However, Niebuhr would have agreed with the general Realist premise that material capabilities are a fundamental tenet of all Realisms and are of fundamental importance in his own analysis given the importance of power thereto. Yet I think he was subtler, his arguments more nuanced, than the rather raw, brute materialism implied in most other Realisms, at least in their structural variants, and he would certainly have rejected any suggestion that it was the structural dimension of materiality that was primary.

Niebuhr might even have embraced a notion of multivariate Realism—in other words, the need for an approach to IR that is rooted in the foibles of human nature and has a strong materialist base and role for power, but that is comfortable with and able to account for many other variables such as ideology, politics, and regime type. I don't believe that this is inconsistent with fellow classical Realist Hans Morgenthau's approach to IR either for that matter. This is particularly true if one revisits his nine dimensions of national power, which include variables such as national morale and the quality of diplomacy, both of which are clearly nonmaterial variables.[20] There has been a fair amount of writing in recent years on the rediscovery or recovery of Realism, and these writings have focused in particular on Hans Morgenthau, making similar points. I note here the work of Michael Williams and William E. Scheuerman in particular.[21] Williams argues that the heart

---

[20] Hans Morgenthau, Hans, *Politics among Nations*, 3rd ed. (New York: Alfred A. Knopf, 1960).

[21] See Michael C. Williams, *Realism Reconsidered: The Legacy of Hans J. Morgenthau in International Relations* (New York: Oxford University Press, 2008); Michael C. Williams, *The Realist Tradition and the Limits of International Relations* (Cambridge, UK: Cambridge University Press, 2005); and William E. Scheuerman, *Morgenthau* (Cambridge, UK: Polity Press, 2009).

of Realism has been lost in recent decades, and he seeks to recover it. He calls this resurrected Realism "willful Realism," with the following characteristics: (1) a "skepticism" rooted in the "rational questioning of the limits of reason"; (2) relationality, or "the relational processes of self and other"; and (3) power politics as Realists have always understood power politics.[22] As Williams notes, "a reduction of 'interest defined as power' to predominantly material forms of each clearly does not do full justice to Morgenthau's Realist understanding of politics."[23] Williams then cites Morgenthau himself; here Morgenthau discusses revisions to the fourth edition of *Politics among Nations*.

> Against the misunderstanding of the central element of power, which, after having been underrated to the point of total neglect, now tends to be equated with material strength, especially of a military nature, I have stressed more than before its immaterial aspects, especially in the form of charismatic power, and have elaborated the discussion of political ideologies.[24]

Niebuhr would have agreed emphatically with Williams and Morgenthau in this sense, noting the many untapped resources of classical Realism that had been all but forgotten with the theoretical hegemony of structural Realism in recent decades.

Consistent with the recent literature arguing for a recovery of Realism, I believe Niebuhr would have liked and agreed heartily with recent arguments like that of Jonathan Kirshner, who argued that Realism should return to its classical Realist essence. Kirshner argued against the reductionism of structural Realism, and for the importance of politics and the simple reality of the seductive nature of power. "Classical realists . . . assume that rising states will want, in a word, more."[25] Discussing the rise of China as a case, he goes on, saying that

> classical realists . . . must be alarmed by the rise of China. A classical realist perspective inherently observes the emergence of new great powers in the system with enormous apprehension, because it expects the ambition

---

[22] Williams, *The Realist Tradition*, pp. 5–6.
[23] Williams, *The Realist Tradition*, p. 110.
[24] Williams, *The Realist Tradition*, p. 110.
[25] Jonathan Kirshner, "The Tragedy of Offensive Realism: Classical Realism and the Rise of China." *European Journal of International Relations* 18/1 (2012): 58.

of rising states to expand along with their capabilities, and also because of the anxiety that this expectation provokes in their neighbors and potential adversaries.[26]

This is indeed what we have observed with China's rise, and it is what Niebuhr would have expected. Although classical Realists expect states to want more, they do not presume to know how much more than that, however. That is an important reason they seek to eschew the determinism in structural Realism, and in particular the offensive Realist variants such as John Mearsheimer's. As Kirshner puts it, "Since politics matters, and policies can be chosen . . . [f]or classical realists, the future is unwritten, and so wise policy matters."[27] Niebuhr couldn't have agreed more. Mearsheimer's determinism, that is, that structural power distribution factors make conflict between China and the United States likely,[28] for example, leaves little room for agency or the roles of nonstructural, nonmaterial variables. Niebuhr's view of Chinese–U.S. relations might in the end be no less pessimistic than Mearsheimer's, but a Niebuhrian analysis leaves more room for agency, good policy, and variables such as politics, ideology, and of course the unavoidable Niebuhrian reality and role of human nature. It would be the latter batch of variables that Niebuhr would expect to drive Chinese–U.S. relations, rather than simply the raw materiality of China's rising power, as important to him as that would be. I conclude that such Niebuhrian insights could contribute to the revival of a progressive Realist research agenda, bringing back in explanatory variables that Realists have too often excluded in the name of parsimony, yet without fundamentally denigrating the explanatory power or analytical advantages of the broader Realist enterprise.

I think Niebuhr would have agreed that the postmodern, critical theory and later constructivist assaults on all the Realisms have posed a serious challenge to the reputation of Realist scholarship as well.[29] The arrival on the scene of Neo-Classical Realist scholarship has remedied some of late Realism's problems, with its move away from overdeterminism and narrow system centrism to a more classical approach that also includes in its analysis the vagaries of domestic political forces in foreign

---

[26] Kirshner, "The Tragedy of Offensive Realism," pp. 53–75.

[27] Kirshner, "The Tragedy of Offensive Realism," p. 65.

[28] Mearsheimer, *The Tragedy of Great Power Politics*.

[29] For a taste, see pieces by Robert Cox, Richard Ashley, and John Ruggie, in Robert Keohane, ed., *Neorealism and Its Critics* (New York: Columbia University Press, 1986), and Wendt, *Social Theory of International Politics*.

policymaking.[30] Niebuhr's Realism always took politics as an important factor in IR theorizing and foreign policymaking. He did not take the politics out of international politics as structural realism arguably did, but he saw it as an ever-present force given the roles of human nature and the will-to-power, among other forces. For Realism to remain vital, as I've argued above, it must return to its more nuanced classical Realist origins, along with the domestic political insights of its Neo-Classical Realist cousin. Moreover, the advantages that Niebuhr's version of human nature-driven classical Realism brings to bear on Realist narratives, analyses, and research agendas are the well-argued ontological truisms of the human condition and the first-level human idiosyncrasies both of which were best captured by Niebuhr's Realist tradition. If indeed Realism needs to return to its roots to remain vital, a return to the work of Reinhold Niebuhr, father of them all, is a good place to start.

Niebuhr, Institutionalisms, Democratic Peace, and Republican IR

Moving beyond Realism, Niebuhr wrote on many topics with an eye to advocating an approach or approaches consistent with what we would today call Liberal IR, defined broadly. He wrote about the importance of institutions, of democratic (and nondemocratic) regime types, about the importance of democracies sticking together in the face of authoritarianism and/or totalitarianism, and other topics that we would classify as Liberal IR. As a Realist, he might not have been given proper credit for his contributions thereto, but let us try, in some small part, to correct that record.

Perhaps it was because he grew up in an immigrant German family in the small-town American Midwest and came from Germany, a land that was culturally and politically authoritarian, with a very strong father figure, Reinhold Niebuhr adored democracy and the democratic freedoms that he found in the United States, from the time he was a young man until his dying days. Going through the first and second world wars, which in both cases

---

[30] For more on Neo-Classical Realism, see Gideon Rose, "Neoclassical Realism and Theories of Foreign Policy," *World Politics* 51/1 (1998): 144–72; and/or see Randall L. Schweller, "The Progressiveness of Neoclassical Realism," in Colin Elman and Miriam Fendius Elman, eds., *Progress in International Relations Theory* (Cambridge, MA: MIT Press, 2003), pp. 311–47. The key players in Neo-Classical Realist scholarship include Thomas Christensen, Aaron Friedberg, Randall Schweller, William Wohlforth, and Fareed Zakaria.

pitted the armies of his own ancestral home against those of his adopted home, he may have felt somewhat on the defensive, having to prove in the eyes of some that he was sufficiently American, sufficiently patriotic, such that he strove to be more American than the Americans, more democratic than the democrats. Whether or not that is part of the reason, it is clear that Reinhold Niebuhr reveled in American freedoms and defended and advocated democracy at every opportunity.

His love of and support for democratic and liberal politics had a strong impact on his writings about politics and foreign affairs throughout his life. While he was a great fan of America, he could also be her greatest critic, often arguing that she was not living up to the ideals he so cherished. During the first and second world wars he argued that America had a duty to stand with the other democracies against the autocracies. He believed that democracy was worth fighting for. He also believed that a league of democracies was good for the world and supported the establishment of the United Nations. What we now call the democratic peace would have come as no surprise for him, nor would he have found anything about it that would challenge any of his cherished beliefs as a Realist. During the Cold War, he saw the conflict not primarily as a bipolar struggle between two powers locked in a material-driven security spiral, but as a contest between two belief systems, two regime types, one of which was democratic, free-market capitalism, and the other of which was Soviet, communist despotism. Niebuhr believed regime type was important. Consequently, I believe it is clear that he would embrace democratic peace theory[31] as articulated in modern IR parlance and would look for ways of spreading the democratic peace, though he also had strong views about the use of force toward such ends. I don't believe he would have supported the 2003 Iraq War, nor would he support initiating any war in the interest of spreading democracy, but he would stand instead on principles consistent with the just war tradition as he understood them, as I argue in Chapter 7.

Niebuhr's Realism was a multivariate Realism. Although material factors clearly mattered for him (power in general, military capabilities, economic might, material interests, etc.), his Realism was not limited to material factors as structural Realism has been or as some Realists in general portray Realism. Regime type mattered, in this case the difference between

---

[31] For the best treatment of democratic peace in the literature, see Michael E. Brown, Sean M. Lynn-Jones, and Steven E. Miller, *Debating the Democratic Peace* (Boston: MIT Press, 1996).

democratic and despotic regime types. Ideology also mattered, in this case the difference between Liberal ideology and communist/Marxist-Leninist ideology. For these reasons, Niebuhr would have welcomed the work of the democratic peace scholars. He would not have assumed that democracies are necessarily led by angels or have angelic foreign policies. To be true to democratic peace, its advocates do not argue as such either. They simply maintain that democracies are highly unlikely to go to war with other democracies. Democracies *do* often go to war with nondemocracies, however. Advocates of democratic peace as an approach to IR do not argue that democracies are necessarily more peaceful than nondemocracies. The empirical evidence suggests they have not been. It simply argues that when the number of democracies increases, the number of dyads consisting of two democracies increases, and this makes war less likely for the myriad reasons democratic peace advocates maintain are important. With these observations, Niebuhr might point out that democratic peace theory, too, has an element of realism (or even Realism)[32] built into it.

In fact, I believe he would like the recent work of Dan Deudney very much, what Duedney calls republican security theory.[33] What Deudney has had to do in reawakening us all to the links between Realism and Liberalism would have come as second nature to Niebuhr, as something assumed and to be taken for granted. Niebuhr would agree with Deudney that artificial and socially constructed is the distinction, even the dichotomy, between Realist and Liberal understandings of IR and security. Historically, in the American tradition there was never a barrier between the two, at least prior to more recent constructions of Realism vs Liberalism in IR discourse, nor should there be a barrier between politics inside and outside the state, to use Walker's terminology.[34] All these dichotomies would seem very strange to Niebuhr, even despite his penchant for dialectics. While surely he could understand that a nation could be Realist without being Liberal, he believed nations that were Liberal and democracies must be Realist, simply because of the political realities in a Hobbesian world. Needed from his perspectives are checks

---

[32] Again here, as I have tried to do throughout the book, I make a distinction between realism (small r), denoting something as being realistic, and Realism (capital R), denoting political realism as found in IR theory circles.

[33] Daniel H. Duedney, *Bounding Power: Republican Security Theory from the Polis to the Global Village* (Princeton, NJ: Princeton University Press, 2007). See also the work of Vibeka Schou Tjalve, *Realist Strategies of Republican Peace: Niebuhr, Morgenthau, and the Politics of Patriotic Dissent* (New York: Palgrave Macmillan, 2008).

[34] R. B. J. Walker, *Inside/Outside: International Relations as Political Theory* (Cambridge, UK: Cambridge University Press, 1993)

and balances because of the capriciousness of human nature, institutional structures to both harness and restrain human impulses, and popular participation in domestic and in some cases international politics, speaking of referenda like the Brexit decision. That the Realist and Liberal approaches have, over time, become competitors and/or mutually exclusive categories in IR, despite the attempts of some like John Ruggie to morph/merge them,[35] is a practical and historical anomaly, at least in the American context. Niebuhr (with Deudney) would maintain that such is the case. I believe he would, again with Deudney, support the notion that there is nothing illogical about considering them potentially as a single approach where logical, especially in the American context, and that doing so, while not necessary, would (again in the American context at least), resolve some of the odd dichotomies that have arisen between Liberal and Realist approaches to IR. This possibility would be particularly attractive (and logical) to Niebuhr given his own proclivities as both a Liberal (in all senses of the word)[36] and a Realist.

Niebuhr, the English School, and Constructivism

Of course, there is no reason to believe that constructivism, the English School, and/or other approaches cannot draw from Niebuhr's insights into human nature and IR either. I would argue that a notion of "human nature constructivism" might be viable. In other words, a scientific realist approach to understanding wherein what Alexander Wendt calls "rump materialism" in his constructivist view of IR could, at least in part, be the stuff of what Niebuhr recognized as the role of human nature, a very material, biological force affecting human behavior. And sitting atop that superstructure (or substructure) would be an interpretivist appropriation of understanding the world in which we live, moving from this "rump material" human nature to human social constructions and the vast social milieu Wendt and other constructivists describe. However, this approach would not be limited

---

[35] John Ruggie, "Continuity and Transformation in the World Polity: Toward a Neorealist Synthesis," *World Politics* 35/02 (January 1983): 261–85.

[36] A liberal might be one supporting the ideology of liberalism (or classical liberalism; in other words, small government, maximum freedom in politics and economics, the importance of individual rights, etc.); or a progressive (highlighting one's attitude toward change, often juxtaposed against conservativism); or someone advocating an approach to IR that emphasizes the importance of regime type (à la democratic peace), institutions (neo-liberal institutionalism), and/or complex interdependence.

to Wendt's preferred third level of analysis,[37] but would by definition include a role for first-level in addition to second- and third-level factors. Like Wendt, however, it would strive to account for the role of other "rump material" forces as they are commingled with ideational and social forces. Daniel Edward Young has made a similar argument, emphasizing that Niebuhrian insights gel well with those of constructivist and English School approaches. They even share a common Christian Realist heritage in the person of Martin Wight, an early Christian Realist as well as a founder of both the English School and an intellectual forebear of constructivism. Wendt's three cultures of anarchy flow directly from Wight's own tripartite breakdown of the world of IR, namely, realism/Hobbes, rationalism/Grotius,[38] and revolutionism/Kant.[39] Many writers have written about the common heritage of constructivist and English School approaches to IR, but there is a Christian Realist nexus as well. Like Hedley Bull,[40] a key progenitor of IR's English School, Niebuhr wrote about the relationship between both order and justice and the importance of the two. He wrote of different cultural and social understandings of order and justice, as well as the clashes between different international societies, such as the European international society and the societies of subjugated colonial peoples.

Constructivists might also find much to like in Niebuhr's work because of the role of ideas and sociopolitical factors in his work. Niebuhr always took ideas and ideology seriously. He believed people acted because of their beliefs, whether religion, political ideologies, the force of culture, or something else. He saw the Cold War as most fundamentally a difference between two opposing belief systems, and not as Waltz and other Realists saw it, as being simply about a distribution of material capabilities. While Niebuhr did not talk about identity in the way today's constructivists do, he understood that the way a person or a people or a nation viewed themselves shaped their view of others as well as their actions toward others. Although the language of constructivism that is so familiar to us today did not exist then, Niebuhr

---

[37] To be fair to Wendt, in conversations with him I have learned that he too is comfortable with his constructivism being applied to the first and second levels of analysis, though that is not the focus of his 1999 book. I have used Wendt's framework at the second-level analysis in some of my work, such as Moore, "The Difference a Day Makes: Understanding the End of the Sino-American 'Tacit Alliance,'" *International Studies Review* 16/4 (December 2014): 540–74.

[38] Wendt prefers to reference Locke instead of Grotius, however.

[39] Daniel Edward Young, "International Institutions and the Problem of Judgment," in Eric Patterson, ed., *Christianity and Power Politics Today: Christian Realism and Contemporary Political Dilemmas* (New York: Palgrave Macmillan, 2008), pp. 153–66.

[40] Bull, *The Anarchical Society*.

was aware enough as a thinker to see forces such as identity and ideology at work in human activity around him and to recognize their importance. His understanding of the lack of certainty, about knowability, also shaped his thinking and will be discussed below; all of this certainly had an impact on the IR field.

A new field of endeavor, located partly between constructivism IR and cognitive science, concerns the role of human nature in IR. Niebuhr has played the most prominent role in making human nature a recognized force in IR, though factors such as human nature were later disparaged and spurned by Waltz's structural approach to IR. Today a new movement in IR is bringing human nature back in, but with a twenty-first-century twist. People like Rose McDermott and Stephen Rosen are studying the relationship between human nature and human activity, or more specifically between human nature and war, drawing from neuroscience and/or social psychology. Christopher Beem's recent work on rationality versus emotions and group behavior provides strong evidence in support of Niebuhr's views of human nature.[41] Even Alex Wendt's recent work on quantum social science and the human mind in the social milieu has its roots in Wendt's understanding of a fundamental, extant human nature.[42] The work of these scholars is on the cutting edge of the most scientific (read that as hard science) approach to IR and has even attracted the likes of James Der Derian, who is presently running a fascinating research program on Quantum IR at the University of Sydney.[43]

Niebuhr might also agree with scholars such as Samuel Barkin,[44] who see a future in a Realist–constructivist nexus. Barkin argues that classical Realism remains the richest Realist variant, and it is from this form of Realism that he draws.[45] Although his 2010 book lacks a nuanced discussion of human

---

[41] See Chapter 3 of this volume for more on Beem's evidence. Christopher Beem, *Democratic Humility: Reinhold Niebuhr, Neuroscience, and America's Political Crisis* (Lanham, MD: Lexington Books, 2015).

[42] For more, see Stephen Rosen, *War and Human Nature* (Princeton, NJ: Princeton University Press, 2009); Peter Hatemi and Rose McDermott, *Man Is by Nature a Political Animal: Evolution, Biology, and Politics* (Chicago: University of Chicago Press, 2011); Beem, *Democratic Humility*; and Alexander Wendt, *Quantum Mind and Social Science: Unifying Physical and Social Ontology* (Cambridge, UK: Cambridge University Press, 2015).

[43] For more, see *Project Q*, University of Sydney, at https://projectqsydney.com.

[44] Samuel Barkin, *Realist Constructivism: Rethinking International Relations Theory* (Cambridge, UK: Cambridge University Press, 2010).

[45] Barkin, *Realist Constructivism*, p. 5.

nature and does not cite Niebuhr or include him in the references section,[46] it is clear that his Realism has much in common with Niebuhr's and that Niebuhr's project, with its emphasis on the importance of ideology, regime type, history, and the like, has much in common with Barkin's project. Niebuhr's Realism was not bound by theoretical strictures that prevented him from analyzing certain variables that were within or outside of the black box of foreign policy decision making.

As should be true of all good social inquiry, Niebuhr's research went wherever the questions/evidence took him, whether the variables he found salient were material, social, ideational, structural, or other. In the same way, while constructivism argues for the importance of the role of things material, particularly in a Hobbesian social milieu (and this is often overlooked), a constructivist approach does not disavow things social, ideational, or structural but, again, should follow wherever the evidence leads. I believe, therefore, that there is no reason an approach characterized as Niebuhrian could not be combined with elements of an approach drawing from constructivist wellsprings as well.

Niebuhr, Existentialist Undertones, and "The Posts"

An underappreciated facet of Niebuhr's work is the existentialist dimension found therein. When we consider Realists, we tend to lump them into materialist, foundationalist, positive categories without much thought or discussion. With the emerging literature on classical Realists like Morgenthau and Niebuhr, however, it is clear that this approach is not helpful.[47] In fact, this only came about because of the hegemony of positivist, material-driven Waltzian structural Realism and perhaps the loss of historical memory of earlier forms of Realism over the decades. As our discipline has advanced and a movement has arisen to "recover" some of our older Realist thinkers, it

---

[46] See Barkin, *Realist Constructivism*, pp. 33, 161, and 184. Barkin mistakenly says, "Realism . . . need not be associated with particular assumptions about human nature" (161). This may be true of structural Realism, but not of Morgenthau and Niebuhr, among others.

[47] See Michael C. Williams, *The Realist Tradition and the Limits of International Relations* (Cambridge, UK: Cambridge University Press, 2005) and *Realism Reconsidered: The Legacy of Hans J. Morgenthau in International Relations* (New York: Oxford University Press, 2008); William E. Sheuerman, *Morgenthau* (Cambridge, UK: Polity Press, 2009); Vibeke Schou Tjalve, *Realist Strategies of Republican Peace: Niebuhr, Morgenthau, and the Politics of Patriotic Dissent* (New York: Palgrave Macmillan, 2008); Richard Ned Lebow, *The Tragic Vision of Politics: Ethics, Interests and Orders* (Cambridge: Cambridge University Press, 2003).

is clear that there is more nuance in these old Realists than we remembered (for those of us who are old enough to remember) or known (for the younger crowd who came to know IR in the Waltzian or post-Waltz world—1979 or later, the year Waltz's seminal *Theory of International Politics* appeared).

A number of existentialist thinkers had an important impact on Niebuhr's thought: notably, Soren Kierkegaard, Fyodor Dostoyevsky, Friedrich Nietzsche, Martin Heidegger, and Paul Tillich.[48] Discussion of this existentialist connection is not new, for as early as 1956, Paul Ramsey called Niebuhr a "theistic existentialist," and a recent work on Niebuhr, by Guilherme Marques Pedro, reaches the same conclusion.[49] While none of the existentialists named above belong to the IR theory pantheon, it remains true that "the posts" in IR (i.e., postpositivism, postmodernism, postcolonialism, and poststructuralism) are indebted to existentialism as the wellspring out of which those writing in the IR tradition of "The Posts" have come. While Niebuhr has not received much credit for it, chronologically speaking at least, Niebuhr brought existentialist/postpositivist thinking into IR before the likes of Walker, Ashley, Der Derian, and the others,[50] whom we normally view as the pathbreakers in postpositivist IR. At least one thinker has characterized Niebuhr (and Morgenthau) as poststructuralist.[51] While I wouldn't agree with that characterization, it does underline my contention that there is something here to discuss.

Any discussion of Niebuhr's exposure to existentialist thought might best begin with Nietzsche. Two things in particular might have drawn Niebuhr to Nietzsche—and three if we include the fact that both were of German heritage, had Lutheran pastors as fathers, and had acute intellectual interests and abilities (though unlike Niebuhr, Nietzsche fell away from his Christian faith,

---

[48] I note that all of these are featured in an excellent reader on the subject: Robert C. Solomon, ed., *Existentialism* (New York: Random House/Modern Library, 1974).

[49] Paul Ramsey, "Love and Law," in Charles Kegley and Robert Bretal, eds., *Reinhold Niebuhr, His Religious, Social and Political Thought* (New York: Macmillan, 1956), pp. 80–123; and Pedro, *Reinhold Niebuhr and International Relations Theory*.

[50] Richard Ashley, "The Poverty of Neorealism," in Robert Keohane, ed., *Neorealism and Its Critics* (New York: Columbia University Press, 1986), pp. 255–300; J. Der Derian and M. J. Shapiro, eds., *International/Intertextual Relations: Postmodern Readings of World Politics* (Lexington, KY: Lexington Books, 1989); David Campbell, *Writing Security: United States Foreign Policy and the Politics of Identity* (Manchester, UK: Manchester University Press, 1992); R.B.J. Walker, *Inside/ Outside: International Relations as Political Theory* (Cambridge, UK: Cambridge University Press, 1993); Steve Smith, Ken Booth, and Marysia Zalewski, *International Theory: Positivism and Beyond* (Cambridge, UK: Cambridge University Press, 1996).

[51] The statement comes from John Patrick Diggins, *The Promise of Pragmatism: Modernism and the Crisis of Modernity* (Chicago: University of Chicago Press, 1994), as found in Tjalve, *Realist Strategies of Republican Peace*, p. 151.

which made all the difference in terms of understanding the lack of deeper alignment between them). First, Niebuhr saw the importance of the individual in political life—perhaps this was the American influence on him in an otherwise very German cultural upbringing, including the role of a typically German strong father figure. So too with Nietzsche. As Niebuhr wrote in his magnum opus, *Nature and Destiny of Man*, "Only in Nietzschean romanticism is the individual preserved; but there he becomes the vehicle of daemonic religion because he knows no law but his own will-to-power and has no God but his own unlimited ambition."[52] In Nietzsche Niebuhr found the free individual, but he also found evil in the unfettered will-to-power, one of the most important elements in Nietzsche's thought, and in Niebuhr's as well.[53] Second, Nietzsche, though a romantic, was not blind to the foibles of human nature, especially to man's potential for evil. In Nietzsche Niebuhr found a healthy skepticism, or even pessimism about human nature and the potential for good in human activity. Again, from *Nature and Destiny of Man*, Niebuhr writes, "One of the modern fruits of Nietzschean thought is Freudian pessimism. Here we have no good opinion about human nature."[54] These are some of the core elements in Niebuhr's thought, and we find them early on in Nietzsche's (earlier) thought as well.

As noted earlier, Niebuhr was also influenced by the Christian existentialists Kierkegaard and Dostoyevsky. Their thought is much closer to Niebuhr's in terms of their still vibrant faith, though they, like Nietzsche, bear the heavy burden of anxiety, self-awareness, and angst that characterizes Nietzsche and the other existentialists. They do so, however, with the freedom that (from the Christian perspective) comes in the Christian understanding of the finished work of Christ; that ultimately makes right what they left wrong; that makes clear what they found murky; that makes peaceful that which they found anxiety-inducing; that brings out truth where they found lies and uncertainty. Niebuhr's thought is very much like theirs in this sense. Niebuhr quotes Kierkegaard at length:

> The determining factor in the self is consciousness, i.e., self-consciousness. The more consciousness, the more self; the more consciousness the more will; the more will, the more self. . . . The self is the conscious synthesis of

---

[52] RN, *The Nature and Destiny of Man: Volume 1* (New York: Charles Scribner's Sons, 1941), p. 92.
[53] RN, *Nature and Destiny of Man* 1, pp. 192–3.
[54] RN, *Nature and Destiny of Man* 1, pp. 24–5.

the limited and the unlimited which is related to itself and the task of which is to become a self, a task which can be realized only in relation to God. To become a self means to become concrete. But to become concrete means to be neither limited nor unlimited, for that which must become concrete is a synthesis. Therefore development consists in this: that in the eternalization of the self one escapes the self endlessly and in the temporalization of the self one endlessly returns to the self.[55]

Both Kierkegaard's *and* Niebuhr's philosophies bear a heaviness and a sobriety, but also a sense of transcendence, of hope in the self, in the human condition, and ultimately the world writ large. For Niebuhr, the very clarity that brings the heaviness and sobriety, when liberated by transcendence, hope, even love, brings peace rather than the despair of Nietzsche. Part of that clarity, however, brings with it "relativity" and an awareness of the limits of human cognition.

What truly marks the existentialist and poststructuralist aspect of Niebuhr's thought is the sense in Niebuhr's writings of a relativism, a realist skepticism suggesting that we are truly limited in what we can know, and therefore we must be humble and tolerant of others' approximations of truth, just as we hope others will be for our own. I do not read Niebuhr's relativism as an absolute relativism, for surely he believed in absolute Truth, with a capital "T," as found in biblical revelation at the least. Yet even in this respect there was a relativism, a humility from Niebuhr in his understanding of the limits of human abilities to comprehend, to fully grasp the truths of biblical revelation. Consequently, Niebuhr railed against the rationalism of the Greeks, Renaissance thinkers, modern liberals, and even Christians who were absolutely sure they had a monopoly on biblical truth in their theological positions. He also railed against all others one might call positivists, with their absolute trust in reason (or their particular reason), and the hubris that in his view went with that rationalist optimism. Speaking specifically of the Renaissance, he said,

The rationalist humanist wing of the Renaissance made its contributions to toleration by challenging particular prejudices with the supposed universalities of reason; and by dissolving the false universalities of

---

[55] Soren Kierkegaard, *Die Krankheit zum Tode* [*A Sickness unto Death*] (Diederich Verlag), p. 27, as cited in RN, *Nature and Destiny of Man* 1, p. 171.

dogmatic religion by the force of empirical observations, proving the wide variety and relativity of all historical forms of culture.[56]

Niebuhr emphasized that we must remain humble, that we could not and should not be too sure of our own approximations of truth, even while we hold to those truths we deem dear, those that to the best of our knowledge and abilities are "true." He would say that we need always to be open to hearing other approximations of "truth" and always remain open to hearing other perspectives. This is something he always modeled in his own life with his willingness to change his mind at times, and this was why he believed so strongly in democracy and intellectual, religious, and political pluralism, as well as toleration.

> This provisional understanding of the relativity of human knowledge, including the relativity of various interpretations of religious revelation, is an integral part of the recovery of the sense of the historical in Renaissance thought. It is in the primary cause of the ability of the Renaissance to meet one of the two tests of the problem of toleration: The willingness to entertain views which oppose our own without rancor and without the effort to suppress them.[57]

The challenge to us remains the same—how to hold to our own convictions while respecting the views of those who hold views very different from our own, and, perhaps just as importantly, how to maintain a political system wherein we can guarantee the same.

A flavor of proto-postcolonial or subaltern approaches is also to be found in Niebuhr's work. He wrote much about colonialism and the pride/chauvinism of the European and American peoples toward the world's people of color. As I wrote in the biographical sketch in Chapter 1, Niebuhr was a race relations activist in Detroit and to some degree in New York, the two places at the center of his professional life. He supported Dr. Martin Luther King's work to gain greater freedoms for African Americans, he supported the Jewish people against oppression whether from Nazi Germany or from their neighbors after the State of Israel was established. He wrote much against colonialism and the hubris of colonialists, arguing that democracy could not be

---

[56] RN, *Nature and Destiny of Man* 2, p. 232.
[57] RN, *Nature and Destiny of Man*, p. 236.

imposed, that all people deserved the same freedoms Americans and Western Europeans enjoyed. His words and actions were very progressive, considering the times in which he wrote and his background as a white male of European descent in the United States in the early to mid-twentieth century, and very much in the interpretivist ontological tradition of postpositivism, postmodernism, postcolonialism, and poststructuralism. One cannot but be surprised that these words, these views, were expressed via the pen (or typewriter, as it were) of a Realist.

My own conclusion is that Niebuhr is actually a foundationalist, ontologically, and a scientific realist, epistemologically.[58] Many aspects of his work, such as human nature or the will-to-power, are treated ontologically as given, in a foundationalist sense. Yet he is not a positivist, for from his perspective there are clearly many aspects of our social milieu for which we have to resign ourselves to an approximate or subjective appropriation of truth and/ or understanding. Given all that has been presented in this volume about Niebuhr's contribution to IR theory, it seems clear that, while he is at heart a classical human nature Realist, nothing in his approach to IR would make it not amenable to working alongside any of the approaches to IR that we have at our disposal today—whether postmodernist, constructivist, feminist, English School, green, or other—in ways that might be consistent with what is called analytic eclecticism.[59]

Closing Thoughts

Niebuhr's analysis, based in the recognition of paradox and the preponderance of moral ambiguity in international policymaking, is not really (nor do I think it was intended to be) a theory of international relations per se, if theory is defined as Ken Waltz defines it, ("theories explain laws," he states)[60] or as explaining causal relations between variables/phenomenon that we have not been able to observe directly. As Ronald Stone has noted, "Reinhold

---

[58] See Gregory Moore, "Research Methods for International Relations Studies: Assembling an Effective Toolkit," (in Chinese), Wang Jianwei, ed., *Handbook of International Relations* (Beijing: Renmin University Press, 2010); 莫凯歌，《国际关系研究方法：组合有效的工具箱》, 王建伟主编，国际关系学，北京：人民大学出版社，2010 ; and (online in English) at International Studies Association's 48th Annual Conference proceedings, Chicago (2007).

[59] Rudra Sil and Peter J. Katzenstein, *Beyond Paradigms: Analytic Eclecticism in the Study of World Politics* (Basingstoke, UK: Palgrave, 2010).

[60] Kenneth Waltz, *Theory of International Politics* (Reading, MA: Addison-Wesley, 1979), p. 4.

Niebuhr has not attempted to construct a theory of international politics"[61] as Ken Waltz has done, for example. Yet Niebuhr's writings on IR writ large *do* provide a coherent approach to IR and foreign policy and *could* provide guidance to academics and policymakers as they think through the theoretical and policy quandaries presented in IR. Niebuhr's work is deserving of a close reading by anyone interested in IR and the intersection of moral and strategic thought. In the end, a realistic national self-conception embodied by an equally realistic vision of practical national potentials, responsibilities, and limitations, tempered by a realistic assessment of both the potentialities and fallibilities of human nature, are perhaps the greatest set of virtues decision makers in the international political milieu can aspire to, from a Niebuhrian perspective.

---

[61] Ronald Stone, *Reinhold Niebuhr: Prophet to Politicians* (Nashville, TN: Abingdon Press), p. 213.

11

Conclusions

Reinhold Niebuhr's writings will be studied for generations to come because of his wisdom, his insights, his humility, and his unusual success at objectivity. Perhaps most impressive, and at the same time most controversial, was the manner in which Niebuhr illuminated the paradoxical dualisms of the human condition. This dualism is the thread that runs throughout his work and, as he believed, begins with the dual nature inherent in each of us. Niebuhr believed that humans are material creatures imbued by their creator with divine qualities and behavioral potentialities due to *imago dei*, their having been created in the image of their creator, as argued and believed in traditional Christendom.

Niebuhrian Dialects and Niebuhr the Conservative Liberal

This dualism is a correlate or perhaps a cause of the dialectics that were central to Niebuhr's work and his worldview. Some criticized Niebuhr for his utilization of dialectics, saying it simply allowed him to take either side of a given argument. Yet in many ways his recognition of the dialectical elements in life is his most brilliant intellectual exercise, a reflection not of his inadequacies as a thinker or of any tendency to find intellectual shortcuts or easy ways out of intellectual conundrums, but rather of his willingness to face the sometimes uncomfortable realities of life's sometimes irreconcilable paradoxes. The only way to deal with some of these issues, in Niebuhr's opinion, was to recognize their dialectical nature: for example, the human being as potentially good, yet unavoidably sinful; God as God of love, yet God of wrath; the peaceful community of humankind as impossible, yet possible. Anyone who has ever had to make a choice between the lesser of two evils or who has ever said to oneself, "Damned if I do; damned if I don't," understands dialectics and the potential dilemma of moral ambiguity in choice making.

Niebuhrian International Relations. Gregory J. Moore, Oxford University Press (2020).
© Oxford University Press.
DOI: 10.1093/oso/9780197500446.001.0001

Dialectics can be a bit disconcerting for most of us. Empiricism, positivism, and cherished notions of objective reality tell us there must be "right" and "wrong." Dialectics, however, tell us that right and wrong can, on occasion, coexist with equal validity. While empiricism generally tells us this is impossible, Niebuhr reveals that this is not only possible, but also not altogether uncommon. Niebuhr's dialectics are by no means akin to postmodernism or its slippery slope to relativism. Nor is Niebuhrian dialectics an argument that all truths are equally valid, that multiple, contradictory "truths" are everywhere, that they are extant in all fields of endeavor, or that there can be no absolute truth. Neither are Niebuhr's dialectics all that much like that of perhaps the most famous dialectician, Hegel, in that Niebuhr did not seem to see dialectics as being quite as teleological or dynamic as Hegel portrayed them. Whereas Hegel's dialectics are dynamic—thesis meeting antithesis with the resultant crisis/conflict/struggle leading to a new synthesis, which over time becomes the new thesis, which meets up against a new antithesis, and on and on—Niebuhr's dialectics seem rather static. He did not see human nature changing, nor, consequently, did he see the nature of human society, politics, or international relations changing significantly. Niebuhr simply argued that dialectics are a part of the human social milieu and that we cannot deny or ignore the existence of dialectical phenomenon but must reserve a place for them in our intellectual toolkit.

Niebuhr's frequent use of dialectics may also explain why he is difficult to categorize and why those on both the progressive left and the conservative right have embraced and quoted him over the years. As Paul Elie put it in 2007,

> the Niebuhr revival has been perplexing, even bizarre, as people with profoundly divergent views of the [Iraq] war have all claimed Niebuhr as their precursor: bellicose neoconservatives, chastened "liberal hawks," and the stalwarts of the antiwar left.[1]

Hawks and conservatives see in Niebuhr one who understands the necessity of force, the darkness of dictatorship, and the reality of evil. Just warriors see in him one who understands the intricacies and importance of using force wisely and with great restraint. Antiwar activists see in him one who

---

[1] Paul Elie, "A Man for All Reasons," *The Atlantic* (November 2007), accessed from https://www.theatlantic.com/magazine/archive/2007/11/a-man-for-all-reasons/306337.

understands the problem of hubris and the dangerous potential of just war turning into ideological crusade. Like the proverbial blind men all describing the same elephant but in terms starkly different and unrecognizable to each other, each of these sorts of understandings of Niebuhr is in fact accurate. What the various invocations of Niebuhr sometimes miss, however, are the nuances in Niebuhr's thought and of course the presence of dialectics.

In reality, while Niebuhr is rightly called a "liberal" politically because of his views on social issues such as race and labor relations and his belief in the role of structural causes of injustice, his arguments about the "sinfulness" of human nature and the existence of evil were and are persuasive and familiar to conservatives. Theologically, along with Karl Barth, he was a defender of a neo-orthodox view of Christianity, a brand of Protestantism critical of liberal Protestantism but "fundamentalist," or the equivalent of today's conservative evangelicalism. Whatever one might call him, he was a Christian who was passionate about his faith and the relevance of Christianity to the human condition. His harsh criticism of the liberal Protestant left and its social gospel endeared him to conservative Christians in his own time and makes him an attractive thinker to many Catholics and evangelical Protestants in our time. A careful review of his actual theology, however, would show that his theology was for the most part too liberal to be a comfortable fit for today's Catholics and evangelicals.[2] For example, he is noted for having criticized evangelicals like Billy Graham, saying their "wholly individualistic conceptions of sin" were "almost irrelevant" to the collective social problems of the age in which he lived,[3] and though he had great reverence for the Bible, he argued that the Bible could not be taken literally.[4] Still, conservatives have found much to like about Niebuhr over the years. Niebuhr has been invoked by Catholic conservatives like Richard John Neuhaus,[5] hawkish Republicans like John McCain,[6] neoconservatives like Michael

---

[2] Eyal Naveh, "Beyond Illusion and Despair: Niebuhr's Liberal Legacy in a Divided American Culture," in Daniel F. Rice, ed., *Reinhold Niebuhr Revisited: Engagements with an American Original* (Grand Rapids, MI: Eerdmens, 2009), pp. 260–85.

[3] Alden Whitman, "Reinhold Niebuhr Is Dead: Protestant Theologian, 78," *The New York Times* (June 2, 1971), p. 1. For more, see RN, "A Proposal for Billy Graham," original manuscript submitted to *The Christian Century* for publication (later published therein on August 8, 1956, p. 921), as found in Box 16, Reinhold Niebuhr Papers, Manuscript Division, Library of Congress, Washington, DC.

[4] Gabriel Fackre, *The Promise of Reinhold Niebuhr*, Third Edition (Grand Rapids, MI: Eerdmen's, 2011).

[5] Richard John Neuhaus, "Internationalisms, etc.," *First Things* (December 2004; accessed March 17, 2012, via http://www.firstthings.com/article/2009/02/internationalisms-etc-50). See also Michael Novak, another Catholic conservative in footnote 7.

[6] John McCain, with Stephen Salter, *Hard Calls: The Art of Great Decisions* (New York: Hachett Book Group, 2007), pp. 319-39.

Novak,[7] evangelicals like Dean Curry,[8] and Jewish conservatives like David Brooks.[9] Commenting on the broad appeal of Niebuhr's work, Brooks said, "Niebuhr was often castigated for being every atheist's favorite theologian and every conservative anti-communist's favorite liberal."[10] His contribution to American social and political thought is nicely summed up by political scientist and IR theorist Hans Morgenthau in a speech he delivered in 1961 for a colloquium honoring Reinhold Niebuhr at the Cathedral Church of St. John the Divine in New York City with Paul Tillich and John Bennett.

> I think if one would want to bring into one formula the contribution which Reinhold Niebuhr has made to the political thinking and the political life of America, one could say that he is responsible for the rediscovery of Political Man. He has rediscovered Political Man in five different respects: He has rediscovered the autonomy of the political sphere. He has rediscovered the intellectual dilemma of understanding politics and acting within the political sphere. He has rediscovered the moral dilemma of political action. He has restored the organic relationship between political thought and political action. Finally, he has rediscovered the tragedy which is inherent in the political act.[11]

In IR today, Niebuhr reminds us that politics matter, both domestic politics and the political dimension of IR. He reminds us that morals, ethics, matter, but he is not an idealist. He does not believe that moral/ethics/ideals alone can guide foreign policy or any other political decision-making. While he was not an idealist, nor was he a consequentialist. He cared too much about morals, ethics, doing "the right thing," to be classified as such. This is perhaps most obvious in Chapter 8 of this book, on humanitarian intervention and the responsibility to protect, but it can be seen throughout this book, and in how he lived his life, in service to his ideals and to other human beings. His service to his ideals and to others can be seen whether in his concern for the plight of workers in his leftist days, his work on behalf of a Jewish homeland

---

[7] Michael Novak, "Father of Neoconservatives," *National Review* (May 11, 1992), p. 39.

[8] Dean Curry, "Where Have All the Niebuhrs Gone? Evangelicals and the Marginalization of Religious Influence in American Public Life," *Journal of Church and State* 97 (1994).

[9] David Brooks, "A Man on a Gray Horse," *Atlantic Monthly* (September, 2002), accessed from https://www.theatlantic.com/magazine/archive/2002/09/a-man-on-a-gray-horse/302558/; David Brooks, "Obama, Gospel and Verse," *The New York Times* (April 26, 2007), p. A25.

[10] Brooks, "A Man on a Gray Horse."

[11] Hans J. Morgenthau, "Niebuhr's Political Thought," in Harold R. Landon, ed., *Reinhold Niebuhr: A Prophetic Voice in Our Time* (Greenwich, CT: Seabury Press, 1962), p. 99.

or against racism, his appeal for the United States to end the Neutrality Act and enter WWII, his campaign against the Vietnam War (which he saw as morally wrong), or simply on behalf of his students whom he served with great self-sacrifice. The apparent contradiction between his moralism and the pragmatism of his politics in some cases illustrates that moral dualism, that inherent tension between morals/ethics and political action. This was of course a key theme in all of his work. He reminds us that foreign policy decision making often involves tragedy, as Morgenthau suggests in his statement above and as Niebuhr himself said in his lifetime. I note here examples such as Niebuhr's own equivocation over the justice and morality of dropping atomic bombs on Hiroshima and Nagasaki, which he in some cases defended as necessary and moral so as to bring an early end to a bloody war, and in other cases he derided as stooping to the level of "Nazi morality."[12] In fact, perhaps both viewpoints were right, and this might just be one of the best examples of the tragedy and the inescapable ethical complexities inherent in political decision making.

Niebuhr on the Rise of Putin's Russia, Donald Trump, and "Post-Truth"

As we enter the third decade of the twenty-first century we find ourselves in a world few would have predicted even five years ago. Russia threatens European security with the invasion of a European state (Ukraine) and threatens to undermine Western European and American democracies via its trolling and other manipulations of public opinion and electoral processes at home and abroad, even while using weapons of mass destruction on British soil to eradicate what Moscow perceives to be an enemy of the Russian state. Referred to here is (1) the use of the radioactive isotope polonium 210 to murder Russian defector Alexander Litvenenko in London in 2006 and (2) the March 2018 attack on Russian double agent Sergei Skripal and his daughter in Salisbury with a nerve agent called *novichok*, a weapon of mass destruction known to be exclusively developed and controlled by Russia. A bit to the west, Americans have elected a president who is perhaps the greatest threat to democracy the United States has ever faced, a

---

[12] RN, "The Atomic Bomb," *Christianity and Society* (Fall 1945); in RN, *Love and Justice*, p. 233; and RN to James B. Conant, letter of March 12, 1946; as described and cited in Richard Wightman Fox, *Reinhold Niebuhr: A Biography* (San Francisco: Harper & Row, 1985), pp. 224–5.

president who does not seem to believe in the virtues of the free press (who believes it propagates "fake news," that the mainstream "fake news" media is "the enemy of the American people"[13]), who appears to be violating the emoluments clause of the U.S. Constitution with his business ties, who does not seem to believe in free trade but rather appears to prefer trade wars and Mexican border walls, who seems to believe he is unbound by constitutional norms in general, desiring to run the country as his personal fiefdom, as a CEO would run a large corporation instead of as the constitutional democracy the United States is. Linked to both Russia and Donald Trump is the rise of a world where "fake news" and "alternative facts" are not just tolerated but celebrated in a way that even Michel Foucault and Jacques Derrida could not have imagined. What would Reinhold Niebuhr have offered us, what does he offer us, in the face of such challenges?

As regards the rise of Putin's authoritarian Russia, much of what was said earlier about China would pertain to any discussion Niebuhr might have about today's Russia as well. While certainly not the Soviet Union of old— with the USSR's "universal creed," its dogmatic belief system that must be spread to the entire world—today's Russia has no creed save for Russia first and, perhaps more importantly, Putin first. Today's Russia under the new czar, Vladimir Putin, is not truly democratic. It is an "illiberal democracy" at best, considering the reports of election irregularities in the recent Russian election and the slow advance of autocratic rule since he took office 20 years ago. Some have even called Russia's autocracy a "kleptocracy,"[14] a nation where political opponents are poisoned abroad and shot at home, even outside the walls of the Kremlin. One prominent example is the murder of Boris Nemtsov, a prominent Russian academic and critic of Putin in 2015. While Russia and the West are not formally in a Cold War at the moment, Russia's relations with the Western powers are at a low point not seen since the lowest moments of the Cold War because of Russia's annexation of Crimea, its incursions into Ukraine, its meddling in Western elections, and its deployment of the toxic nerve agent, *novichok,* on British soil in early 2018, among other ills.

Were Niebuhr observing these events, he would point to the political system of Russia, its lack of accountability to its people, as a key problem for

---

[13] Michael G. Grynbaum, "Trump Calls the News Media the 'Enemy of the American People,'" *The New York Times* (February 17, 2017).

[14] Karen Dawisha, *Putin's Kleptocracy: Who Owns Russia?* (New York: Simon and Schuster, 2012).

Russia and Russia's adversaries. Putin's manipulation of the electoral system, which has extended his stay as supreme leader for 20 years to date,[15] with five years to go following the recent election, is a problem from a Niebuhrian perspective and is a problem made more acute because of the role of human nature, Niebuhr would remind us. Power corrupts, Lord Acton warned us, and absolute power such as Putin increasingly wields is likely to corrupt absolutely, as Dawisha and others[16] have warned us is already the case with Putin. There are also worries that Putin may be influenced by an alternative nativist Russian ideology advocated by Moscow State University professor and right-wing nationalist, Alexandr Dugin, who has gained influence over Putin according to some analysts.[17] Dugin is influenced by a combination of fascist, Slavophile, Aryan, Occult, Orthodox Christian, antiglobalist, Eurasianist, and Russian nativist philosophical narratives. Niebuhr would see neo-imperialist Russian activities in Ukraine, Transnistria, Moldova, Georgia, its numerous acts of poisoning Russian dissidents in the UK, and its penchant for using trolls and other tools to manipulate U.S. and other Western elections as signs that Russia is a potentially dangerous power under the leadership of Vladimir Putin. He would argue for a strong Western stand against Putin's aggressions and assaults on truth.

In the same way, I believe Niebuhr would have been a critic of the politics, presidency, and person of Donald J. Trump, president of the United States, after his 2016 election. He would have found fault with Trump's apparent narcissism, his inability to admit mistakes or weaknesses, his tendency to belittle and marginalize anyone who criticizes him, and the revolving door of the Trump cabinet. Niebuhr believed in the wisdom of humility and railed against the dangers of hubris. Trump apparently does not, at least as it regards himself. From Niebuhr's perspective, this makes Trump more liable to folly than humbler leaders might be, for it is clear that he does not like to hear criticism and has an inflated view of his own omniscience and abilities. This means that, whatever merits he might have, he would be highly vulnerable

---

[15] One might rightly note that Putin has only been president formally for 15 years to date. However, I might respond that Dmitry Medvedev's five-year tenure in the midst of Putin's second and third terms was simply a continuation of Putin's czarist reign given Putin's sway over Medvedev.

[16] Masha Gessen, *The Future Is History: How Totalitarianism Reclaimed Russia* (New York: Riverhead Books, 2017); Steve LeVine, *Putin's Labyrinth: Spies, Murder, and the Dark Heart of the New Russia* (New York: Random House, 2008); Edward Lucas, *The New Cold War: Putin's Russia and the Threat to the West* (New York: St. Martin's Griffin, 2014).

[17] Marlene Laruelle, *Alexandr Dugin: A Russian Version of the European Radical Right?* Occasional Paper No. 294, The Kennan Institute (Washington, DC: Woodrow Wilson International Center for Scholars, 2014)

to groupthink[18] and to having a chorus of "yes-men" (and women) around him rather than a team who could give him wise, truly objective counsel. In like manner, his management of the American media is highly problematic. Anything said about him that he finds unfavorable is deemed "fake news." He seems to find the free press, one of the most cherished principles of American democracy, a burden and a nuisance, seeming to prefer authoritarian power structures in how he operates and in certain statements such as "maybe we'll give that a try some day" in a discussion about the removal of term limits for the Chinese president in March 2018.[19] Niebuhr would have found that highly problematic and would have gone on record in the media circles in which he traveled to raise the issue, as he did about other politicians of his era.[20] By his denunciations of the American media and his apparent disdain for democratic structures of accountability, Niebuhr would have likely recognized in Donald Trump illiberal (or non-Liberal) trends presenting a clear and present danger to American democracy.

Both Vladimir Putin and Donald Trump have something important in common—they both have disdain for a media that would hold them accountable and call them out when they engage in questionable acts, and they both enjoy contributing to an almost postmodern world of "alternative facts," as Trump advisor Kellyann Conway famously put it. The political systems behind them are vastly different, but this common theme unites them: both argue that they are besieged by hurtful narratives by agents of ill will. Russia (i.e., Putin) has, of course, made this narrative production an art, both with its state-run media and its state-led trolling and election guidance mechanisms in Russia and around the Western world, perhaps the best-known example abroad being its role in the 2016 U.S. presidential elections. While President Trump does not have the state-run media at his beck and call as Putin does, he does seem to have an alliance of sorts with Fox News to the point that he has selected members of his team from Fox News commentators (e.g., John Bolton as National Security Advisor). The White House and Fox News seem to have come to share and sustain a common narrative production mechanism of their own, perhaps more powerful than

---

[18] Irving Janus, *Groupthink: Psychological Studies of Policy Decisions and Fiascoes*, second edition (New York: Cengage Learning, 1982).

[19] See Amanda Erickson, "In a Jokey Speech, Trump Praised Xi," *The Washington Post*, March 4, 2018 (www.washingtonpost.com).

[20] He was particularly hard on John F. Kennedy, whose affairs in particular he found unsavory and unbecoming of a president.

Putin's because it is ostensibly part of the free press tradition in the United States. [21] Were Niebuhr around to contribute to a discussion of this phenomenon, without doubt he would add his voice to the chorus of critics of the recent turn in American politics and in European politics as well. Here I speak of Farage, Erdogan, Orban, the Le Pens, Wilders, and so on, who have put together nativist, xenophobic, alarmist constituencies built on this new media trend of constructed news that challenges traditional definitions of media objectivity. Niebuhr called out the Soviet Union on its production of false narratives via state-run propaganda campaigns, [22] and he would certainly be sensitive to the production of false narratives in any political environment today, whether in Russia, China, or the United States. He was a scholar and an influential public intellectual who believed he had a duty to speak truth to power, and that is precisely what he did, whether critiquing the U.S. policy of neutrality in the opening stages of World War II, the policy of racial segregation in southern U.S. states, or the U.S. military involvement in Vietnam, all of which he vocally opposed. As many commentators phrased it in his day, he was like a voice crying in the wilderness, and so I believe he would be today were he still with us.

Final Thoughts on Reinhold Niebuhr

Having lived through World War I, the Fordist era, the Great Depression, World War II, the Cold War, the civil rights movement, the Vietnam War, and other pivotal events of his era, Niebuhr must have found solace and respite from the dialectics and frustrations of life in his understanding that

> the hope of Christian faith that the divine power which bears history can complete what even the highest human striving must leave incomplete, and can purify the corruptions which appear in even the purest human aspirations, is an indispensable prerequisite for diligent fulfillment of our historic tasks. Without it we are driven to alternate moods of sentimentality and despair; trusting human powers too much in one moment and

---

[21] Michael M. Grynbaum, "John Bolton, Fresh from Fox News, Joins the Trump Cast," *The New York Times* (March 22, 2018; www.nytimes.com).

[22] RN, "The Quaker Way," *Christianity and Society* (Winter, 1949-1950); and *Love and Justice*, edited by D. B. Robertson (Westminster, UK: John Knox Press, 1957), p. 297.

losing all faith in the meaning of life when we discover the limits of human possibilities.[23]

This faith in a divine role leading to the potential for an occasional transcendence of human fallibility and self-interest underlies Niebuhr's thought and provides the source of optimism (and even a measure of idealism) in his work, in what is otherwise a very sober, realist view of human nature, human interrelations and, ultimately, international relations. The statement quoted above again reflects the Niebuhrian dialectic, here pointing to the great potential for wisdom and good in humanity, which in the Niebuhrian understanding of human nature coexists with the perhaps more common human potential for folly and evil.

In what is perhaps the best-known saying attributed to him, and one that is used daily in Alcoholics Anonymous meetings around the world, Niebuhr puts in perspective his own role in human affairs, and by extension our own, in his "Serenity Prayer."

> God, give us grace to accept with serenity
> the things that cannot be changed,
> courage to change the things that should be changed,
> and wisdom to distinguish the one from the other.[24]

Niebuhr seemed to have lived out these words, for he understood what he could not change—most importantly humankind's fallible, self-interested nature, and all its limitations. He certainly had courage, for he challenged the Washington establishment and others when he saw something amiss, as he believed was the case with the Vietnam War, which led to all of his opposition thereto. And it would seem that he had the wisdom to know the difference, for he remained faithful, humble, and at the same time intellectually and politically engaged until the end of his days.

---

[23] RN, *The Children of Light and the Children of Darkness* (New York: Charles Scribner's Sons, 1944), p. 189.

[24] This saying was used by RN in a sermon in 1943, and some say was attributed to RN as early as 1937, but first found its way into print in 1950 (and is attributed to RN) as a part of an Alcoholics Anonymous newsletter called the *Grapevine* (Wikipedia, "Serenity Prayer," http://en.wikipedia.org/wiki/Serenity_Prayer#cite_note-4; accessed October 7, 2011). See also his daughter Elisabeth Sifton's excellent treatment of this prayer and the life work of her father in *The Serenity Prayer: Faith and Politics in Times of Peace and War* (New York: W. W. Norton, 2005). Another, briefer, better known form is as follows: "God, grant me the serenity to accept the things I cannot change, Courage to change the things I can, And wisdom to know the difference."

Bibliography

Allen-Ebrahimian, Bethany, "How China Won the War against Western Media," *Foreign Policy* (March 4, 2016; https://foreignpolicy.com/2016/03/04/china-won-war-western-media-censorship-propaganda-communist-party).

Allison, Graham, "The Thucydides Trap: Are the US and China Headed for War?" *The Atlantic* (September 24, 2015; http://www.theatlantic.com/international/archive/2015/09/united-states-china-war-thucydides-trap/406756).

Amstutz, Mark, "Reinhold Niebuhr's Christian Realism and the Bush Doctrine," in Eric Patterson (ed.), *Christianity and Power Politics Today: Christian Realism and Contemporary Political Dilemmas* (New York: Palgrave Macmillan, 2008): 117–35.

Arendt, Hannah, *The Origins of Totalitarianism* (New York: Schocken Books, 1951).

Ashley, Richard, "The Poverty of Neorealism," in Robert Keohane (ed.), *Neorealism and Its Critics* (New York: Columbia University Press, 1986).

Bacevich, Andrew, "Introduction," in Reinhold Niebuhr (ed.), *The Irony of American History* (Chicago: University of Chicago Press, 2008).

Barbour, John D., "Niebuhr vs. Niebuhr," *The Christian Century* 101 (November. 21, 1984): 1096–9.

Barkin, Samuel, *Realist Constructivism: Rethinking International Relations Theory* (Cambridge, UK: Cambridge University Press, 2010).

Barkow, Jerome, Leda Cosmides, and John Tooby (eds.), *The Adapted Mind: Evolutionary Psychology and the Generation of Culture*, Revised Ed. (Oxford: Oxford University Press, 1995).

Beckley, Michael, "China's Century? Why America's Edge Will Endure," *International Security* 36/3 (Winter 2011/2012): 41–78.

Beem, Christopher, *Democratic Humility: Reinhold Niebuhr, Neuroscience, and America's Political Crisis* (Lanham, MD: Lexington Books, 2015).

Bellamy, Alex J., *Responsibility to Protect* (Cambridge, UK; Polity Press, 2009).

Bennett, John C., "Reinhold Niebuhr's Contribution to Social Ethics," in Harold R. Landon (ed.), *Reinhold Niebuhr: A Prophetic Voice in Our Time* (Greenwich, CT: Seabury Press, 1962).

Biddle, Stephen, *Military Power: Explaining Victory and Defeat in Modern Battle* (Princeton, NJ: Princeton University Press, 2006).

Bingham, June, *Courage to Change* (New York: Scribner's, 1961).

Branigan, Tania, "Xi Jinping, China's Expected Future Leader, Has Not Been Seen for 10 days," *The Guardian* (September 11, 2012; https://www.theguardian.com/world/2012/sep/11/xi-jinping-china-not-seen).

Breslin, Shaun, "The 'China Model' and the Global Crisis: From Friedrich List to a Chinese Mode of Governance?" *International Affairs* 87/6 (2011): 1323–43.

Brooks, David, "A Man on a Gray Horse," *Atlantic Monthly* (September 2002), accessed from https://www.theatlantic.com/magazine/archive/2002/09/a-man-on-a-gray-horse/302558/.

Brooks, David, "Obama, Gospel and Verse," *New York Times* (April 26, 2007): A25.

Brown, Charles C., *Niebuhr and His Age: Reinhold Niebuhr's Prophetic Role in the Twentieth Century* (Philadelphia: Trinity Press International, 1992).

Brown, Kerry, *CEO, China: The Rise of Xi Jinping* (New York: I. B. Tauris, 2016).

Brown, Michael E., Sean M. Lynn-Jones, and Steven E. Miller, *Debating the Democratic Peace* (Boston: MIT Press, 1996).

Buckley, Chris, "China Is Detaining Muslims in Vast Numbers. The Goal: 'Transformation.'" *New York Times* (September 8, 2018; https://www.nytimes.com/2018/09/08/world/asia/china-uighur-muslim-detention-camp.html).

Bull, Hedley, *The Anarchical Society: A Study of Order in World Politics* (New York: Columbia University Press, 1977/2012).

Burnham, Gilbert, Riyadh Lafta, Shannon Doocy, and Les Roberts, "Mortality after the 2003 Invasion of Iraq: A Cross-Sectional Cluster Sample Survey," *The Lancet* 368 (October 21, 2006): 1426.

Bush, George W., "Threats and Responses: Bush's Speech at the Start of the War," delivered March 19, 2003. *New York Times* (March 20, 2003).

Callahan, William A., "Sino-Speak: Chinese Exceptionalism and Politics of History," *The Journal of Asian Studies*, 71/1 (2012): 33–55.

Campbell, David, *Writing Security: United States Foreign Policy and the Politics of Identity* (Manchester, UK: Manchester University Press, 1992).

Carr, Edward Hallet, *Twenty Years' Crisis, 1919–1939: An Introduction to International Relations* (New York: Palgrave MacMillan, 2001[1939]).

Carter, Jimmy, Letter to Ursula Niebuhr, August 1, 1976, Box 46, Reinhold Niebuhr Papers, Manuscript Division, Library of Congress, Washington, DC.

Chang, Iris, *The Rape of Nanking: The Forgotten Holocaust of WW II* (New York: Basic Books, 1997).

Chen, Liang, *From a Christian Socialist to a Christian Realist: Reinhold Niebuhr and the Soviet Union, 1930–1945*, doctoral dissertation (Singapore: National University of Singapore, 2007).

Childress, James, "Reinhold Niebuhr's Realistic-Pragmatic Approach to War and 'The Nuclear Dilemma,'" in Richard Harries (ed.), *Reinhold Niebuhr and the Issues of Our Time* (Grand Rapids, MI: Eerdmans, 1986).

China Digital Times, "WeChat Banned from Australian Defense Staff's Work Phones" (March 17, 2018; https://chinadigitaltimes.net/2018/03/wechat-banned-from-australian-defense-staffs-work-phones).

Chrystal, William G., *Niebuhr Studies* (Reno, Nevada: Empire for Liberty LLC, 2012), Kindle version.

Coll, Alberto, "The Relevance of Christian Realism to the Twenty-First Century," in Eric Patterson (ed.), *Christianity and Power Politics Today: Christian Realism and Contemporary Political Dilemmas* (New York: Palgrave Macmillan, 2008).

Conant, James B., Letter of March 12, 1946, to RN; as cited in Fox, *Reinhold Niebuhr: A Biography*, p. 224.

Cowan, Wayne, *Christianity and Crisis* Editor, to RN, April 13, 1970, RN Papers; as found in Fox, *Reinhold Niebuhr: A Biography*, p. 283.

Craig, Campbell, *Glimmer of a New Leviathan: Total War in the Realism of Niebuhr, Morgenthau, and Waltz* (New York: Columbia University Press, 2003).

Crouter, Richard (ed.), *Reinhold Niebuhr: On Politics, Religion and Christian Faith* (Oxford: Oxford University Press, 2010).

Curry, Dean, "Where Have All the Niebuhrs Gone? Evangelicals and the Marginalization of Religious Influence in American Public Life," *Journal of Church and State*, 97 (1994): 97–114.

Davis, Harry R., and Robert C. Good (eds.), *Reinhold Niebuhr on Politics* (New York: Charles Scribner's Sons, 1960).

Dawisha, Karen, *Putin's Kleptocracy: Who Owns Russia?* (New York: Simon and Schuster, 2012).

Der Derian, James, and M. J. Shapiro (eds.), *International/Intertextual Relations: Postmodern Readings of World Politics* (Lexington, KY: Lexington Books, 1989).

Dershowitz, Alan M., *Preemption: A Knife that Cuts Both Ways* (New York: W. W. Norton, 2006).

Diamond, Larry, and Orville Schell, co-chairs, *Chinese Influence and American Interests: Promoting Constructive Vigilance,* a Report of the Working Group on Chinese Influence Activities in the United States (Stanford, CA: Hoover Institution Press, 2018).

Diggins, John Patrick, *The Promise of Pragmatism: Modernism and the Crisis of Modernity* (Chicago: University of Chicago Press, 1994); as found in Tjalve (2008).

Diggins, John Patrick, *Why Niebuhr Now?* (Chicago: University of Chicago Press, 2011).

Doblmeier, Martin, "An American Conscience: The Reinhold Niebuhr Story," PBS Video, Journey Films (April 2, 2017; http://www.pbs.org/video/mpt-presents-american-conscience-reinhold-niebuhr-story).

Dodds, Laurence, "Chinese Businesswoman Accused of Jaywalking after AI Camera Spots Her Face on an Advert," *The Telegraph* (November 25, 2018; https://www.telegraph.co.uk/technology/2018/11/25/chinese-businesswoman-accused-jaywalking-ai-camera-spots-face).

Dollar, David, "Xi's Power Grab Gives a Short-term Boost with Long-term Ramifications," *Order from Chaos*, Brookings Institution (February 27, 2018; https://www.brookings.edu/blog/order-from-chaos/2018/02/27/xis-power-grab-gives-a-short-term-boost-with-long-term-ramifications).

Dorrien, Gary, "Introduction," in Reinhold Niebuhr, *The Children of Light and the Children of Darkness: A Vindication of Democracy and a Critique of its Traditional Defense* (Chicago: University of Chicago Press, 2011[1944]), Kindle edition.

Duedney, Daniel H., *Bounding Power: Republican Security Theory from the Polis to the Global Village* (Princeton, NJ: Princeton University Press, 2007).

Economy, Elizabeth, "China's Imperial President: Xi Jinping Tightens His Grip," *Foreign Affairs* (November/December, 2014): 80–91.

Economy, Elizabeth, *The Third Revolution: Xi Jinping and the New Chinese State* (New York: Oxford University Press, 2018).

Elie, Paul, "A Man for All Reasons," *The Atlantic* (November, 2007), accessed from https://www.theatlantic.com/magazine/archive/2007/11/a-man-for-all-reasons/306337/.

Elshtain, Jean Bethke, *Just War against Terror* (New York: Basic Books, 2003/2004).

Erickson, Amanda, "In a Jokey Speech, Trump Praised Xi," *Washington Post*, March 4, 2018 (www.washingtonpost.com).

Fackre, Gabriel, *The Promise of Reinhold Niebuhr*, 3rd ed. (Grand Rapids, MI: Eerdmans, 2011).

Federal Council of Churches, "Atomic Warfare and the Christian Faith," excerpted in "Theology and the Bomb," *The Christian Century*, April 10, 1946; as cited in Fox, *Reinhold Niebuhr: A Biography*, p. 224.

Fox, Richard Wightman, *Reinhold Niebuhr: A Biography* (San Francisco: Harper & Row, 1985).

Fox, Richard Wightman, "Who Can but Prophesy? The Life of Reinhold Niebuhr," in Charles W. Kegley (ed.), *Reinhold Niebuhr, His Religious, Social and Political Thought* (New York: Pilgrim Press, 1984).

Fulda, Andreas, "Beijing Is Weaponizing Nationalism against Hong Kongers: Hong Kong's Unique Identity Threatens Xi Jinping's Rhetoric of Greatness," *Foreign Policy* (https://foreignpolicy.com/2019/07/29/beijing-is-weaponizing-nationalism-against-hong-kongers/; July 29, 2019).

Garnaut, John, *The Rise and Fall of the House of Bo* (New York: Penguin, 2012).

Gessen, Masha, *The Future Is History: How Totalitarianism Reclaimed Russia* (NewYork: Riverhead Books, 2017).

GlobalSecurity.org, "China's Defense Budget" (accessed October 13, 2018; https://www.globalsecurity.org/military/world/china/budget.htm).

Gries, Peter Hays, *China's New Nationalism: Pride, Politics, and Diplomacy,* Berkeley: University of California Press, 2004.

Grigg, Angus, "WeChat's Privacy Issues Mean You Should Delete China's No. 1 Messaging App," *Australian Financial Review* (February 22, 2018; https://www.afr.com/news/world/asia/wechats-privacy-issues-mean-you-should-delete-chinas-no1-messaging-app-20180221-h0wgct).

Grynbaum, Michael G., "Trump Calls the News Media the 'Enemy of the American People,'" *New York Times* (Feb. 17, 2017).

Grynbaum, Michael M., "John Bolton, Fresh from Fox News, Joins the Trump Cast," *New York Times* (March 22, 2018; www.nytimes.com).

Hass, Ryan, and Zach Balin, *US-China Relations in the Age of Artificial Intelligence* (Washington, DC: Brookings Institution; Thursday, January 10, 2019).

Halperin, Stephen, *The Beijing Consensus: How China's Authoritarian Model Will Dominate the Twenty-First Century* (New York: Basic Books, 2010).

Hampson, Daphne, "Reinhold Niebuhr on Sin: A Critique," in Richard Harries (ed.), *Reinhold Niebuhr and the Issues of Our Time* (Grand Rapids, MI: Eerdmans, 1986).

Harries, Richard (ed.), *Reinhold Niebuhr and the Issues of Our Time* (Grand Rapids, MI: Eerdmans, 1986).

Harries, Richard "Reinhold Niebuhr's Critique of Pacifism and his Pacifist Critics," in Richard Harries (ed.), *Reinhold Niebuhr and the Issues of Our Time* (Grand Rapids, MI: Eerdmans, 1986).

Harries, Richard, and Stephen Platten (eds.), *Reinhold Niebuhr and Contemporary Politics: God and Power* (Oxford: Oxford University Press, 2010).

Hayton, Bill, *The South China Sea: The Struggle for Power in Asia* (New Haven, CT: Yale University Press, 2014).

Holder, R. Ward, and Peter B. Josephson, *The Irony of Barack Obama: Barack Obama, Reinhold Niebuhr and the Problem of Christian Statecraft* (Surrey, UK: Ashgate, 2012).

Holy Bible, English Standard Version (Wheaton, IL: Crossway Publishers, 2001).

Horsley, Jamie, "China's Orwellian Social Credit Score Isn't Real," *Foreign Policy* (November 16, 2018; https://foreignpolicy.com/2018/11/16/chinas-orwellian-social-credit-score-isnt-real).

Hulsether, Mark, *Building a Protestant Left: Christianity and Crisis Magazine, 1941–1993* (Knoxville: University of Tennessee Press, 1999).

International Institute of Strategic Studies, *The Military Balance 2013, The Military Balance 2014, The Military Balance 2015, The Military Balance 2016, The Military*

Balance 2017, The Military Balance 2018 (London: Taylor & Francis, 2013, 2014, 2015, 2016, 2017, 2018).

IraqBodyCount.com, "Iraqi Deaths from Violence, 2003–2011," via http://www.iraqbodycount.org/analysis/numbers/2011/ (January 2, 2012; accessed March 12, 2012).

Janus, Irving L., *Groupthink: Psychological Studies of Policy Decisions and Fiascoes* 2nd ed. (New York: Cengage Learning, 1982).

Johnston, Douglas M., *Religion: The Missing Dimension of Statecraft* (Oxford: Oxford University Press, 1994).

Joske, Alex, *Picking Flowers, Making Honey: The Chinese Military's Collaboration with Foreign Universities*, Australian Strategic Policy Institute Policy Brief 10 (Canberra: Australian Strategic Policy Institute, October 2018).

Kaczmarski, Marcin, "The Sino-Russian Relationship: Fellow Travelers in the West-dominated World," *China Quarterly* 236 (December 2018): 1197–1205.

Kagan, Robert, *The World America Made,* New York: Alfred A. Knopf, 2012.

Kant, Immanuel, *Kant: Political Writings*, Hans Reiss (ed.) (New York: Cambridge University Press, 1991).

Kegley, Charles W. (ed.), *Reinhold Niebuhr, His Religious, Social and Political Thought* (New York: Pilgrim Press, 1984).

Kegley, Charles W. *Politics, Religion and Modern Man* (Quezon City: University of the Philippines Press, 1969).

Kegley, Charles W., and Robert Bretal (eds.), *Reinhold Niebuhr, His Religious, Social and Political Thought* (New York: Macmillan Company, 1956).

Keohane, Robert O. (ed.), *Neorealism and Its Critics* (New York: Columbia University Press, 1986).

Keohane, Robert O., and Joseph S. Nye, *Power and Interdependence: World Politics in Transition* (Boston: Little Brown, 1977).

Kennan, George F. *Memoirs: 1925–1950* (Boston: Little, Brown, 1967).

Kennan, George F. (known as "X" here). "The Sources of Soviet Conduct," *Foreign Affairs* XXV (July, 1947): 566–82.

Kennan, George F. "Reinhold Niebuhr: 1892–1971" (no further citation information available about this small booklet); as found in Box 49, Reinhold Niebuhr Papers, Manuscript Division, Library of Congress, Washington, DC.

Kennedy, Scott, "The Myth of the Beijing Consensus," *Journal of Contemporary China* 19/65 (June 2010): 461–77.

Kierkegaard, Soren, *Die Krankheit zum Tode* [A Sickness unto Death] (Diederich Verlag), p. 27, as cited in RN, *Nature and Destiny of Man*, Volume 1, p. 171.

Kirshner, Jonathan, "The Tragedy of Offensive Realism: Classical Realism and the Rise of China," *European Journal of International Relations*, 18/1(2012): 53–75.

Korolev, Alexander, "The Strategic Alignment between Russia and China: Myths and Reality," *The Asan Forum* (May 04, 2015), accessed from http://www.theasanforum.org/the-strategic-alignment-between-russia-and-china-myths-and-reality/.

Lafeber, Walter, *America, Russia, and the Cold War: 1945–1971* (New York: John Wiley & Sons, 1972).

Landon, Harold R. (ed.). *Reinhold Niebuhr: A Prophetic Voice in Our Time* (Greenwich, CT: Seabury Press, 1962).

Langer, Gary, and Jon Cohen, "Poll: Broad Optimism in Iraq, But Also Deep Divisions Among Groups," *ABC News* (December 12, 2005; http://abcnews.go.com/International/PollVault/story?id=1389228).

Lardy, Nicholas, *The State Strikes Back: The End of the Economic Reform in China?* (Washington: Peterson Institute for International Economics, 2019).

Laruelle, Marlene, *Alexandr Dugin: A Russian Version of the European Radical Right?* Occasional Paper No. 294, The Kennan Institute (Washington, DC: Woodrow Wilson International Center for Scholars, 2014).

Lebow, Richard Ned, *The Tragic Vision of Politics: Ethics, Interests and Orders* (Cambridge: Cambridge University Press, 2003).

Lefever, Ernest W. (ed.), *World Crisis and American Responsibility: Nine Essays* (New York: Association Press, 1958).

Legro, Jeffrey, and Andrew Moravscik, "Is Anybody Still a Realist?" *International Security*, 24/2 (Fall 1999): 5–55.

Leibholz, Sabine, Letters to RN and from RN to Sabine Leibholz (Dietrich Bonhoeffer's twin sister), in Boxes 49 and 55 in the Reinhold Niebuhr Papers, Manuscript Division, Library of Congress, Washington, DC.

Lemert, Charles, *Why Niebuhr Matters* (New Haven, CT: Yale University Press, 2011).

LeVine, Steve, *Putin's Labyrinth: Spies, Murder, and the Dark Heart of the New Russia* (New York: Random House, 2008).

Lewis, C. S., *That Hideous Strength* (New York: Scribner, 2003[1945]).

Library of Congress, Reinhold Niebuhr Papers, Manuscript Division, Washington, DC.

Lord, Charles, Lee Ross, and Mark Lepper, "Biased Assimilation and Attitude Polarization: The Effects of Prior Theories on Subsequently Considered Evidence," *Journal of Personality and Social Psychology* 37/11 (1979): 2098–2109.

Lovin, Robin, *Reinhold Niebuhr and Christian Realism* (Cambridge, UK: Cambridge University Press, 1995).

Lucas, Edward, *The New Cold War: Putin's Russia and the Threat to the West* (New York: St. Martin's Griffin, 2014).

Ma, Alexandra, "China Has Started Ranking Citizens," *Business Insider* (October 29, 2018; https://www.businessinsider.com/china-social-credit-system-punishments-and-rewards-explained-2018-4).

Marsh, David, and Jerry Stoker (eds.), *Theory and Methods in Political Science*, 2nd ed. (New York: Palgrave Macmillan, 2002).

Mazzetti, Mark, "C.I.A. Said to Find No Hussein Link to Terror Chief," *New York Times* (September 9, 2006).

McCain, John, with Stephen Salter, *Hard Calls: The Art of Great Decisions* (New York: Hachett Book Group, 2007), pp. 319–39.

McClay, Wilfred, "The Continuing Irony of American History," *First Things* (February, 2002; accessed March 17, 2012 via http://www.firstthings.com/article/2007/06/001-the-continuing-irony-of-american-history-36).

McCorkle, Mac, "On Recent Political Uses of Reinhold Niebuhr: Toward a New Appreciation of His Legacy," in Richard Harries and Stephen Platten (eds.), *Reinhold Niebuhr and Contemporary Politics: God and Power* (Oxford: Oxford University Press, 2010).

Mearsheimer, John J., "The Gathering Storm: China's Challenge to US Power in Asia," *The Chinese Journal of International Politics* 3(2010): 381–396.

Mearsheimer, John J., *The Tragedy of Great Power Politics* (New York: W. W. Norton, 2001/2014).

Metaxes, Eric, *Bonhoeffer: Pastor, Martyr, Prophet, Spy* (Nashville, TN: Thomas Nelson, 2010; Kindle Location 1955–1962).

Miles, Rebekah, "Was Ursula Niebuhr Reinhold's Coauthor?" *The Christian Century* (January 19, 2012; https://www.christiancentury.org/article/2012-01/uncredited, accessed August 11, 2018).

Moore, Gregory J., "Avoiding a Thucydides Trap in Sino-American Relations . . . and 7 Reasons Why That Might Be Difficult," *Asian Security* 13/2 (2017): 98–115.

Moore, Gregory J., "Bismarck or Wilhelm? China's Peaceful Rise and the South China Sea," *Asian Perspective* 42/2 (April–June, 2018).

Moore, Gregory J., "Christian Views of War: The Case of Iraq," Council on Faith and International Affairs (January 4, 2008; http://rfiaonline.org/extras/articles/310-the-case-of-iraq).

Moore, Gregory J., "The Difference a Day Makes: Understanding the End of the Sino-American 'Tacit Alliance,'" *International Studies Review* 16/4 (December, 2014): 540–74.

Moore, Gregory J., *Human Nature, Collective Society and International Relations in the Thought of Reinhold Niebuhr*, Master's Thesis 1991.M66 (Charlottesville: University of Virginia, 1991).

Moore, Gregory J., "Research Methods for International Relations Studies: Assembling an Effective Toolkit," (in Chinese), Wang Jianwei (ed.), *Handbook of International Relations* (Beijing: Renmin University Press, 2010); 莫凯歌，《国际关系研究方法：组合有效的工具箱》，王建伟主编，国际关系学，北京：人民大学出版社，2010；and (online in English) at International Studies Association's 48th Annual Conference proceedings, Chicago, IL (2007).

Morgenthau, Hans, *Politics Among Nations*, 3rd ed. (New York: Alfred A. Knopf, 1960).

Morgenthau, Hans, "Niebuhr's Political Thought," in Harold R. Landon (ed.), *Reinhold Niebuhr: A Prophetic Voice in Our Time* (Greenwich, CT: Seabury Press, 1962).

Mozur, Paul, "Inside China's Dystopian Dreams: A. I., Shame and Lots of Cameras," *New York Times* (July 8, 2018; https://www.nytimes.com/2018/07/08/business/china-surveillance-technology.html).

Mullen, Jethro, "China Posts Weakest Annual Economic Growth in 26 Years," *CNN Money* (January 27, 2017; http://money.cnn.com/2017/01/19/news/economy/china-fourth-quarter-gdp-economic-growth/index.html).

Naveh, Eyal, "Beyond Illusion and Despair: Niebuhr's Liberal Legacy in a Divided American Culture," in Daniel F. Rice (ed.), *Reinhold Niebuhr Revisited: Engagements with an American Original* (Grand Rapids, MI: Eerdmens, 2009).

Neuhaus, Richard John, "Internationalisms, etc.," *First Things* (December, 2004; accessed March 17, 2012, via http://www.firstthings.com/article/2009/02/internationalisms-etc-50).

Niebuhr, H. Richard, "The Grace of Doing Nothing," *The Christian Century* (March 23, 1932).

Niebuhr, Reinhold, "America and the War in China," *The Christian Century* (September 29, 1937), pp. 1195–6; as found in Box 56, Reinhold Niebuhr Papers, Manuscript Division, Library of Congress, Washington, DC.

Niebuhr, Reinhold, "Anti-Semitism," *Radical Religion* 3 (Summer 1938).

Niebuhr, Reinhold, "The Atomic Bomb," *Christianity and Society* (Fall 1945).

Niebuhr, Reinhold, *Beyond Tragedy* (New York: Charles Scribner's Sons, 1937).

Niebuhr, Reinhold, "The Bombing of Germany," *Christianity and Society* (Summer 1943).

Niebuhr, Reinhold, "British Experience and American Power," *Christianity and Crisis* 16 (May 14, 1956): 57; Good and Davis, 303.

Niebuhr, Reinhold, "Can We Organize the World?" *Christianity and Crisis* 13 (Feb. 2, 1953).

Niebuhr, Reinhold, "Caribbean Blunder," *Christianity and Crisis* 25 (May 31, 1965).

Niebuhr, Reinhold, *The Children of Light and the Children of Darkness: A Vindication of Democracy and a Critique of Its Traditional Defense* (Chicago: University of Chicago Press, 2011[1944]), Kindle Version.

Niebuhr, Reinhold, *The Children of Light and the Children of Darkness* (New York: Charles Scribner's Sons, 1944).

Niebuhr, Reinhold, "China and the United Nations," original manuscript sent to *The New Leader* for publication on March 26, 1957; as found in Box 15, Reinhold Niebuhr Papers, Manuscript Division, Library of Congress, Washington, DC.

Niebuhr, Reinhold, "Christian Faith and Political Controversy," *Christianity and Crisis* (July 21, 1952).

Niebuhr, Reinhold, "The Christian Faith and the World Crisis," *Christianity and Crisis* (inaugural issue, February 10, 1941).

Niebuhr, Reinhold, *Christian Realism and Political Problems* (New York: Charles Scribner's Sons, 1952).

Niebuhr, Reinhold, "Christianity and Darwin's Revolution," written for a 100-year anniversary symposium on Darwin at the University of Pittsburgh, convened by Prof. Ralph Buchsbaum (submitted by RN on February 28, 1957), as found in Box 15, Reinhold Niebuhr Papers, Manuscript Division, Library of Congress, Washington, DC.

Niebuhr, Reinhold, *Christianity and Power Politics* (New York: Charles Scribner's Sons, 1940).

Niebuhr, Reinhold, "The Communist Party and Russia," *Christianity and Society* 9 (Spring, 1944): 8; and in Davis and Good, p. 261.

Niebuhr, Reinhold, "The Dilemma in China," *Messenger* 14 (January 4, 1949): 4, as found in Charles C. Brown, *Niebuhr and His Age: Reinhold Niebuhr's Prophetic Role in the Twentieth Century* (Philadelphia: Trinity Press International, 1992), p. 148.

Niebuhr, Reinhold, "The Ethic of Jesus and the Social Problem," *Religion in Life* (Spring, 1932), in D.B. Robertson (ed.), *Love and Justice* (Lousville, KY: Westminster/John Knox Press, 1957), pp. 29–40.

Niebuhr, Reinhold, "The Failure of German Americanism" (*The Atlantic*, July, 1916): 16–18.

Niebuhr, Reinhold, *Faith and Politics* (New York: George Braziller, 1968).

Niebuhr, Reinhold, to Waldo Frank, June 1, 1939, Frank Papers, University of Pennsylvania; as quoted in Fox, *Reinhold Niebuhr: A Biography*, p. 186.

Niebuhr, Reinhold, to Felix Frankfurter, March 31, 1948, Frankfurter Papers, Library of Congress; as found in Fox, *Reinhold Niebuhr: A Biography*, p. 296.

Niebuhr, Reinhold, "The Germans Must Be Told!" *The Christian Century* (August 9, 1933); as found in Box 15, Reinhold Niebuhr Papers, Manuscript Division, Library of Congress, Washington, DC.

Niebuhr, Reinhold, "Hazards and Resources," *Virginia Quarterly Review* 25 (Spring 1949): 204; and Good and Davis, 262.

Niebuhr, Reinhold, "History (God) Has Overtaken Us," *Christianity and Society* (Winter 1941).

Niebuhr, Reinhold, "Human Nature and Social Change," *The Christian Century* 50 (1933): 363.

Niebuhr, Reinhold, to Hubert Humphrey (Vice President of the United States), dated July 26, 1968; as found in Box 49, Reinhold Niebuhr Papers, Manuscript Division, Library of Congress, Washington, DC.

Niebuhr, Reinhold, *The Irony of American History* (New York: Charles Scribner's Sons, 1952; and Chicago: University of Chicago Press, 2008; page numbers in text refer to 1952 version unless otherwise indicated).

Niebuhr, Reinhold, "Jews after the War," *The Nation* (February 21 and 28, 1942); as found in Box 17, Reinhold Niebuhr Papers, Manuscript Division, Library of Congress, Washington, DC.

Niebuhr, Reinhold, Letter to the Editor, *The Christian Century* (May 27, 1936); as cited in Fox, *Reinhold Niebuhr: A Biography*, p. 210.

Niebuhr, Reinhold, Letter to the Editor, "MacArthur Statements Contrasted," *New York Times*, December 6, 1950; as found in Fox, *Reinhold Niebuhr: A Biography*, p. 241.

Niebuhr, Reinhold, Letter to the Editor, "Our Position in Asia," *New York Times*, December 23, 1950; and found in Fox, *Reinhold Niebuhr: A Biography*, p. 241.

Niebuhr, Reinhold, *Love and Justice*, edited by D. B. Robertson (Westminster, UK: John Knox Press, 1957).

Niebuhr, Reinhold, "Love of Country," *Evangelical Herald* (April 18, 1918).

Niebuhr, Reinhold, *Man's Natures and His Communities* (New York: Charles Scribner's Sons, 1965).

Niebuhr, Reinhold, "Montgomery Savagery," *Christianity in Crisis* (June 12, 1961): 103; as found in Fox, *Reinhold Niebuhr: A Biography*, p. 282.

Niebuhr, Reinhold, "The Moral Issue in International Relations," manuscript submitted to Kenneth Thompson of the Rockefeller Foundation for a conference sponsored by the same, submitted April 2, 1954.

Niebuhr, Reinhold, *Moral Man and Immoral Society* (New York: Charles Scribner's Sons, 1932).

Niebuhr, Reinhold, "The Nation's Crime against the Individual," *The Atlantic* (November, 1916).

Niebuhr, Reinhold, *The Nature and Destiny of Man: Volumes 1 & 2* (New York: Charles Scribner's Sons, 1941 and 1943, respectively).

Niebuhr, Reinhold, "A Negotiated Peace," *Christianity and Crisis* (April 7, 1941).

Niebuhr, Reinhold, "Our Chances for Peace," *Christianity and Crisis* (February 17, 1947).

Niebuhr, Reinhold, "Our Moral and Spiritual Resources for International Cooperation," *Social Action*, 22 (Feb., 1956): 18–9.

Niebuhr, Reinhold, "Pacifism and 'America First,'" *Christianity and Crisis* (June 16, 1941); as found in Robertson, *Love and Justice* (1957): 286.

Niebuhr, Reinhold, "Peace Lessons from the Orient," *The Christian Advocate* (May 19, 1932), p. 524; as found in Box 56, Reinhold Niebuhr Papers, Manuscript Division, Library of Congress, Washington, DC.

Niebuhr, Reinhold, "Plans for World Reorganization," *Christianity and Crisis*, 2 (October 19, 1942): 3–6.

Niebuhr, Reinhold, "The Problem of Nuclear Warfare," an original manuscript submitted to Rev. Angus Dun, Bishop of the Diocese of Washington, on May 1, 1957 (for a conference of the College or Preachers on nuclear energy, held in conjunction with the 50th anniversary of the laying of the cornerstone of the Washington Cathedral), p. 7; as found in Box 16, Reinhold Niebuhr Papers, Manuscript Division, Library of Congress, Washington, DC.

Niebuhr, Reinhold, "A Proposal for Billy Graham," original manuscript submitted to *The Christian Century* for publication (later published therein on August 8, 1956, p. 921); as found in Box 16, Reinhold Niebuhr Papers, Manuscript Division, Library of Congress, Washington, DC.

Niebuhr, Reinhold, "The Quaker Way," *Christianity and Society* (Winter 1949–1950); and *Love and Justice*, p. 297.

Niebuhr, Reinhold, "Radical Religion," in the inaugural issue of *Radical Religion*, 1 (Fall 1935): 4–5.

Niebuhr, Reinhold, *Radical Religion*, 13/4 (Autumn 1948).

Niebuhr, Reinhold, "Repeal the Neutrality Act!" *Christianity and Crisis* (October 20, 1941).

Niebuhr, Reinhold, "Report of the Mayor's Committee on Race Relations, Detroit, Michigan," The Mayor's Office, City of Detroit, 1926; as found in Box 16, Reinhold Niebuhr Papers, Manuscript Division, Library of Congress, Washington, DC.

Niebuhr, Reinhold, "Reinhold Niebuhr Discusses the War in Vietnam," *The New Republic* (January 29, 1966), p. 16; as found in Box 56, Reinhold Niebuhr Papers, Manuscript Division, Library of Congress, Washington, DC.

Niebuhr, Reinhold, Reinhold Niebuhr Papers, Manuscript Division, Library of Congress, Washington, DC.

Niebuhr, Reinhold, "The Rising Tide of Color," original manuscript found in Box 17, Reinhold Niebuhr Papers, Manuscript Division, Library of Congress, Washington, DC. No further information on date or whether it was published is available in the box/folder.

Niebuhr, Reinhold, "Seven Great Errors of U.S. Foreign Policy," *The New Leader* 39(December 24–31, 1956): 3–5.

Niebuhr, Reinhold, "Should We Be Consistent?" *Christianity and Crisis* 10 (February 6, 1950): 1; Good and Davis, 309.

Niebuhr, Reinhold, "The Social Myths of the 'Cold War,'" *Journal of International Affairs* 21 (1967): 40–56; as found in Box 56, Reinhold Niebuhr Papers, Manuscript Division, Library of Congress, Washington, DC.

Niebuhr, Reinhold, "Streaks of Dawn in the Night," *The Christian Century* (December 12, 1949): 162–64.

Niebuhr, Reinhold, *The Structure of Nations and Empires* (New York: Charles Scribner's Sons, 1959).

Niebuhr, Reinhold, "Universal Government," *The Center Magazine* 18 (November/December, 1985).

Niebuhr, Reinhold, "Vietnam and the Imperial Conflict," *The New Leader* 49/12 (June 6, 1966).

Niebuhr, Reinhold, "What Chance has Gandhi?" *The Christian Century* (October 14, 1931): 1274–76; as found in Box 17, Reinhold Niebuhr Papers, Manuscript Division, Library of Congress, Washington, DC.

Niebuhr, Reinhold, "The West and Asia," p. 5, original manuscript found in Box 17, Reinhold Niebuhr Papers, Manuscript Division, Library of Congress, Washington, DC. No further information on date or whether it was published is available in the box/folder, but a handwritten note on page one says, "The New Leader," in which it may have been published (The discussion of the fall of Dien Bien Phu suggests the date may have been 1954).

Niebuhr, Reinhold, "Why Is Barth Silent on Hungary?" *The Christian Century* (January 23, 1957): 109.

Niebuhr, Reinhold, "Why Sanctions Are Good," *Radical Religion* (Fall, 1935).

Niebuhr, Reinhold, "World Community and World Government," *Christianity and Crisis* 6 (March 4, 1946): 5.

Niebuhr, Reinhold, *"World Crisis and American Responsibility; Nine Essays,"* Ernest W. Lefever (ed.) (New York: Association Press, 1958).

Niebuhr, Reinhold, and Bishop Angus Dun, "God Wills Both Justice and Peace," *Christianity and Crisis* 15 (June 13, 1955), as found in Campbell Craig, *Glimmer of a New Leviathan: Total War in the Realism of Niebuhr, Morgenthau, and Waltz* (New York: Columbia University Press, 2003).

Niebuhr, Reinhold, and Hans Morgenthau, "The Ethics of War and Peace in a Nuclear Age" (informal discussion), *War/Peace Report* (February 1967).

Niebuhr, Ursula M. (ed.), *Remembering Reinhold Niebuhr: Letters of Reinhold and Ursula M. Niebuhr* (New York: Bloomsbury, 2001).

Nye, Joseph S., Jr., *The Future of Power* (New York: Public Affairs, 2011).

Oral History Research Office, Columbia University, "Interview with R. Niebuhr," in *The Reminiscences of Reinhold Niebuhr* (New York, 1954).

Orwell, George, *1984* (New York: Plume, 2003[1949]).

Patterson, Eric (ed.), *Christianity and Power Politics Today: Christian Realism and Contemporary Political Dilemmas* (New York: Palgrave Macmillan, 2008).

Pattison, James, *Humanitarian Intervention and the Responsibility to Protect: Who Should Intervene?* (New York: Oxford University Press, Kindle Edition, 2010).

Pavlischek, Keith, "Reinhold Niebuhr, Christian Realism, and Just War Theory: A Critique," in Eric D. Patterson, *Christianity and Power Politics Today* (Palgrave Macmillan, 2008), and also available on the website of the Ethics and Public Policy Center (www.eppc.org/docLib/20080205_palpatterson03.pdf).

Pedro, Guilherme Marques, *Reinhold Niebuhr and International Relations Theory: Realism Beyond Thomas Hobbes* (Basingstoke, UK: Routledge, 2017).

Phillips, Tom, "China Universities Must Become Communist Party 'Strongholds,' Says Xi Jinping," *The Guardian* (December 9, 2016; https://www.theguardian.com/world/2016/dec/09/china-universities-must-become-communist-party-strongholds-says-xi-jinping).

Pillsbury, Michael, *The Hundred Year Marathon: China's Secret Strategy to Replace America as the Global Superpower* (New York: Henry Holt, 2015).

Pollack, Kenneth M., *The Threatening Storm: The Case for Invading Iraq* (New York: Random House, 2002).

Power, Samantha, *A Problem from Hell—America and the Age of Genocide* (New York: Basic Books, 2013 [2002]).

Qin, Yaqing, "A Chinese School of International Relations Theory: Possibility and Inevitability," in William A. Callahan and Elena Barabantseva (eds.), *China Orders the World? Soft Power, Norms and Foreign Policy* (Washington, DC: Woodrow Wilson Center Press, 2011), pp. 37–53.

Ramo, Joshua Cooper, *The Beijing Consensus* (London: Foreign Policy Centre, 2004).

Ramsey, Paul, *The Just War: Force and Political Responsibility* (Lanham, MD: Rowman & Littlefield, 2002).

Ramsey, Paul, "Love and Law," in Charles W. Kegley and Robert Bretal (eds.), *Reinhold Niebuhr, His Religious, Social and Political Thought* (New York: Macmillan Company, 1956).

Rand, Ayn, *Atlas Shrugged* (New York: Plume 1999 [1957]).

Rasmussen, Larry, "Empire or Global Community?" in Daniel F. Rice (ed.), *Reinhold Niebuhr Revisited: Engagements with an American Original* (Grand Rapids, MI: Eerdmans, 2009).

Rice, Daniel F., *Reinhold Niebuhr and His Circle of Influence* (Cambridge, UK: Cambridge University Press, 2012).

Rice, Daniel F., (ed.), *Reinhold Niebuhr Revisited: Engagements with an American Original* (Grand Rapids, MI: Eerdmans, 2009).

Rose, Gideon, "Neoclassical Realism and Theories of Foreign Policy," *World Politics*, 51/1 (1998): 144–172.

Rosen, Stephen, *War and Human Nature* (Princeton, NJ: Princeton University Press, 2009).

Royce, Marie, US Assistant Secretary of State for Educational and Cultural Affairs, "The U.S. Welcomes Chinese Students," EducationUSA Forum, Washington, DC Tuesday, July 30, 2019.

Ruggie, John, "Continuity and Transformation in the World Polity: Toward a Neorealist Synthesis," *World Politics* 35/2 (January 1983): 261–85.

Scheuerman, William E., *Morgenthau* (Cambridge, UK: Polity Press, 2009).

Schlesinger, Arthur, Jr., "Forgetting Reinhold Niebuhr," *New York Times* (September 18, 2005): 12.

Schlesinger, Arthur, Jr., "The Political Conscience of Reinhold Niebuhr," *Esquire,* 100 (December 1983): 394–6.

Schweller, Randall, "The Progressiveness of Neoclassical Realism," in Colin Elman and Miriam Fendius Elman (eds.), *Progress in International Relations Theory* (Cambridge, MA: MIT Press, 2003).

Shambaugh, David, *China's Future* (Cambridge, UK: Polity Press, 2016).

Shambaugh, David, "The Coming Chinese Crack-up," *Wall Street Journal* (March 6, 2015), accessed from https://www.wsj.com/articles/the-coming-chinese-crack-up-1425659198.

Shirk, Susan, "China in Xi's 'New Era': The Return to Personalistic Rule," *Journal of Democracy* 29/2 (April 2018; https://www.journalofdemocracy.org/article/china-xi's-"new-era"-return-personalistic-rule), pp. 22–36.

Sifton, Elisabeth, *The Serenity Prayer: Faith and Politics in Times of Peace and War* (New York: W. W. Norton, 2005).

Smith, Michael J., *Realist Thought from Weber to Kissinger* (Baton Rouge: Louisiana State University Press, 1986).

Smith, Steve, Ken Booth, and Marysia Zalewski, *International Theory: Positivism and Beyond* (Cambridge, UK: Cambridge University Press, 1996).

Solomon, Robert C. (ed.), *Existentialism* (New York: Random House/Modern Library, 1974).

Stein, Jeff, "U.S. Military Spending Inches Closer to $1 Trillion Mark as Concerns over Federal Deficit Grow," *Washington Post*, June 19, 2018 (accessed October 13, 2018; https://www.washingtonpost.com/news/wonk/wp/2018/06/19/u-s-military-budget-inches-closer-to-1-trillion-mark-as-concerns-over-federal-deficit-grow/?noredirect=on&utm_term=.1de75d32fd31).

Stoessinger, John G., *Crusaders and Pragmatists: Movers of Modern American Foreign Policy*, 2nd ed. (New York: W. W. Norton, 1985).

Stone, Ronald H. *Prophet to Politicians* (Nashville, TN: Abingdon Press, 1972).

Stone, Ronald H. "The Contribution of Reinhold Niebuhr to the Late Twentieth Century," in Charles W. Kegley (ed.), *Reinhold Niebuhr, His Religious, Social and Political Thought* (New York: Pilgrim Press, 1984).

Stone, Ronald H. *Professor Reinhold Niebuhr: A Mentor to the Twentieth Century* (Louisville: Westminster, UK: John Knox Press, 1992).

Stone, Ronald H. *Prophet to Politicians* (Nashville, TN: Abingdon Press, 1972).

St. Augustine, *City of God* (New York: Image Books, 1958).

St. Petersburg [Florida] Times, "A Senate Committee Finds That, Contrary to What President Bush Has Said, Saddam Hussein Repulsed Overtures From al-Qaida" (September 9, 2006).

Talmadge, Caitlin, *The Dictator's Army: Battlefield Effectiveness in Authoritarian Regimes* (Ithaca, NY: Cornell University Press, 2015).

Thompson, Kenneth W., "Europe's Crisis and America's Dilemma," *Christianity and Crisis* 16 (January 7, 1957): 181–6.

Thompson, Kenneth W., "Niebuhr and the Foreign Policy Realists," in Daniel F. Rice (ed.), *Reinhold Niebuhr Revisited: Engagements with an American Original* (Grand Rapids, MI: Eerdmans, 2009).

Thompson, Kenneth W., "Niebuhr's Conception of Politics in the United States and the World," article handed out as part of class reading material by Mr. Thompson, University of Virginia, 1990, no further citation.

Thompson, Kenneth W., "The Political Philosophy of Reinhold Niebuhr," in Charles W. Kegley (ed.), *Reinhold Niebuhr, His Religious, Social and Political Thought* (New York: Pilgrim Press, 1984).

Tippet, Krista (host), "Obama's Theologian: David Brooks and E. J. Dionne on Reinhold Niebuhr and the American Present," American Public Media's National Public Radio program, "On Being," with journalists David Brooks (*New York Times*) and E. J. Dionne (*Washington Post*), (February 12, 2009; accessed March 13, 2012, via http://being.publicradio.org/programs/2009/obamas-theologian/).

Tippet, Krista (host), "Moral Man and Immoral Society: The Public Theology of Reinhold Niebuhr," American Public Media's National Public Radio program, "On Being," with Paul Ellie, Jean Bethke Elshtain, and Robin Lovin, (October 25, 2007; accessed March 14, 2012, via http://being.publicradio.org/programs/niebuhr-rediscovered/index.shtml).

Tjalve, Vibeke Schou, *Realist Strategies of Republican Peace: Niebuhr, Morgenthau, and the Politics of Patriotic Dissent* (New York: Palgrave Macmillan, 2008).

Tooby, John, and Leda Cosmides, "Introduction," in Jerome Barkow, Leda Cosmides and John Tooby (eds.), *The Adapted Mind: Evolutionary Psychology and the Generation of Culture*, Revised Ed. (Oxford: Oxford University Press, 1995).

United Nations, *2005 World Summit Outcome*, A/RES/60/1 (http://www.un.org/summit2005/documents.html; 2005).

USAToday/CNN/Gallup, "Key findings: Nationwide survey of 3,500 Iraqis," *USA Today* (May 20, 2005; http://www.usatoday.com/news/world/iraq/2004-04-28-gallup-iraq-findings.htm).

Van Ness, Peter, *Revolution and Foreign Policy: Peking's Support for Wars of National Liberation* (Berkeley: University of California Press, 1970).

Walker, R. B. J, *Inside/Outside: International Relations as Political Theory* (Cambridge, UK: Cambridge University Press, 1993).

Waltz, Kenneth, *Theory of International Politics* (Reading, MA: Addison-Wesley, 1979).

Walzer, Michael, *Just and Unjust Wars: A Moral Argument with Historical Illustrations*, 3rd ed. (New York: Basic Books, [1977] 2000).

Wang, Zheng, *Never Forget National Humiliation: Historical Memory in Chinese Politics and Foreign Relations* (New York: Columbia University Press, 2012).

Wason, P. E., "On the Failure to Eliminate Hypotheses in a Conceptual Task," *Quarterly Journal of Experimental Psychology* 12 (1960): 129–40.

Weigel, George, "Exorcising Wilson's Ghost: Morality and Foreign Policy in America's Third Century," *Washington Quarterly* 10 (Autumn, 1987): 31–40.

Wendt, Alexander, *Quantum Mind and Social Science: Unifying Physical and Social Ontology* (Cambridge, UK: Cambridge University Press, 2015).

Wendt, Alexander, *Social Theory of International Politics* (Cambridge, UK: Cambridge University Press, 1999).

Whitman, Alden, "Reinhold Niebuhr is Dead: Protestant Theologian, 78," *New York Times* (June 2, 1971): 1.

Wikipedia, "Serenity Prayer," http://en.wikipedia.org/wiki/Serenity_Prayer#cite_note-4; accessed October 7, 2011).

Williams, Michael C., *Realism Reconsidered: The Legacy of Hans J. Morgenthau in International Relations* (New York: Oxford University Press, 2008).

Williams, Michael C., *The Realist Tradition and the Limits of International Relations* (Cambridge, UK: Cambridge University Press, 2005).

Winter, Don, "The Carter-Niebuhr Connection—The Politician as Philosopher," *National Journal* (February 4, 1978): 188–92.

Wolf, William John, "Reinhold Niebuhr's Doctrine of Man," in Charles W. Kegley (ed.), *Reinhold Niebuhr, His Religious, Social and Political Thought* (New York: Pilgrim Press, 1984).

XE Corporation, "USD to CNY Chart" (Accessed July 27, 2017; https://www.xe.com/currencycharts/?from=USD&to=CNY&view=5Y).

Yan, Xuetong, *Ancient Chinese Thought, Modern Chinese Power*, (Princeton, NJ: Princeton University Press, 2011).

Yoder, John Howard, *The Politics of Jesus: Vicit Agnus Noster* ("Our Lamb Has Conquered"), 2nd ed. (Carlisle, UK: Paternoster and Eerdmans, 1994).

Young, Daniel Edward, "International Institutions and the Problem of Judgment," in Eric Patterson (ed.), *Christianity and Power Politics Today: Christian Realism and Contemporary Political Dilemmas* (New York: Palgrave Macmillan, 2008).

Yu, Keping, *Democracy Is a Good Thing: Essays on Politics, Society and Culture in Contemporary China* (Washington, DC: Brookings Institution, 2011).

Zhao, Suisheng, "A State-led Nationalism: The Patriotic Education Campaign in Post-Tiananmen China," *Communist and Post-Communist Studies,* 31/3 (September 1998): 287–302.

Index

For the benefit of digital users, indexed terms that span two pages (e.g., 52–53) may, on occasion, appear on only one of those pages.